3 9635 1032 7327 7
D1402951

SCHLOW
CENTRE
REGION
LIBRARY

# PLANET OF THE APES

# THE DEVIL'S PAWN

# PLANE

ROSS RICHIE Chief Executive Officer • MATT GAGNON Editor-in-Chief • WES HARRIS VP-Publishing • LANCE KREITER VP-Licensing & Merchandising • PHIL BARBARO Director of Finance
BRYCE CARLSON Managing Editor • DAFNA PLEBAN Editor • SHANNON WATTERS Editor • ERIC HARBURN Assistant Editor • ADAM STAFFARONI Assistant Editor • CHRIS ROSA Assistant Editor
STEPHANIE GONZAGA Graphic Designer • EMILY MCGUINESS Marketing Coordinator • DEVIN FUNCHES Marketing & Sales Assistant • JASMINE AMIRI Operations Assistant

PLANET OF THE APES Volume Two — April 2012. Published by BOOM! Studios, a division of Boom Entertainment, Inc. PLANET OF THE APES TM & © 2012 Twentieth Century Fox Film Corporation. All Rights Reserved. Originally published in single magazine form as PLANET OF THE APES 5-8. Copyright © 2011 Twentieth Century Fox Film Corporation. All rights reserved. BOOM! Studios™ and the BOOM! Studios logo are trademarks of Boom Entertainment, Inc., registered in various countries and categories. All characters, events, and institutions depicted herein are fictional. Any similarity between any of the names, characters, persons, events, and/or institutions in this publication to actual names, characters, and persons, whether living or dead, events, and/or institutions is unintended and purely coincidental. BOOM! Studios does not read or accept unsolicited submissions of ideas, stories, or artwork.

A catalog record of this book is available from OCLC and from the BOOM! Studios website, www.boom-studios.com, on the Librarians Page.

BOOM! Studios, 6310 San Vicente Boulevard, Suite 107, Los Angeles, CA 90048-5457. Printed in China. First Printing. ISBN: 978-1-60886-669-4

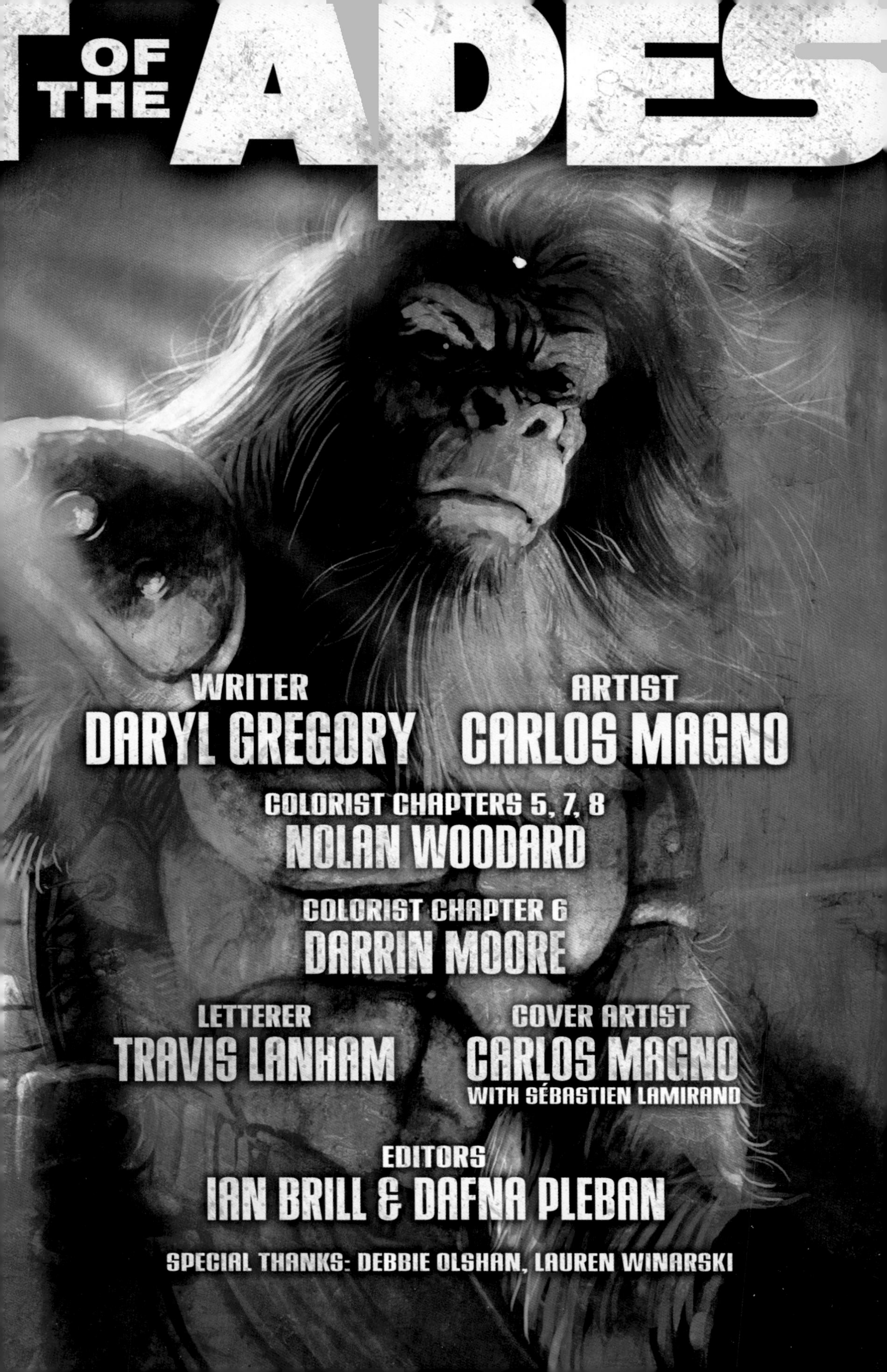
OF THE APES

WRITER
DARYL GREGORY

ARTIST
CARLOS MAGNO

COLORIST CHAPTERS 5, 7, 8
NOLAN WOODARD

COLORIST CHAPTER 6
DARRIN MOORE

LETTERER
TRAVIS LANHAM

COVER ARTIST
CARLOS MAGNO
WITH SÉBASTIEN LAMIRAND

EDITORS
IAN BRILL & DAFNA PLEBAN

SPECIAL THANKS: DEBBIE OLSHAN, LAUREN WINARSKI

# CHAPTER FIVE

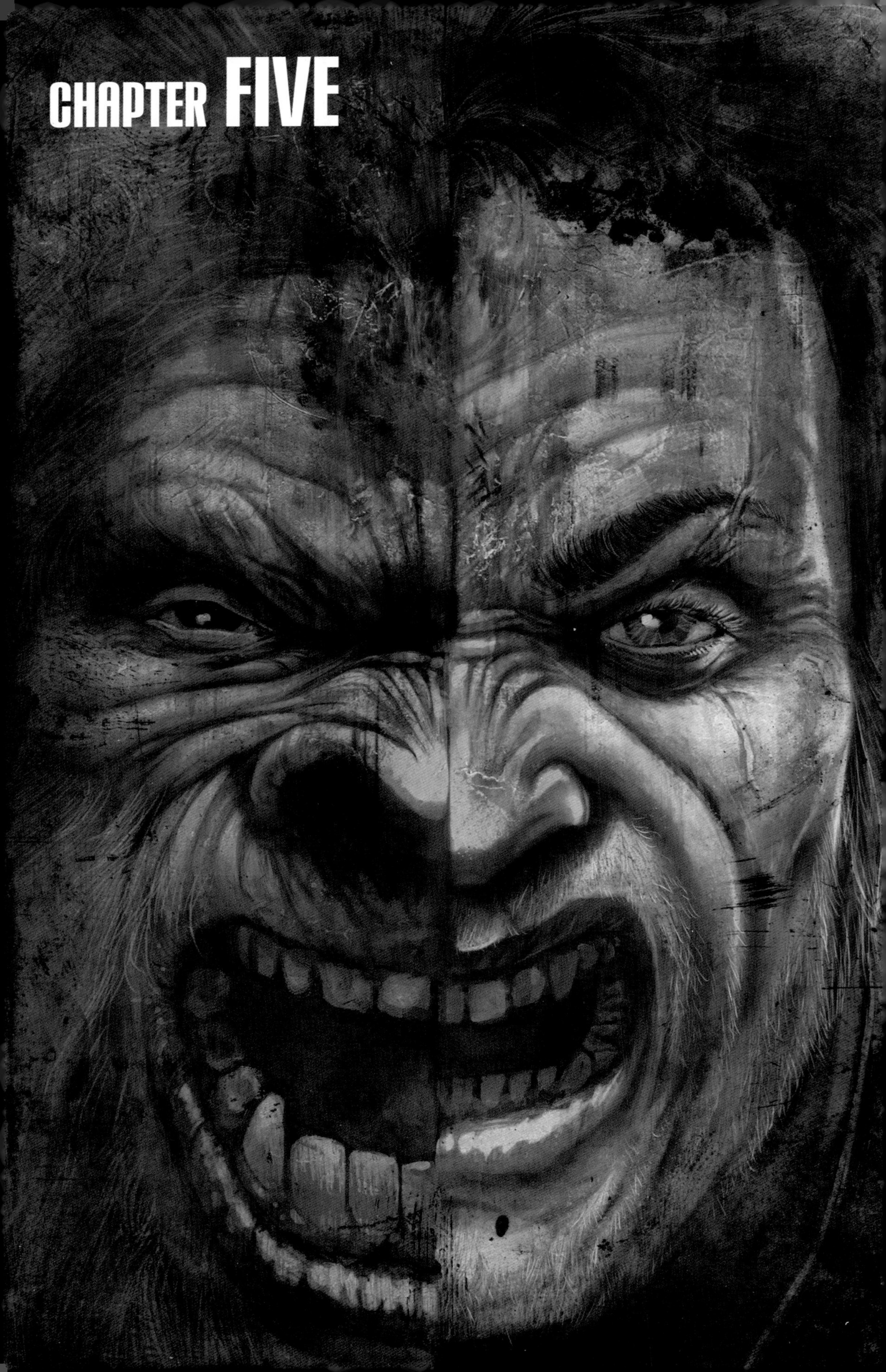

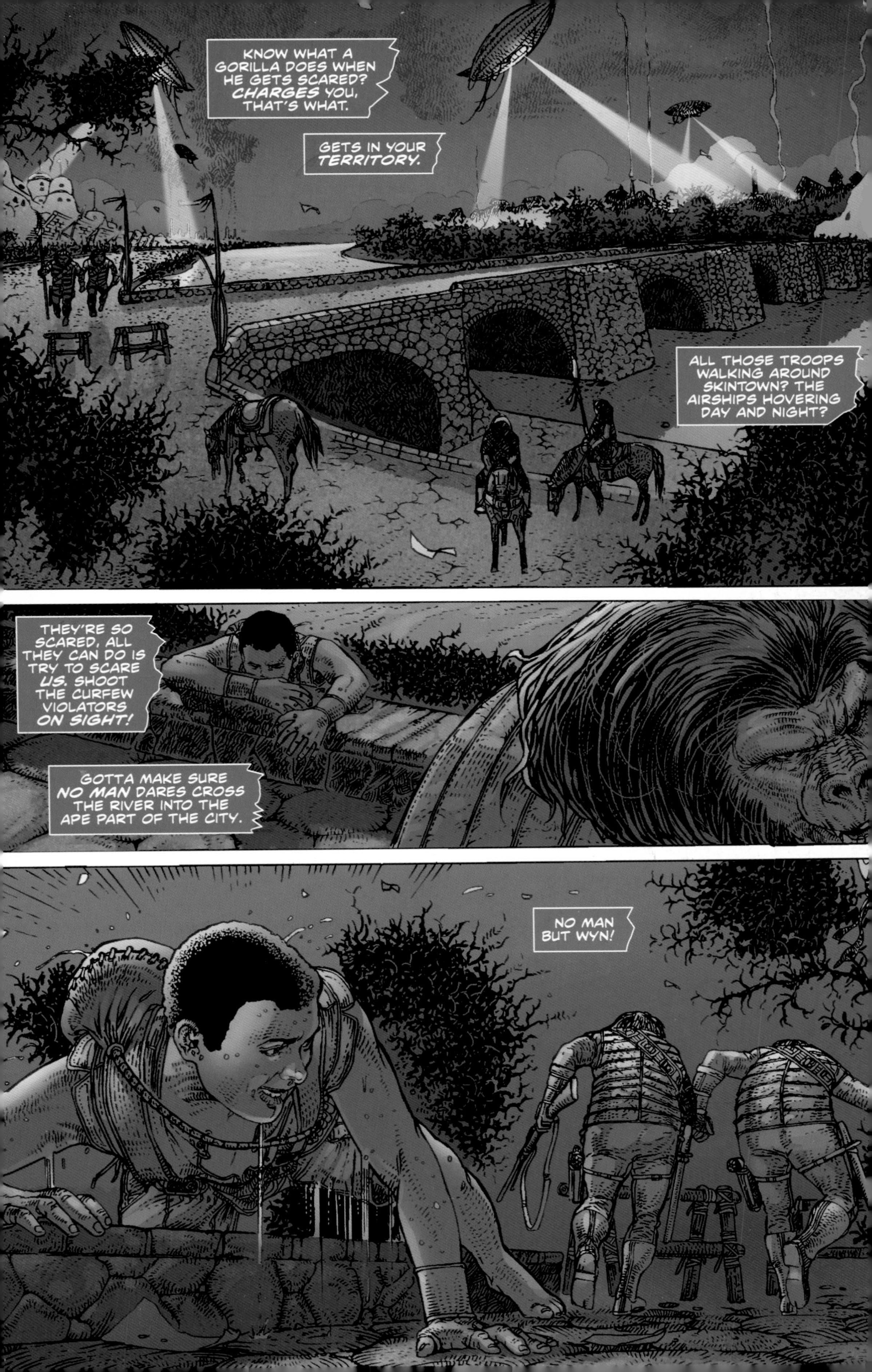
KNOW WHAT A GORILLA DOES WHEN HE GETS SCARED? CHARGES YOU, THAT'S WHAT.
GETS IN YOUR TERRITORY.
ALL THOSE TROOPS WALKING AROUND SKINTOWN? THE AIRSHIPS HOVERING DAY AND NIGHT?
THEY'RE SO SCARED, ALL THEY CAN DO IS TRY TO SCARE US. SHOOT THE CURFEW VIOLATORS ON SIGHT!
GOTTA MAKE SURE NO MAN DARES CROSS THE RIVER INTO THE APE PART OF THE CITY.
NO MAN BUT WYN!

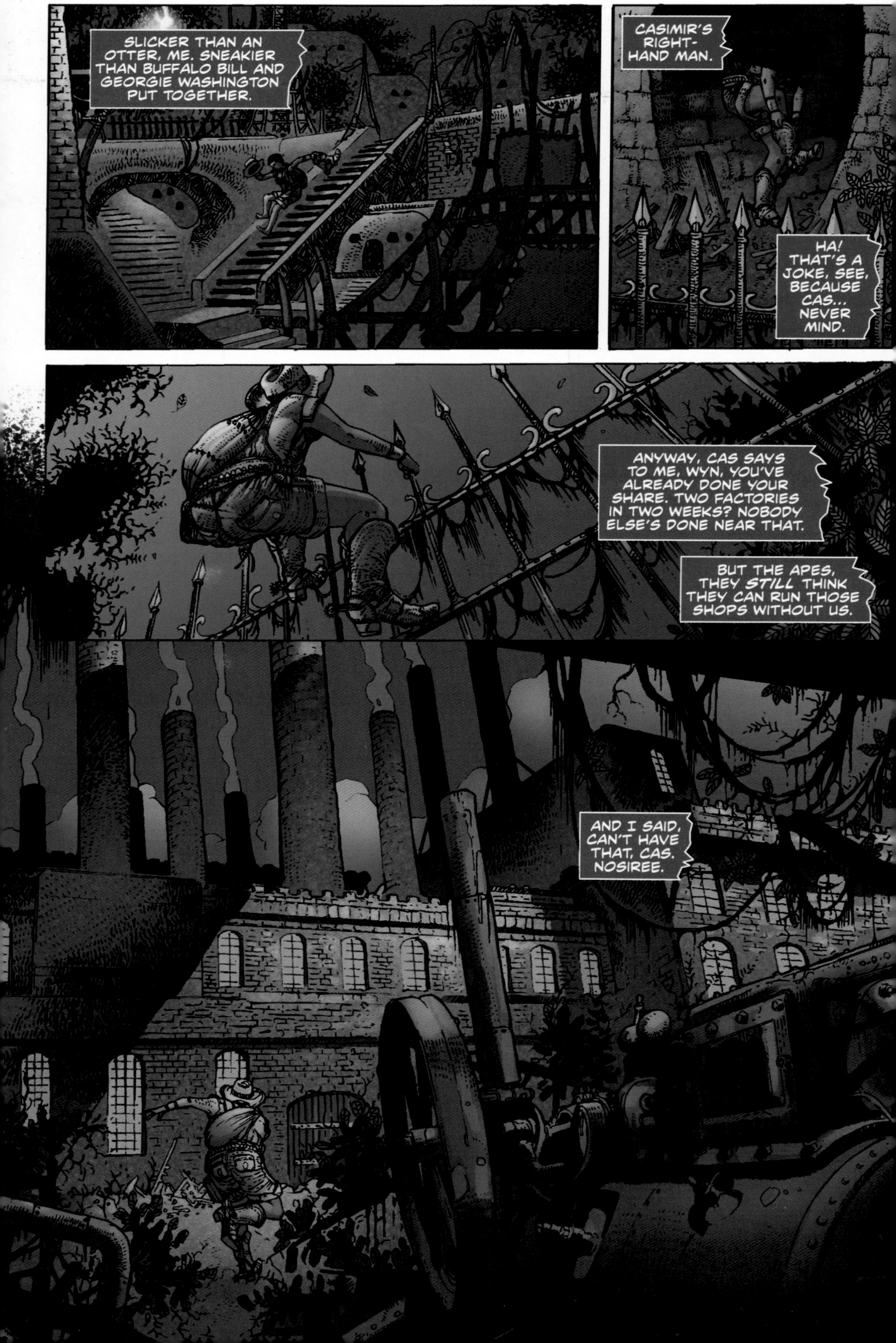
SLICKER THAN AN OTTER, ME. SNEAKIER THAN BUFFALO BILL AND GEORGIE WASHINGTON PUT TOGETHER.
CASIMIR'S RIGHT-HAND MAN.
HA! THAT'S A JOKE, SEE, BECAUSE CAS... NEVER MIND.
ANYWAY, CAS SAYS TO ME, WYN, YOU'VE ALREADY DONE YOUR SHARE. TWO FACTORIES IN TWO WEEKS? NOBODY ELSE'S DONE NEAR THAT.
BUT THE APES, THEY *STILL* THINK THEY CAN RUN THOSE SHOPS WITHOUT US.
AND I SAID, CAN'T HAVE THAT, CAS. NOSIREE.

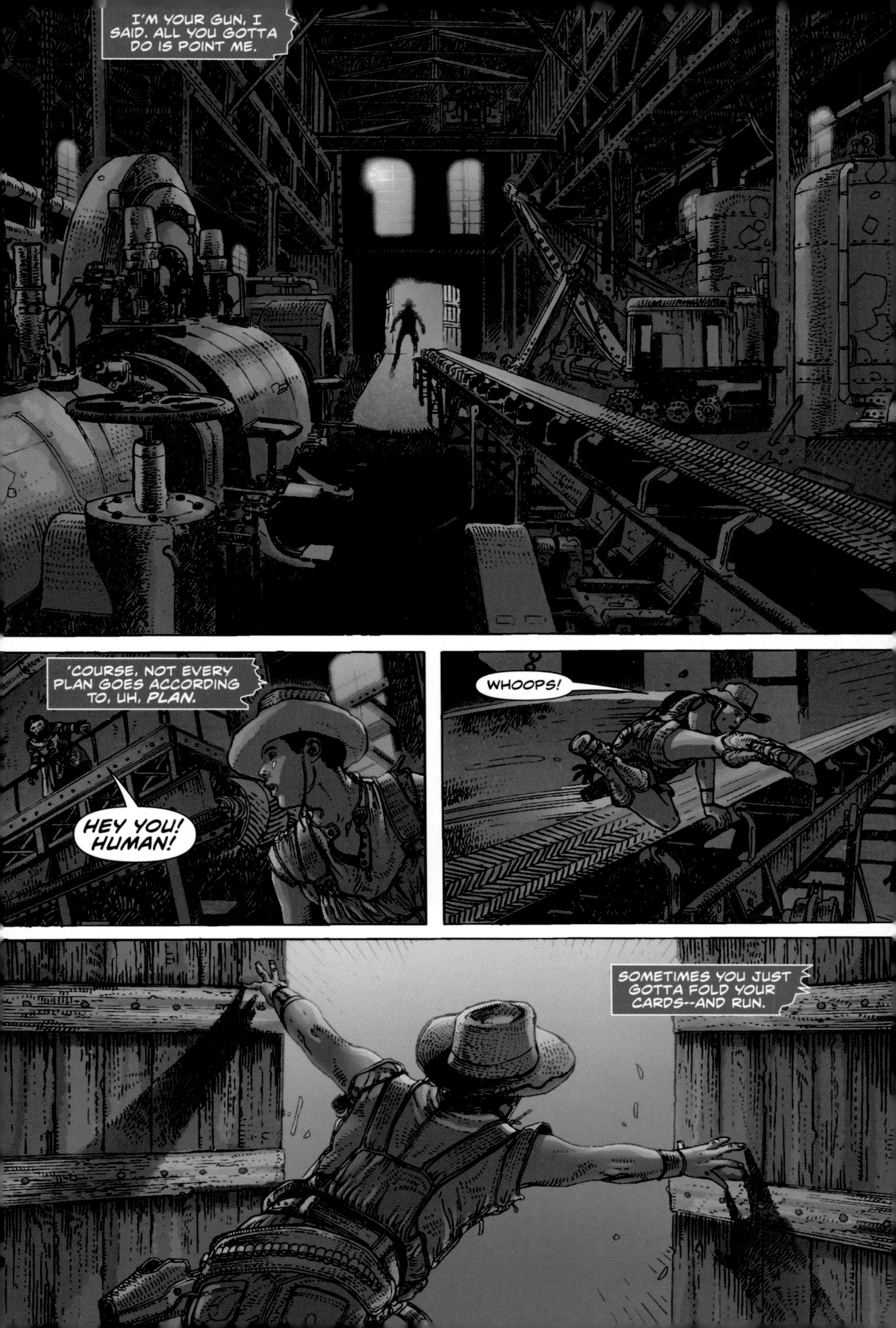
I'M YOUR GUN, I SAID. ALL YOU GOTTA DO IS POINT ME.
'COURSE, NOT EVERY PLAN GOES ACCORDING TO, UH, *PLAN*.
*HEY YOU! HUMAN!*
WHOOPS!
SOMETIMES YOU JUST GOTTA FOLD YOUR CARDS--AND RUN.

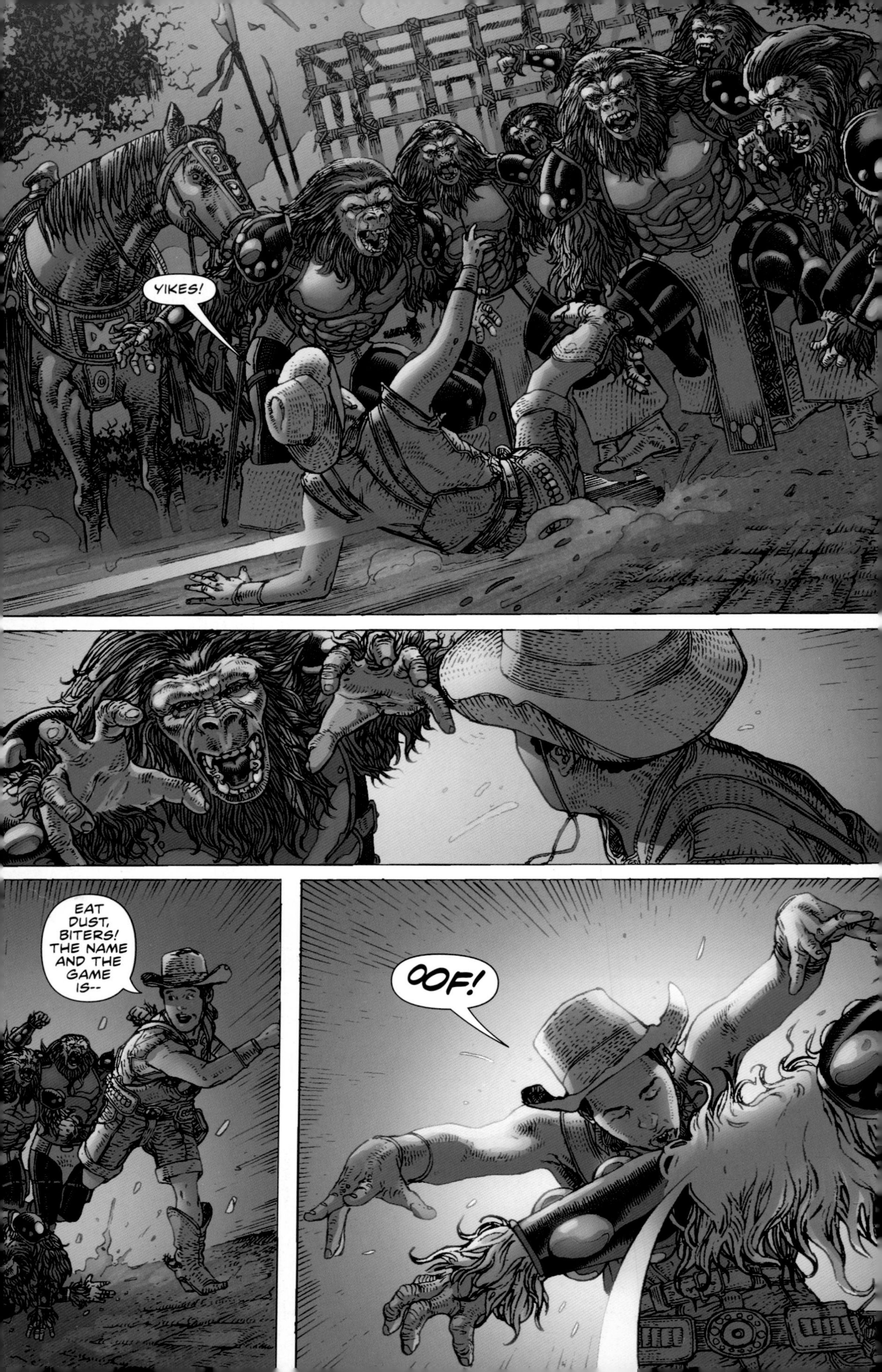
YIKES!
EAT DUST, BITERS! THE NAME AND THE GAME IS--
OOF!

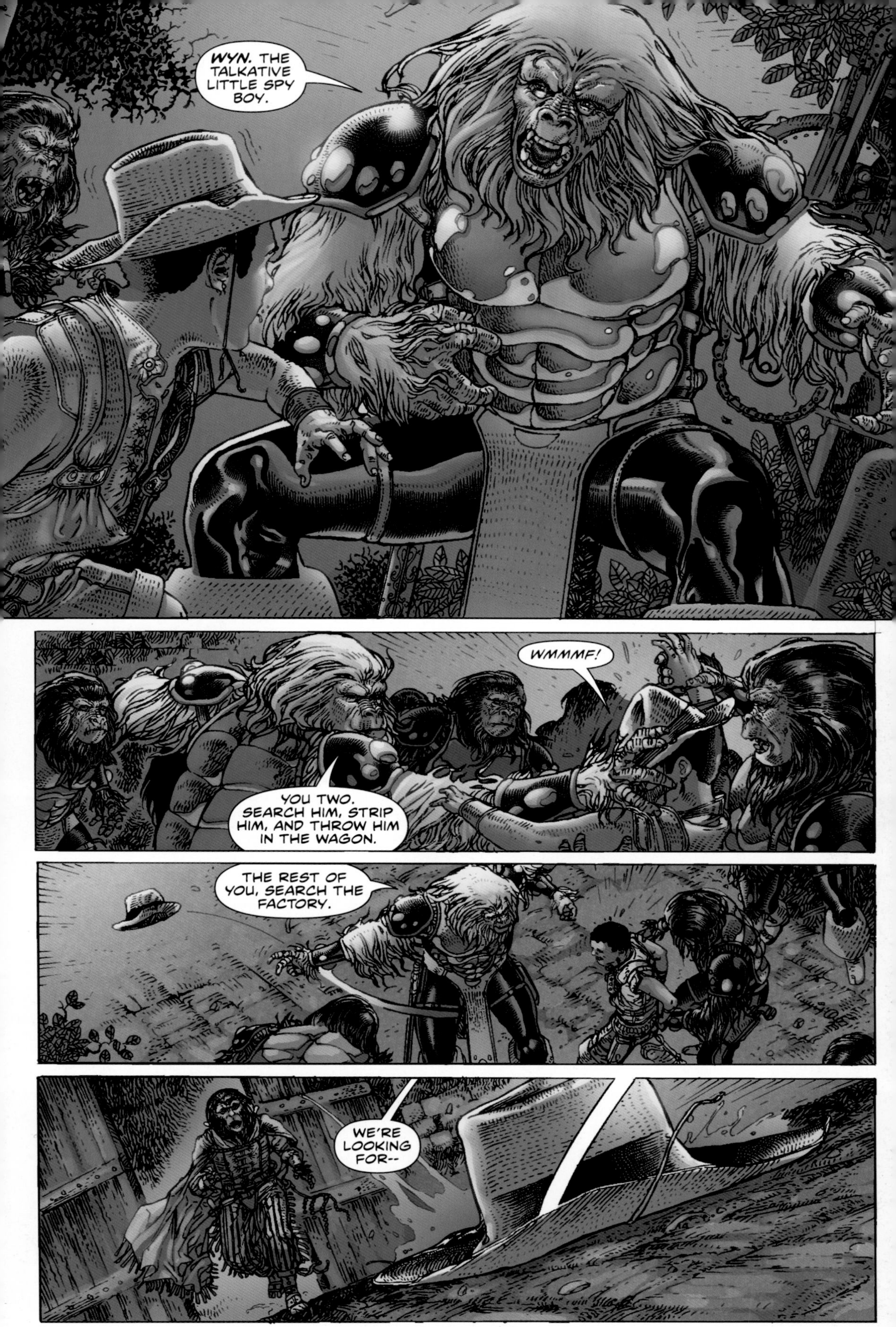
WYN. THE TALKATIVE LITTLE SPY BOY.
WMMMF!
YOU TWO. SEARCH HIM, STRIP HIM, AND THROW HIM IN THE WAGON.
THE REST OF YOU, SEARCH THE FACTORY.
WE'RE LOOKING FOR--

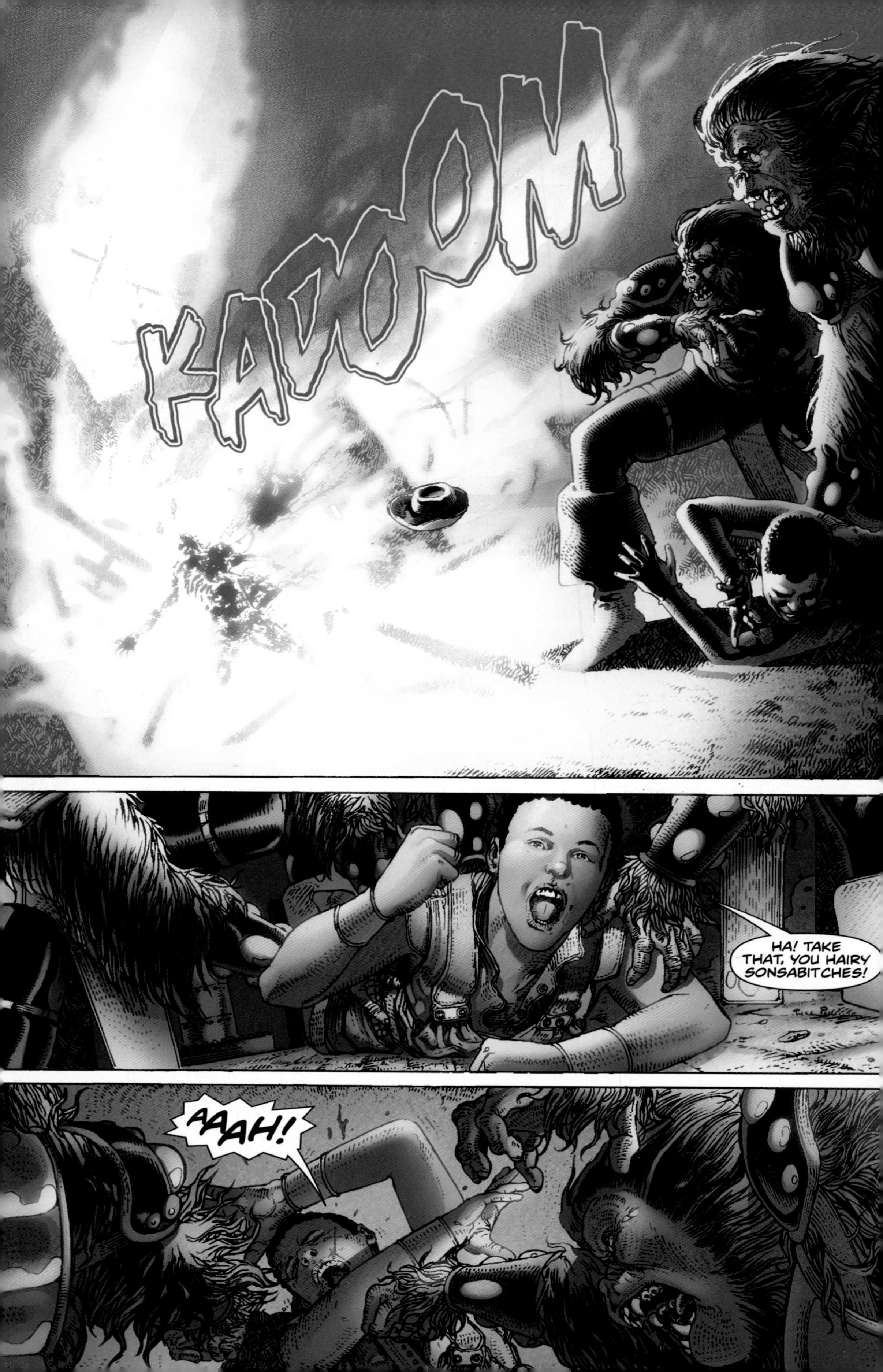
KADOOM
HA! TAKE THAT, YOU HAIRY SONSABITCHES!
AAAH!

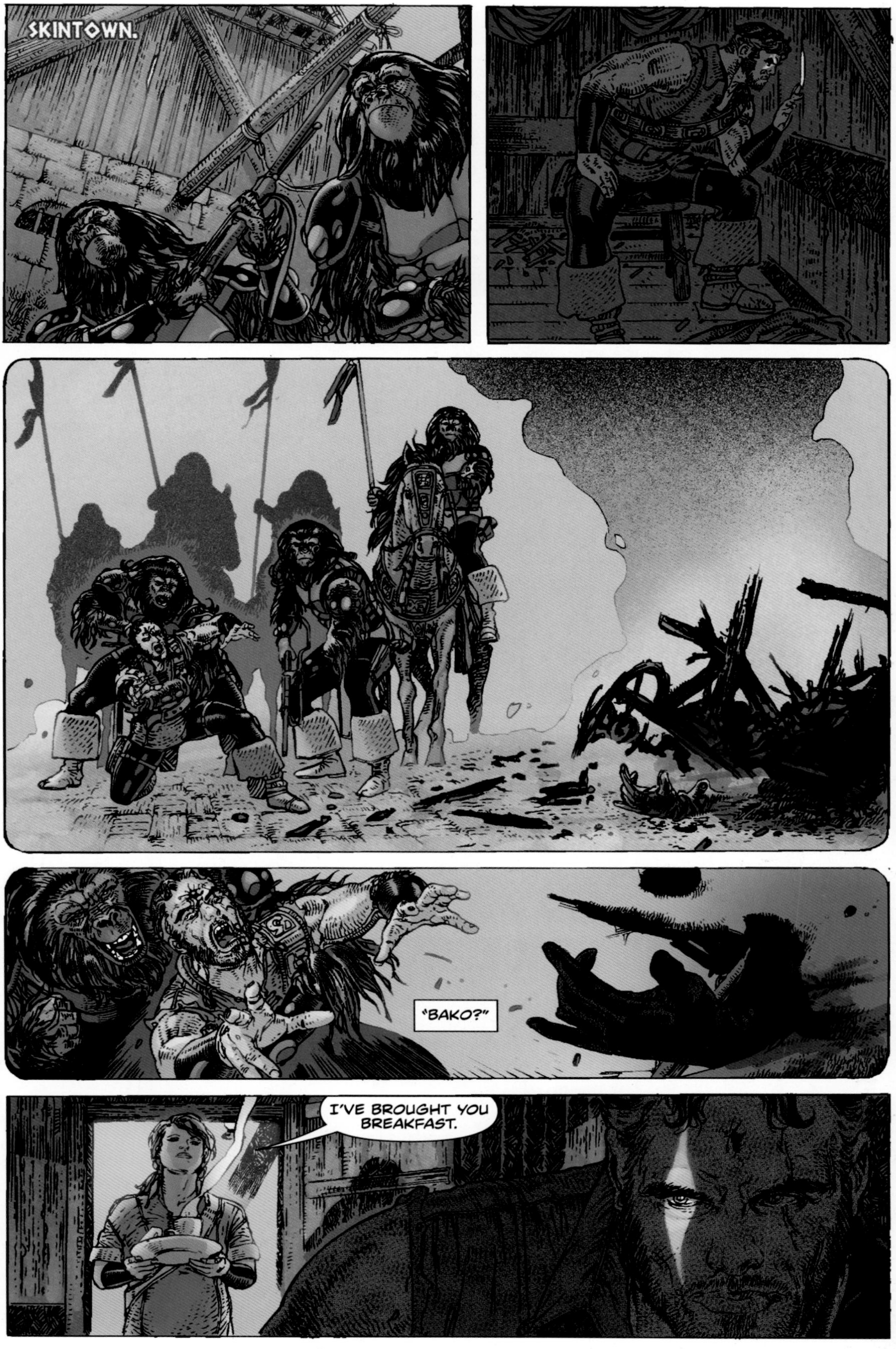
SKINTOWN.
"BAKO?"
I'VE BROUGHT YOU BREAKFAST.

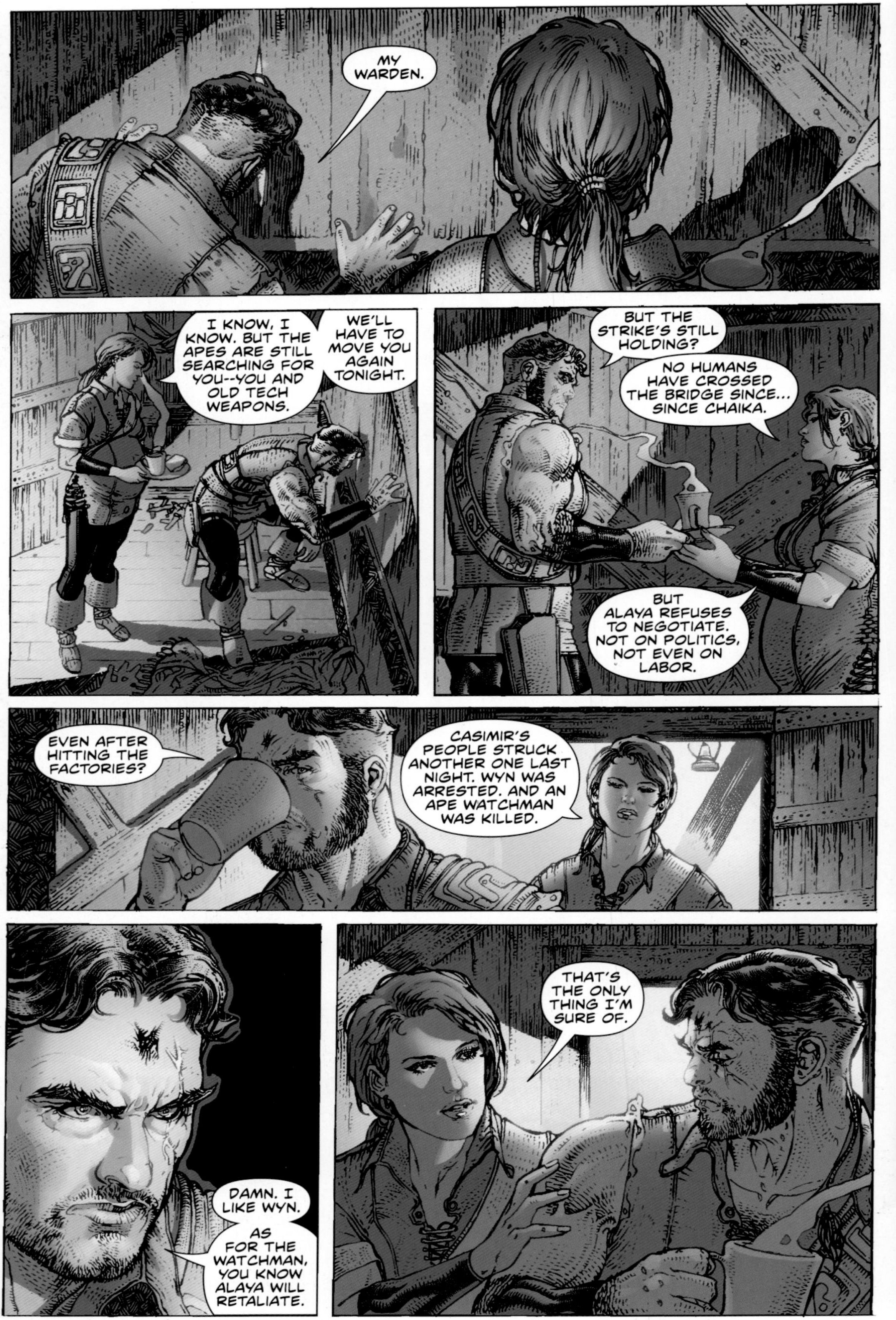
MY WARDEN.
I KNOW, I KNOW. BUT THE APES ARE STILL SEARCHING FOR YOU--YOU AND OLD TECH WEAPONS.
WE'LL HAVE TO MOVE YOU AGAIN TONIGHT.
BUT THE STRIKE'S STILL HOLDING?
NO HUMANS HAVE CROSSED THE BRIDGE SINCE... SINCE CHAIKA.
BUT ALAYA REFUSES TO NEGOTIATE. NOT ON POLITICS, NOT EVEN ON LABOR.
EVEN AFTER HITTING THE FACTORIES?
CASIMIR'S PEOPLE STRUCK ANOTHER ONE LAST NIGHT. WYN WAS ARRESTED. AND AN APE WATCHMAN WAS KILLED.
DAMN. I LIKE WYN.
AS FOR THE WATCHMAN, YOU KNOW ALAYA WILL RETALIATE.
THAT'S THE ONLY THING I'M SURE OF.

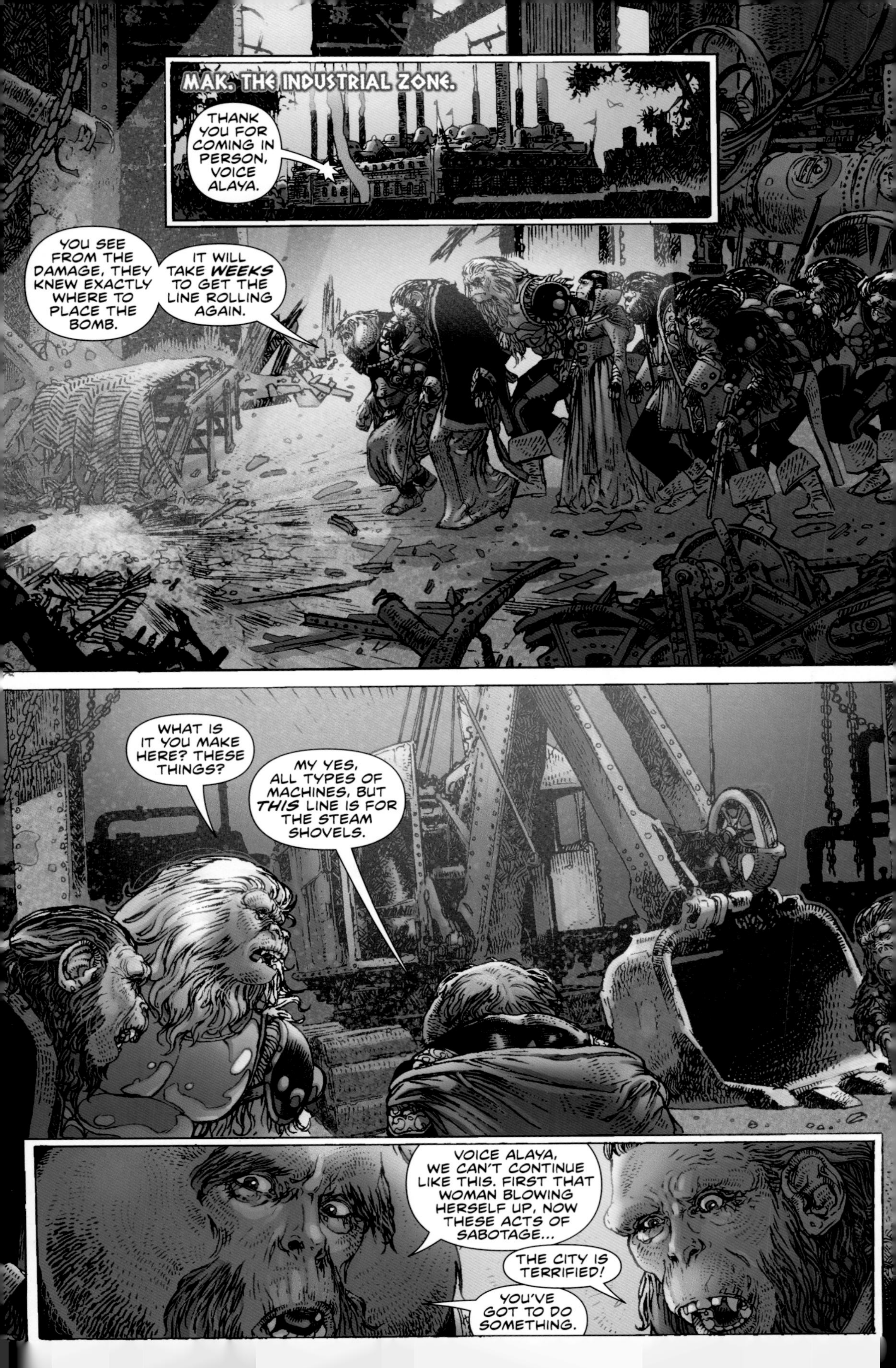
MAK. THE INDUSTRIAL ZONE.
THANK YOU FOR COMING IN PERSON, VOICE ALAYA.
YOU SEE FROM THE DAMAGE, THEY KNEW EXACTLY WHERE TO PLACE THE BOMB.
IT WILL TAKE *WEEKS* TO GET THE LINE ROLLING AGAIN.
WHAT IS IT YOU MAKE HERE? THESE THINGS?
MY YES, ALL TYPES OF MACHINES, BUT *THIS* LINE IS FOR THE STEAM SHOVELS.
VOICE ALAYA, WE CAN'T CONTINUE LIKE THIS. FIRST THAT WOMAN BLOWING HERSELF UP, NOW THESE ACTS OF SABOTAGE...
THE CITY IS TERRIFIED!
YOU'VE GOT TO DO SOMETHING.

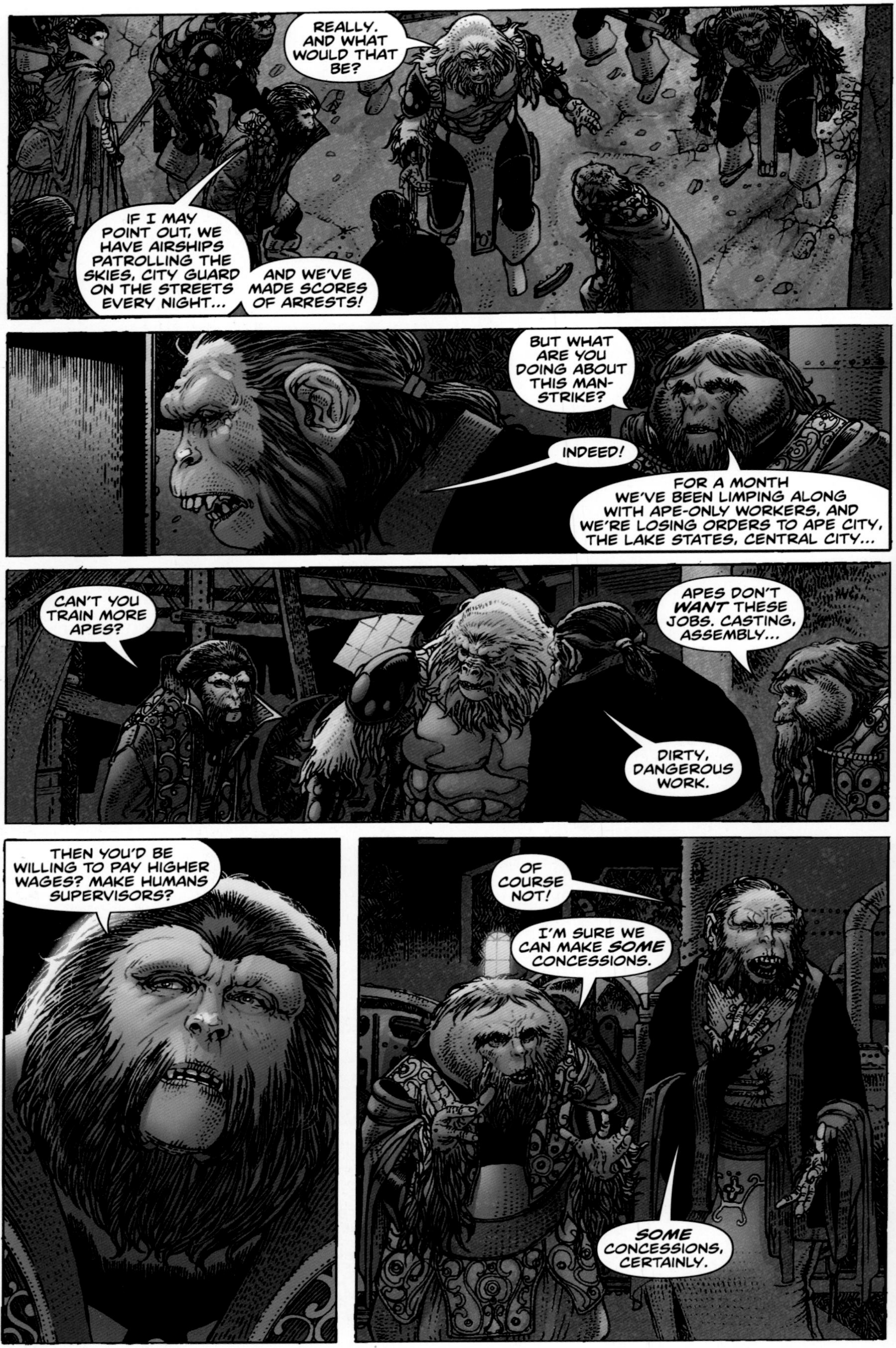
REALLY. AND WHAT WOULD THAT BE?
IF I MAY POINT OUT, WE HAVE AIRSHIPS PATROLLING THE SKIES, CITY GUARD ON THE STREETS EVERY NIGHT...
AND WE'VE MADE SCORES OF ARRESTS!
BUT WHAT ARE YOU DOING ABOUT THIS MAN-STRIKE?
INDEED!
FOR A MONTH WE'VE BEEN LIMPING ALONG WITH APE-ONLY WORKERS, AND WE'RE LOSING ORDERS TO APE CITY, THE LAKE STATES, CENTRAL CITY...
CAN'T YOU TRAIN MORE APES?
APES DON'T *WANT* THESE JOBS. CASTING, ASSEMBLY...
DIRTY, DANGEROUS WORK.
THEN YOU'D BE WILLING TO PAY HIGHER WAGES? MAKE HUMANS SUPERVISORS?
OF COURSE NOT!
I'M SURE WE CAN MAKE *SOME* CONCESSIONS.
*SOME* CONCESSIONS, CERTAINLY.

HOW ABOUT GIVING THEM A SPOT ON THE COUNCIL?

PARDON?

THAT'S WHAT THEY WANT--FULL REPRESENTATION. VOTING RIGHTS EQUAL TO AN APE'S.

RIDICULOUS!

WE ALREADY GIVE HUMANS TWO CHAIRS AT THE MERCHANT COMMISSION. BUT GOVERNMENT SEATS?

HA! WHAT NEXT, THEIR OWN CITYSTATE?

IT'LL BE DELPHI ALL OVER AGAIN.

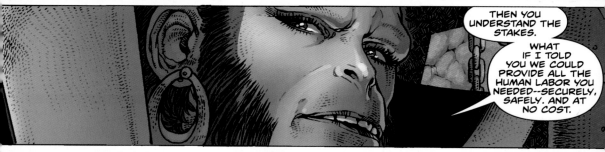

THEN YOU UNDERSTAND THE STAKES.

WHAT IF I TOLD YOU WE COULD PROVIDE ALL THE HUMAN LABOR YOU NEEDED--SECURELY, SAFELY. AND AT NO COST.

FREE?

PERHAPS YOU SHOULD EXPLAIN, VOICE ALAYA.

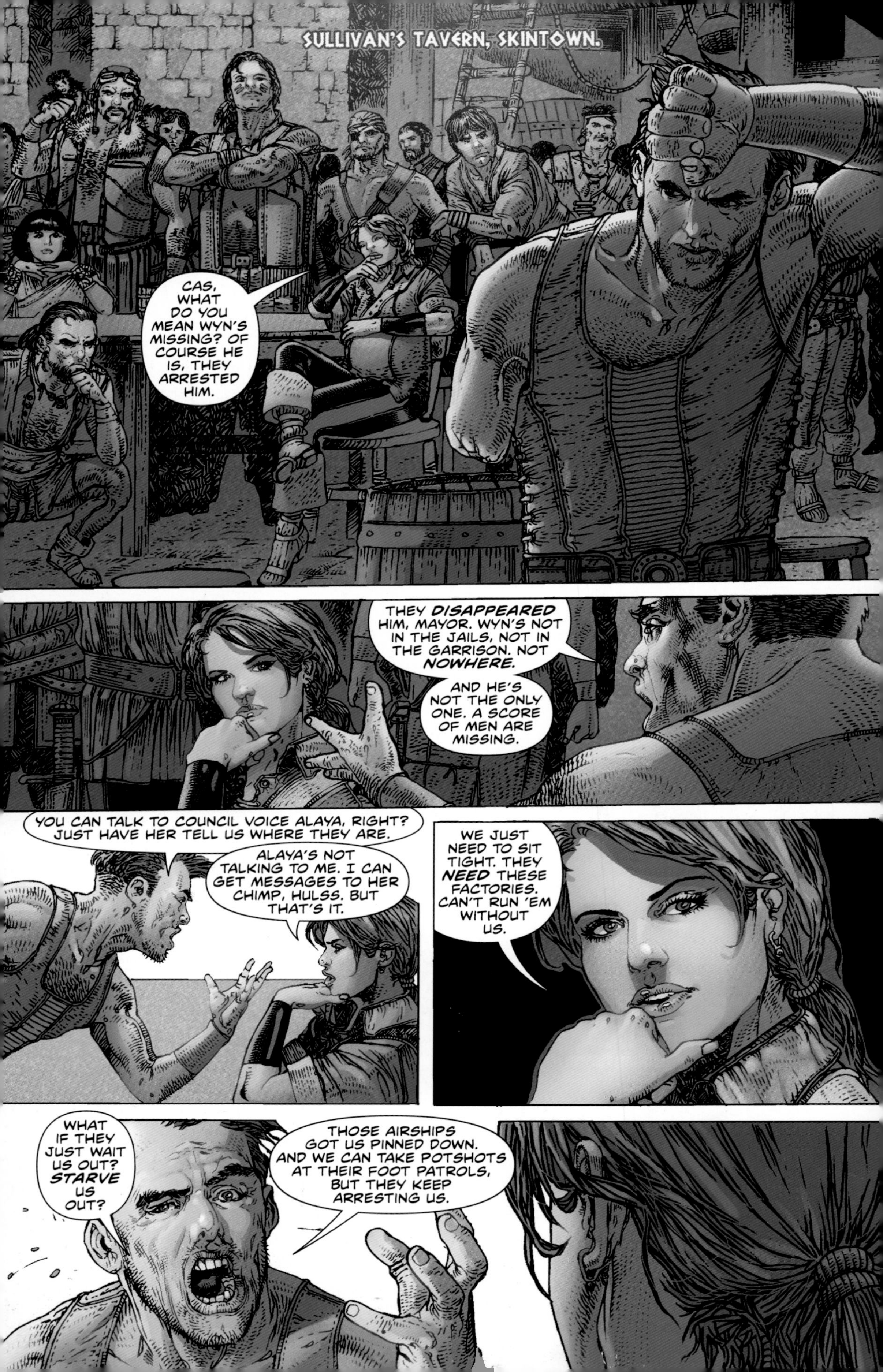
SULLIVAN'S TAVERN, SKINTOWN.
CAS, WHAT DO YOU MEAN WYN'S MISSING? OF COURSE HE IS, THEY ARRESTED HIM.
THEY DISAPPEARED HIM, MAYOR. WYN'S NOT IN THE JAILS, NOT IN THE GARRISON. NOT NOWHERE.
AND HE'S NOT THE ONLY ONE. A SCORE OF MEN ARE MISSING.
YOU CAN TALK TO COUNCIL VOICE ALAYA, RIGHT? JUST HAVE HER TELL US WHERE THEY ARE.
ALAYA'S NOT TALKING TO ME. I CAN GET MESSAGES TO HER CHIMP, HULSS. BUT THAT'S IT.
WE JUST NEED TO SIT TIGHT. THEY NEED THESE FACTORIES. CAN'T RUN 'EM WITHOUT US.
WHAT IF THEY JUST WAIT US OUT? STARVE US OUT?
THOSE AIRSHIPS GOT US PINNED DOWN. AND WE CAN TAKE POTSHOTS AT THEIR FOOT PATROLS, BUT THEY KEEP ARRESTING US.

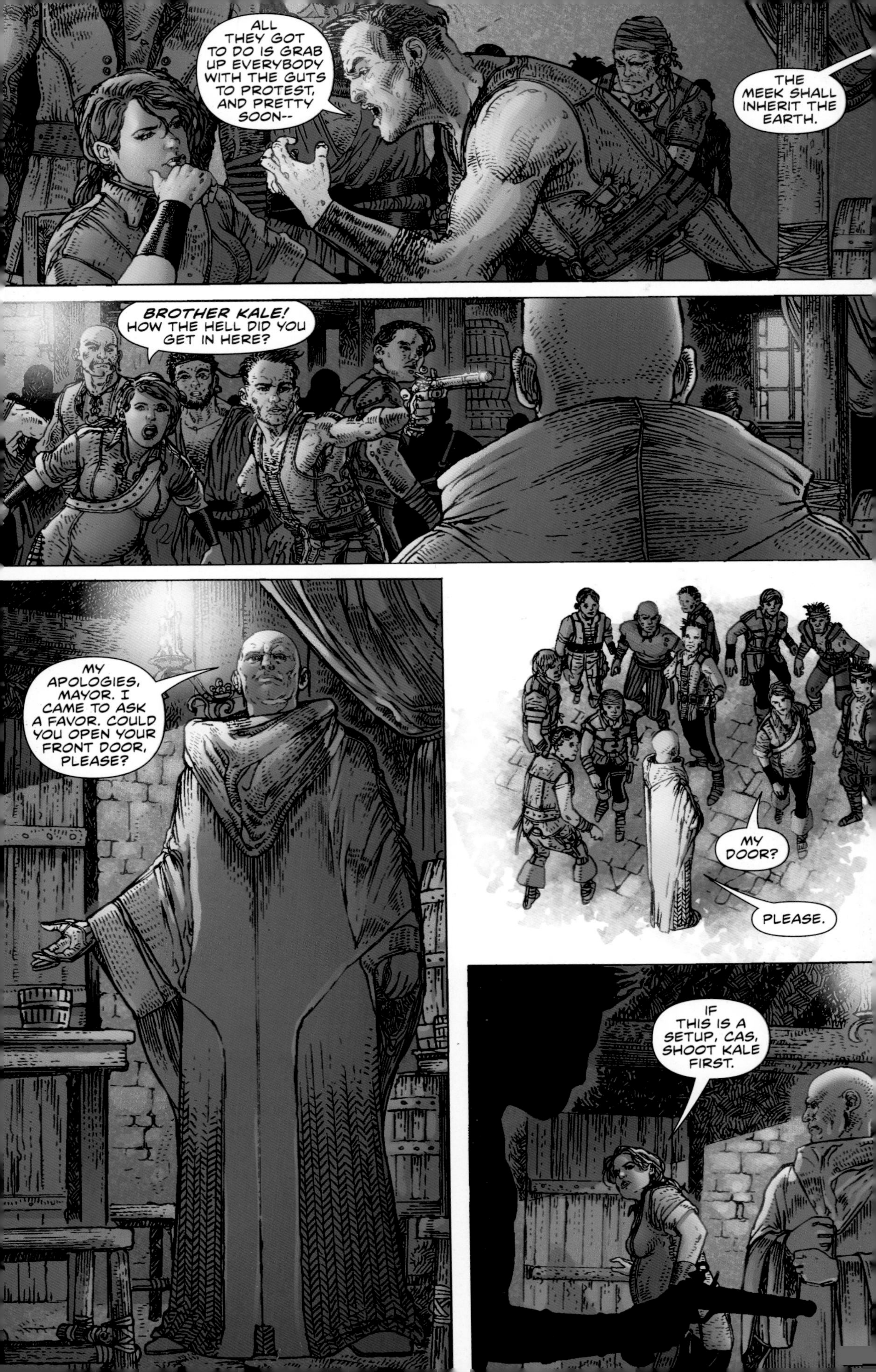
ALL THEY GOT TO DO IS GRAB UP EVERYBODY WITH THE GUTS TO PROTEST, AND PRETTY SOON--
THE MEEK SHALL INHERIT THE EARTH.
*BROTHER KALE!* HOW THE HELL DID YOU GET IN HERE?
MY APOLOGIES, MAYOR. I CAME TO ASK A FAVOR. COULD YOU OPEN YOUR FRONT DOOR, PLEASE?
MY DOOR?
PLEASE.
IF THIS IS A SETUP, CAS, SHOOT KALE FIRST.

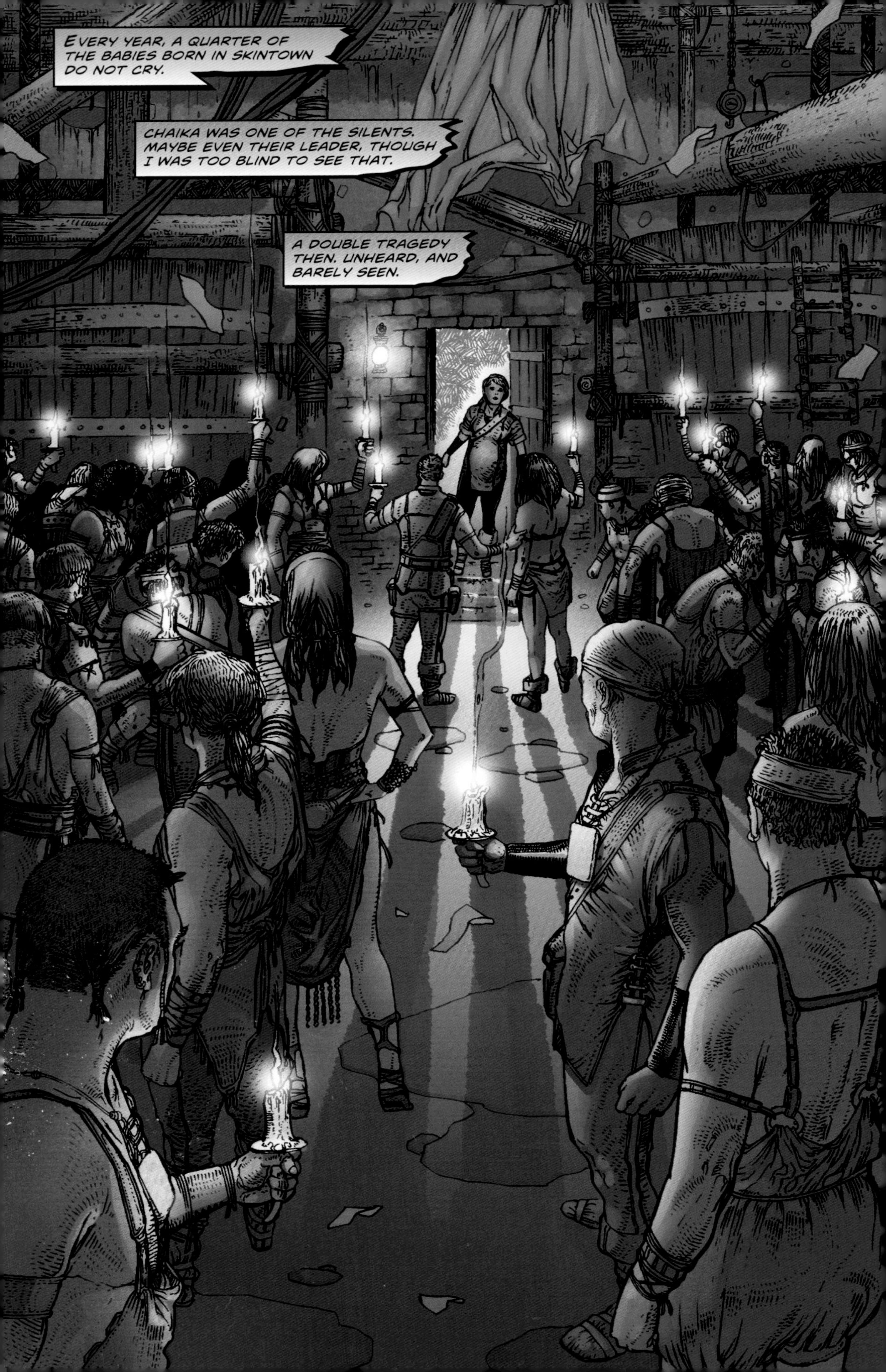
EVERY YEAR, A QUARTER OF THE BABIES BORN IN SKINTOWN DO NOT CRY.
CHAIKA WAS ONE OF THE SILENTS. MAYBE EVEN THEIR LEADER, THOUGH I WAS TOO BLIND TO SEE THAT.
A DOUBLE TRAGEDY THEN. UNHEARD, AND BARELY SEEN.

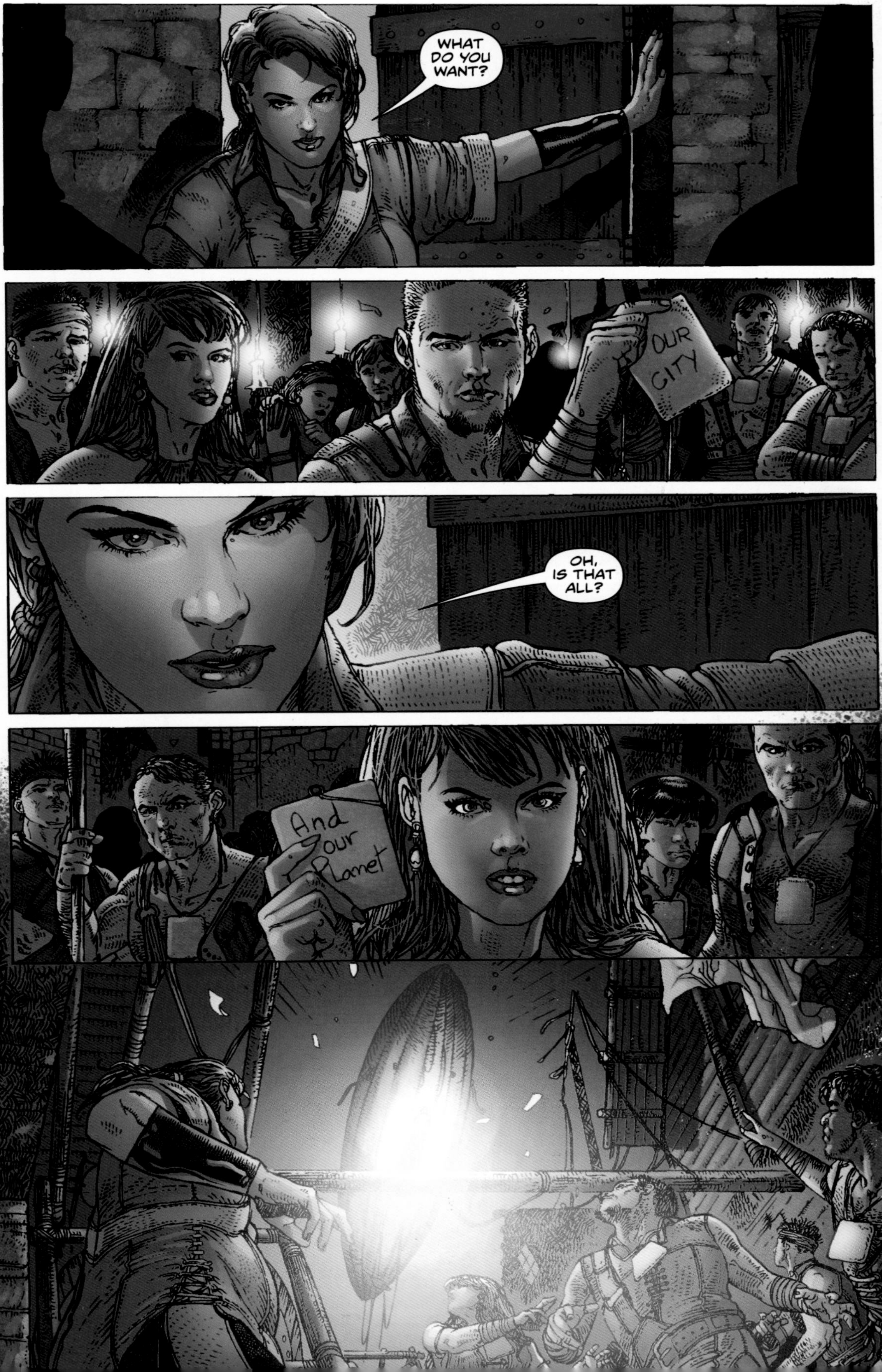
WHAT DO YOU WANT?
OUR CITY
OH, IS THAT ALL?
And our Planet

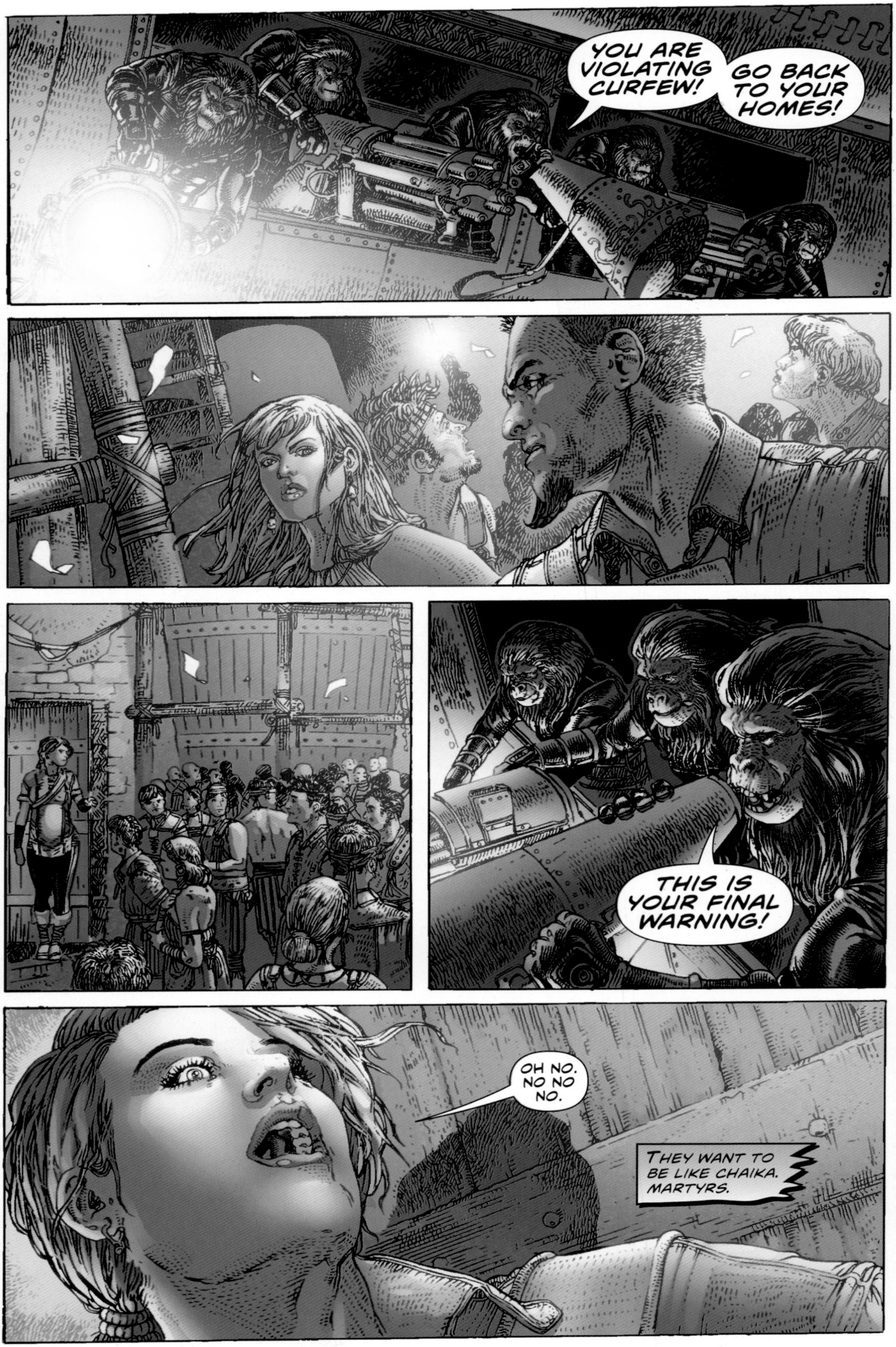
YOU ARE VIOLATING CURFEW!
GO BACK TO YOUR HOMES!
THIS IS YOUR FINAL WARNING!
OH NO. NO NO NO.
THEY WANT TO BE LIKE CHAIKA. MARTYRS.

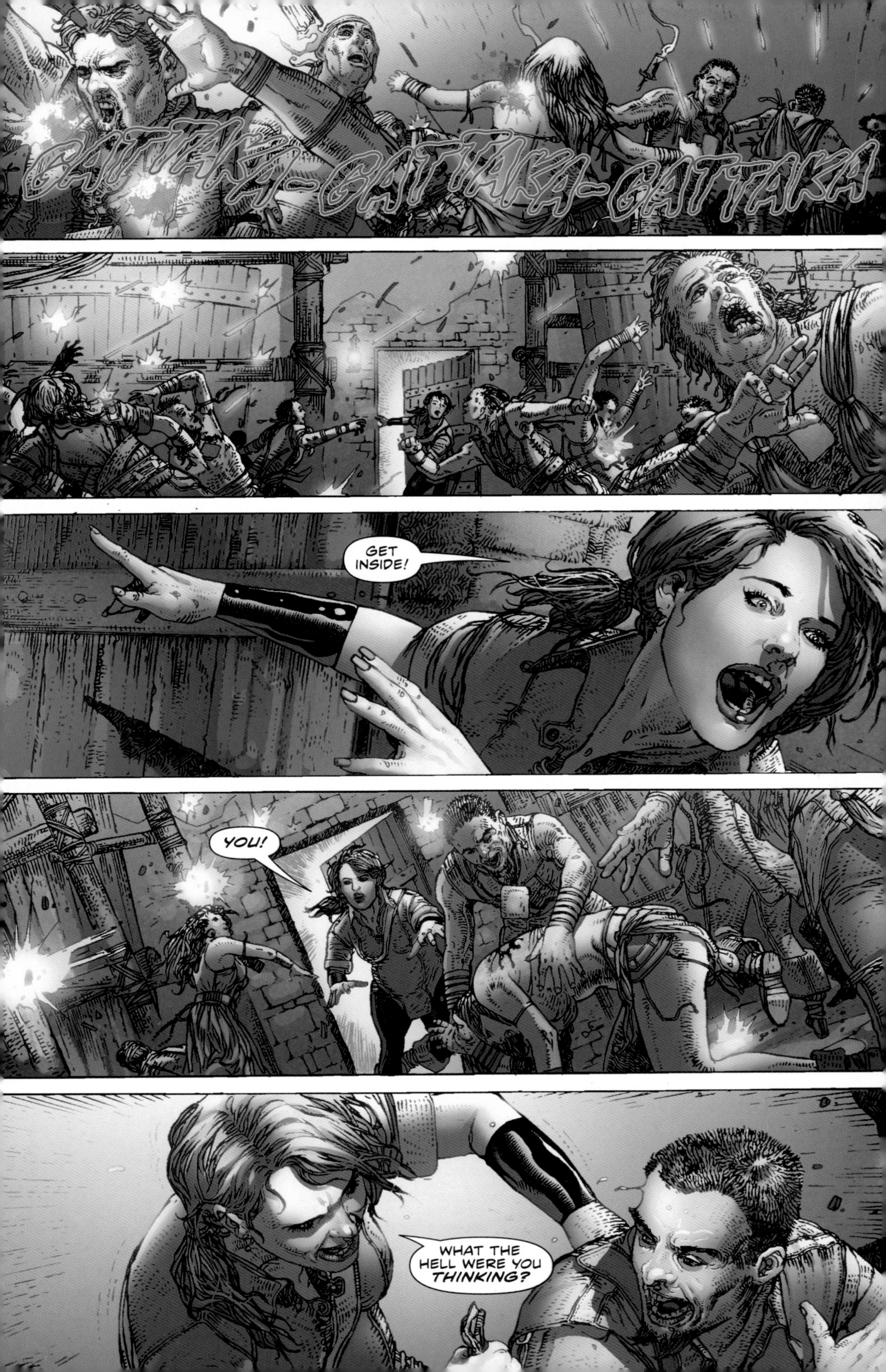
GATTAKA-GATTAKA-GATTAKA
GET INSIDE!
YOU!
WHAT THE HELL WERE YOU *THINKING?*

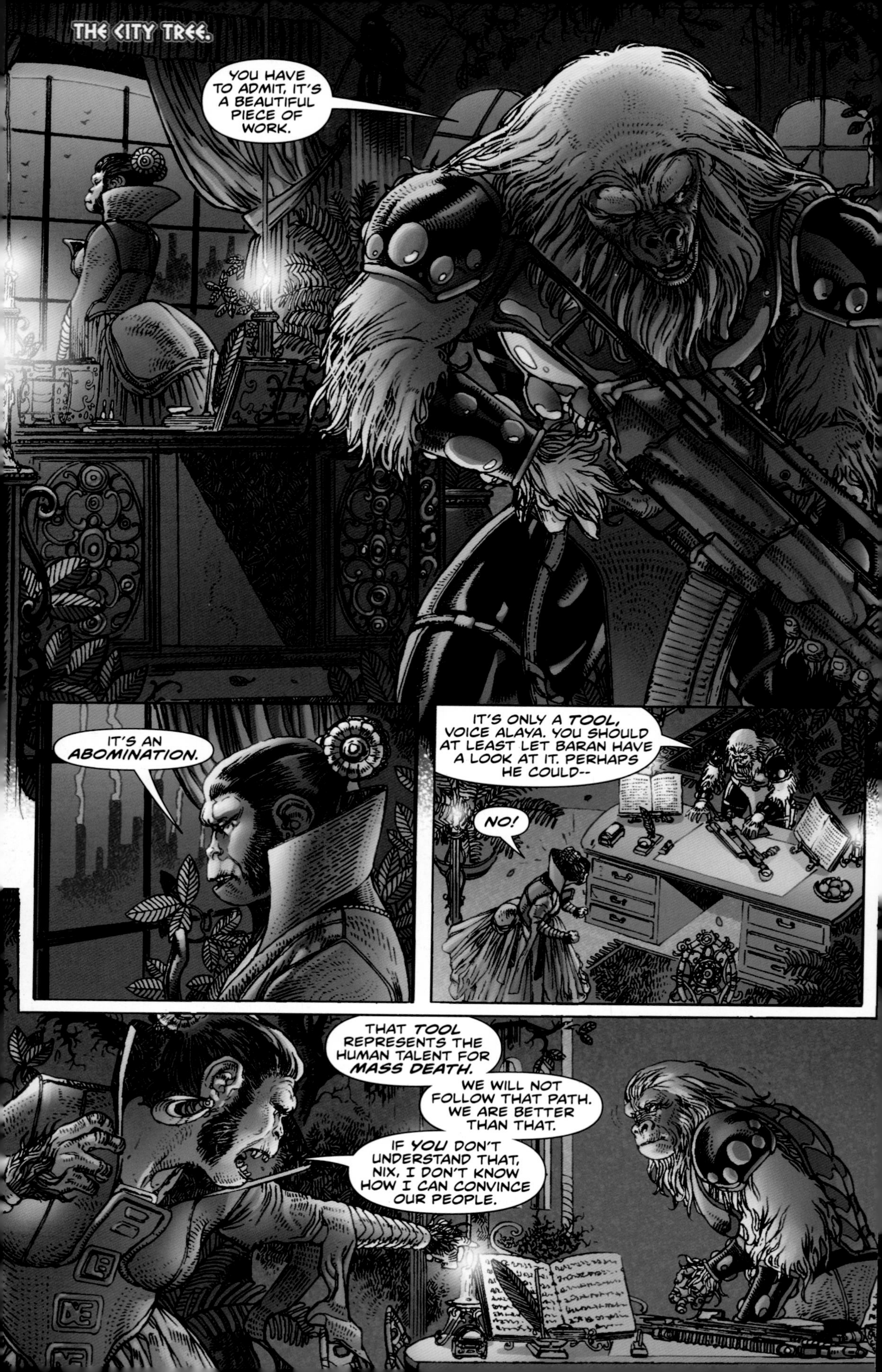
THE CITY TREE.
YOU HAVE TO ADMIT, IT'S A BEAUTIFUL PIECE OF WORK.
IT'S AN *ABOMINATION.*
IT'S ONLY A *TOOL,* VOICE ALAYA. YOU SHOULD AT LEAST LET BARAN HAVE A LOOK AT IT. PERHAPS HE COULD--
*NO!*
THAT *TOOL* REPRESENTS THE HUMAN TALENT FOR *MASS DEATH.*
WE WILL NOT FOLLOW THAT PATH. WE ARE BETTER THAN THAT.
IF *YOU* DON'T UNDERSTAND THAT, NIX, I DON'T KNOW HOW I CAN CONVINCE OUR PEOPLE.

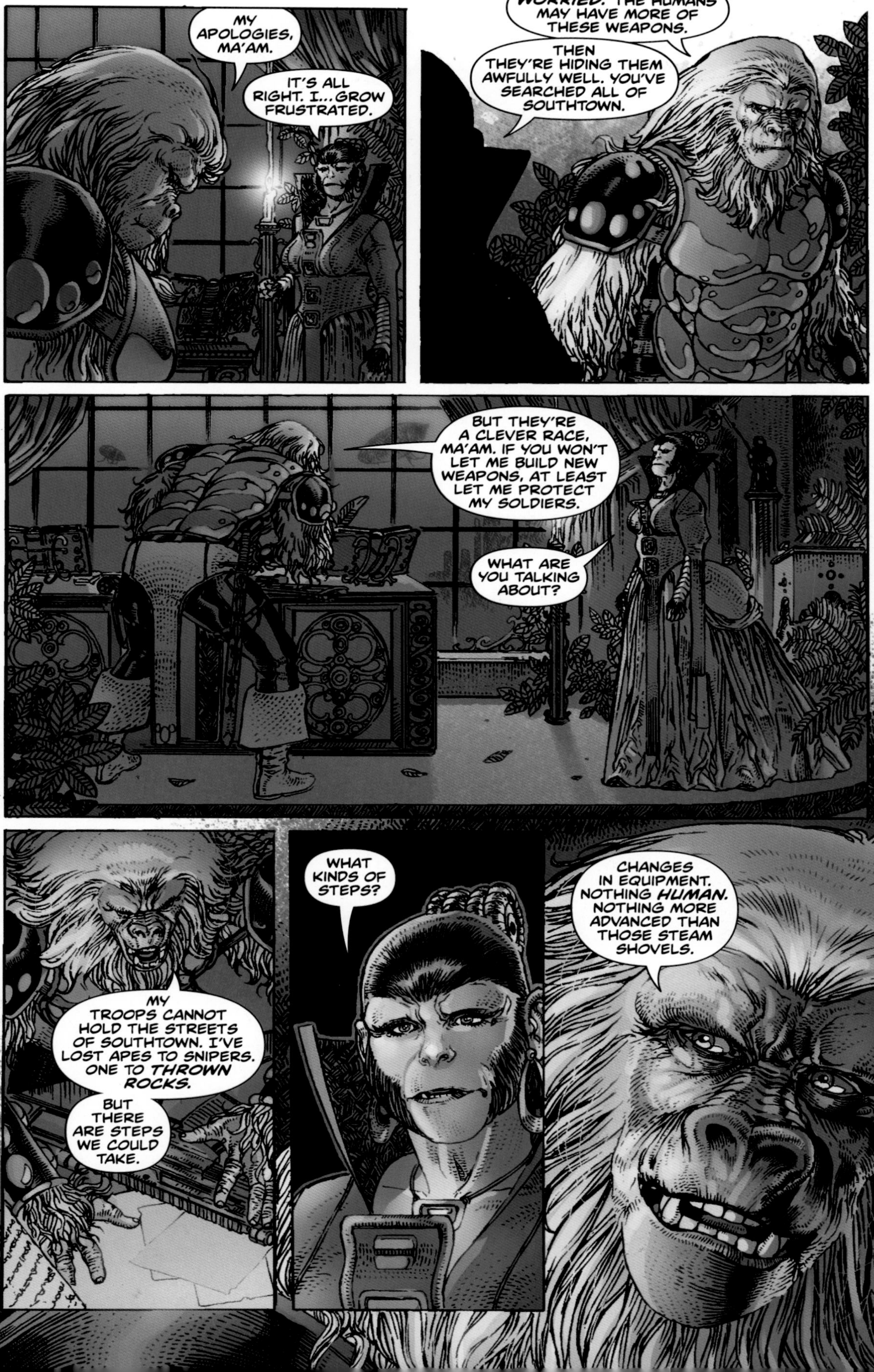
MY APOLOGIES, MA'AM.
IT'S ALL RIGHT. I...GROW FRUSTRATED.
AND I GROW WORRIED. THE HUMANS MAY HAVE MORE OF THESE WEAPONS.
THEN THEY'RE HIDING THEM AWFULLY WELL. YOU'VE SEARCHED ALL OF SOUTHTOWN.
BUT THEY'RE A CLEVER RACE, MA'AM. IF YOU WON'T LET ME BUILD NEW WEAPONS, AT LEAST LET ME PROTECT MY SOLDIERS.
WHAT ARE YOU TALKING ABOUT?
MY TROOPS CANNOT HOLD THE STREETS OF SOUTHTOWN. I'VE LOST APES TO SNIPERS. ONE TO THROWN ROCKS.
BUT THERE ARE STEPS WE COULD TAKE.
WHAT KINDS OF STEPS?
CHANGES IN EQUIPMENT. NOTHING HUMAN. NOTHING MORE ADVANCED THAN THOSE STEAM SHOVELS.

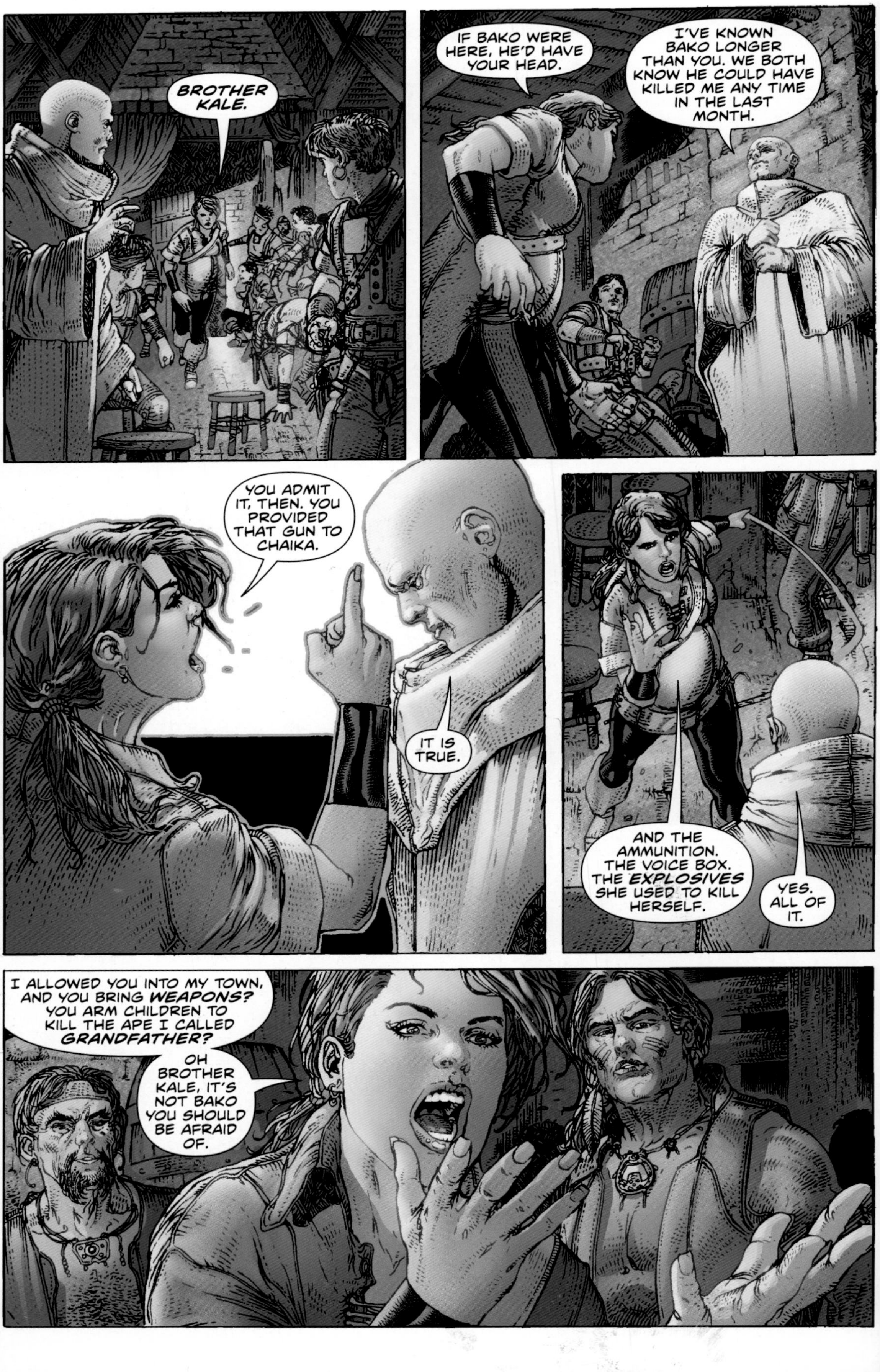
BROTHER KALE.
IF BAKO WERE HERE, HE'D HAVE YOUR HEAD.
I'VE KNOWN BAKO LONGER THAN YOU. WE BOTH KNOW HE COULD HAVE KILLED ME ANY TIME IN THE LAST MONTH.
YOU ADMIT IT, THEN. YOU PROVIDED THAT GUN TO CHAIKA.
IT IS TRUE.
AND THE AMMUNITION. THE VOICE BOX. THE EXPLOSIVES SHE USED TO KILL HERSELF.
YES. ALL OF IT.
I ALLOWED YOU INTO MY TOWN, AND YOU BRING WEAPONS? YOU ARM CHILDREN TO KILL THE APE I CALLED GRANDFATHER?
OH BROTHER KALE, IT'S NOT BAKO YOU SHOULD BE AFRAID OF.

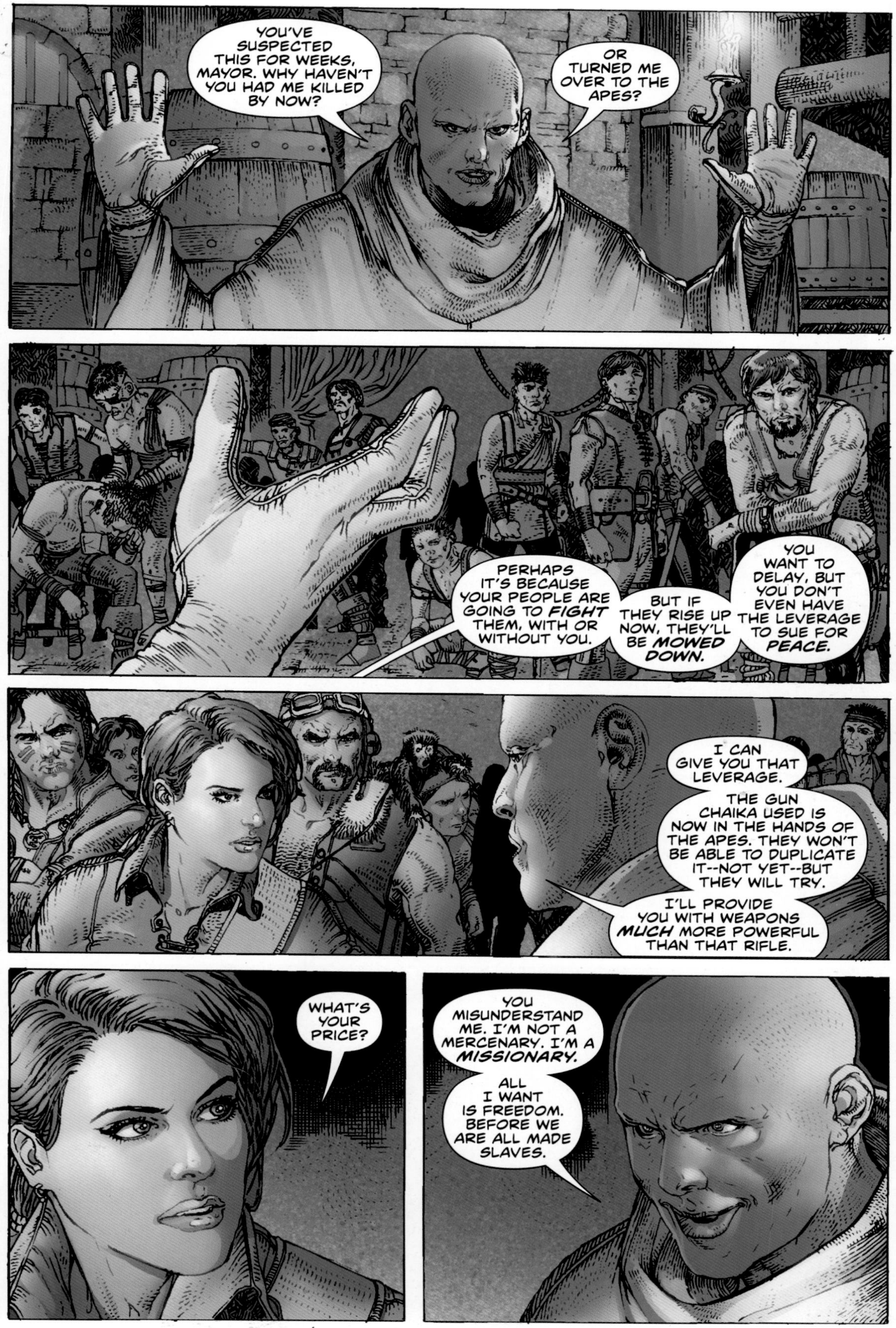
YOU'VE SUSPECTED THIS FOR WEEKS, MAYOR. WHY HAVEN'T YOU HAD ME KILLED BY NOW?
OR TURNED ME OVER TO THE APES?
PERHAPS IT'S BECAUSE YOUR PEOPLE ARE GOING TO FIGHT THEM, WITH OR WITHOUT YOU.
BUT IF THEY RISE UP NOW, THEY'LL BE MOWED DOWN.
YOU WANT TO DELAY, BUT YOU DON'T EVEN HAVE THE LEVERAGE TO SUE FOR PEACE.
I CAN GIVE YOU THAT LEVERAGE.
THE GUN CHAIKA USED IS NOW IN THE HANDS OF THE APES. THEY WON'T BE ABLE TO DUPLICATE IT--NOT YET--BUT THEY WILL TRY.
I'LL PROVIDE YOU WITH WEAPONS MUCH MORE POWERFUL THAN THAT RIFLE.
WHAT'S YOUR PRICE?
YOU MISUNDERSTAND ME. I'M NOT A MERCENARY. I'M A MISSIONARY.
ALL I WANT IS FREEDOM. BEFORE WE ARE ALL MADE SLAVES.

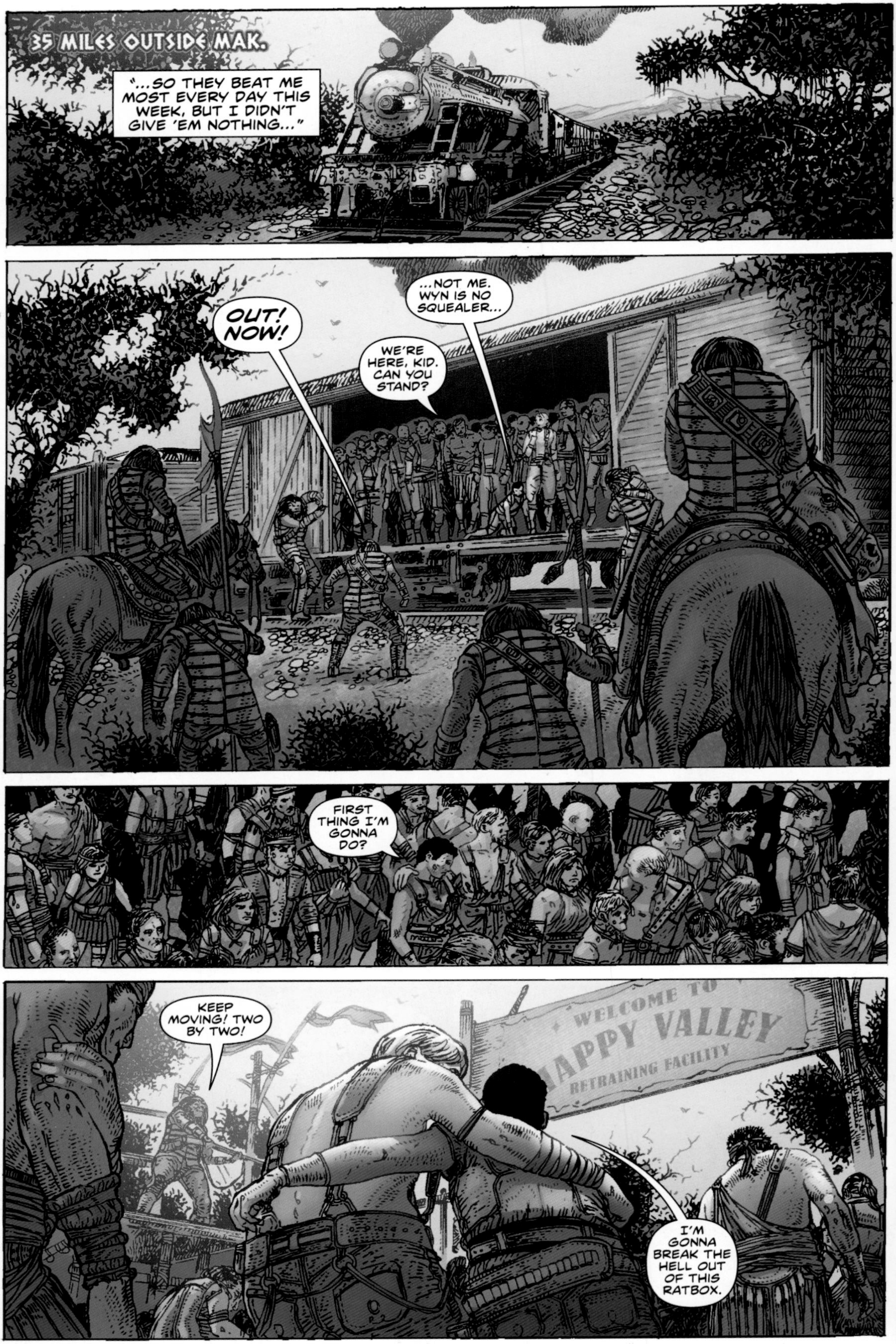
35 MILES OUTSIDE MAK.
"...SO THEY BEAT ME MOST EVERY DAY THIS WEEK, BUT I DIDN'T GIVE 'EM NOTHING..."
OUT! NOW!
...NOT ME. WYN IS NO SQUEALER...
WE'RE HERE, KID. CAN YOU STAND?
FIRST THING I'M GONNA DO?
KEEP MOVING! TWO BY TWO!
WELCOME TO
HAPPY VALLEY
RETRAINING FACILITY
I'M GONNA BREAK THE HELL OUT OF THIS RATBOX.

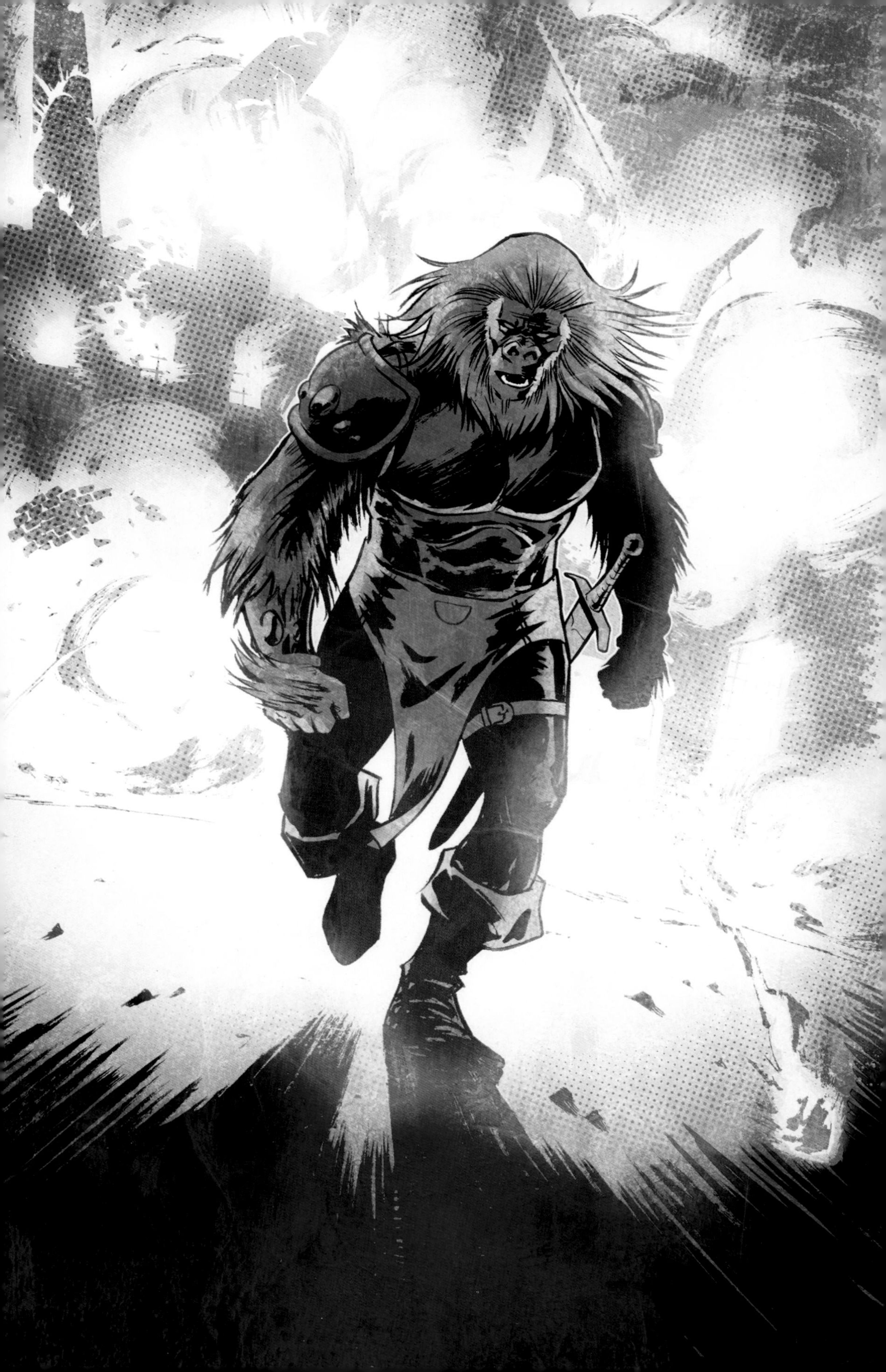

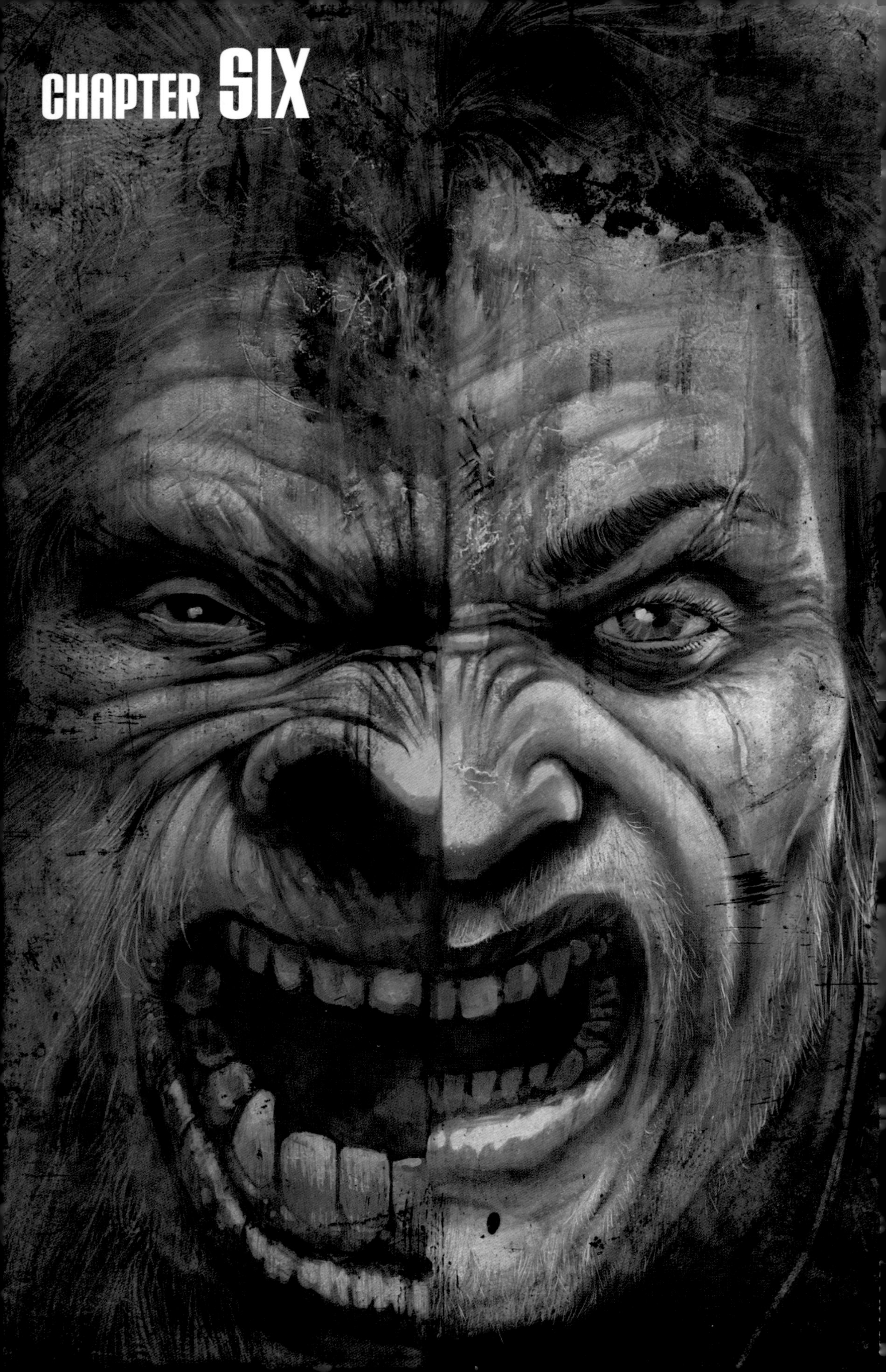
CHAPTER SIX

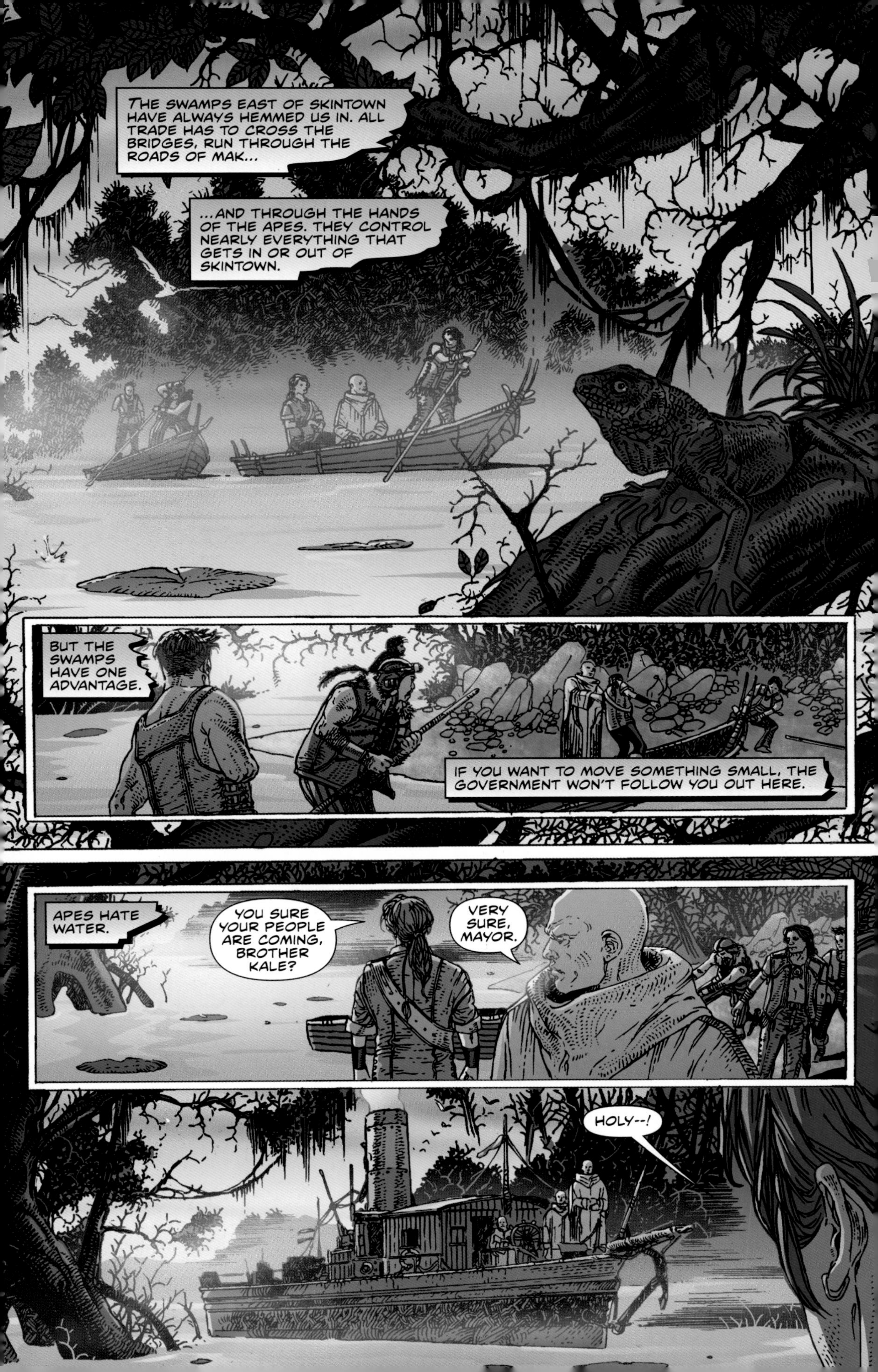
THE SWAMPS EAST OF SKINTOWN HAVE ALWAYS HEMMED US IN. ALL TRADE HAS TO CROSS THE BRIDGES, RUN THROUGH THE ROADS OF MAK...
...AND THROUGH THE HANDS OF THE APES. THEY CONTROL NEARLY EVERYTHING THAT GETS IN OR OUT OF SKINTOWN.
BUT THE SWAMPS HAVE ONE ADVANTAGE.
IF YOU WANT TO MOVE SOMETHING SMALL, THE GOVERNMENT WON'T FOLLOW YOU OUT HERE.
APES HATE WATER.
YOU SURE YOUR PEOPLE ARE COMING, BROTHER KALE?
VERY SURE, MAYOR.
HOLY--!

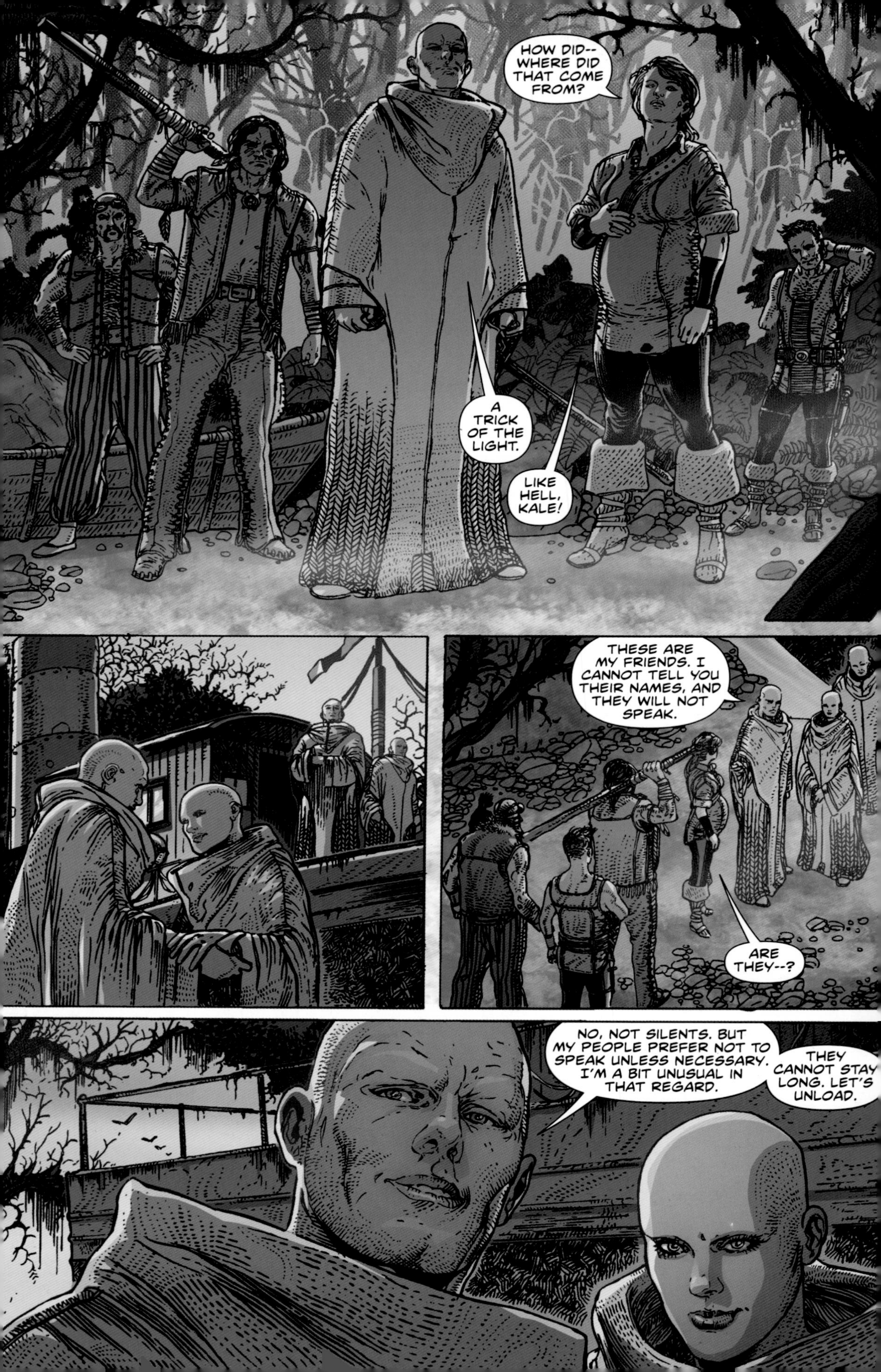
HOW DID-- WHERE DID THAT COME FROM?
A TRICK OF THE LIGHT.
LIKE HELL, KALE!
THESE ARE MY FRIENDS. I CANNOT TELL YOU THEIR NAMES, AND THEY WILL NOT SPEAK.
ARE THEY--?
NO, NOT SILENTS. BUT MY PEOPLE PREFER NOT TO SPEAK UNLESS NECESSARY. I'M A BIT UNUSUAL IN THAT REGARD.
THEY CANNOT STAY LONG. LET'S UNLOAD.

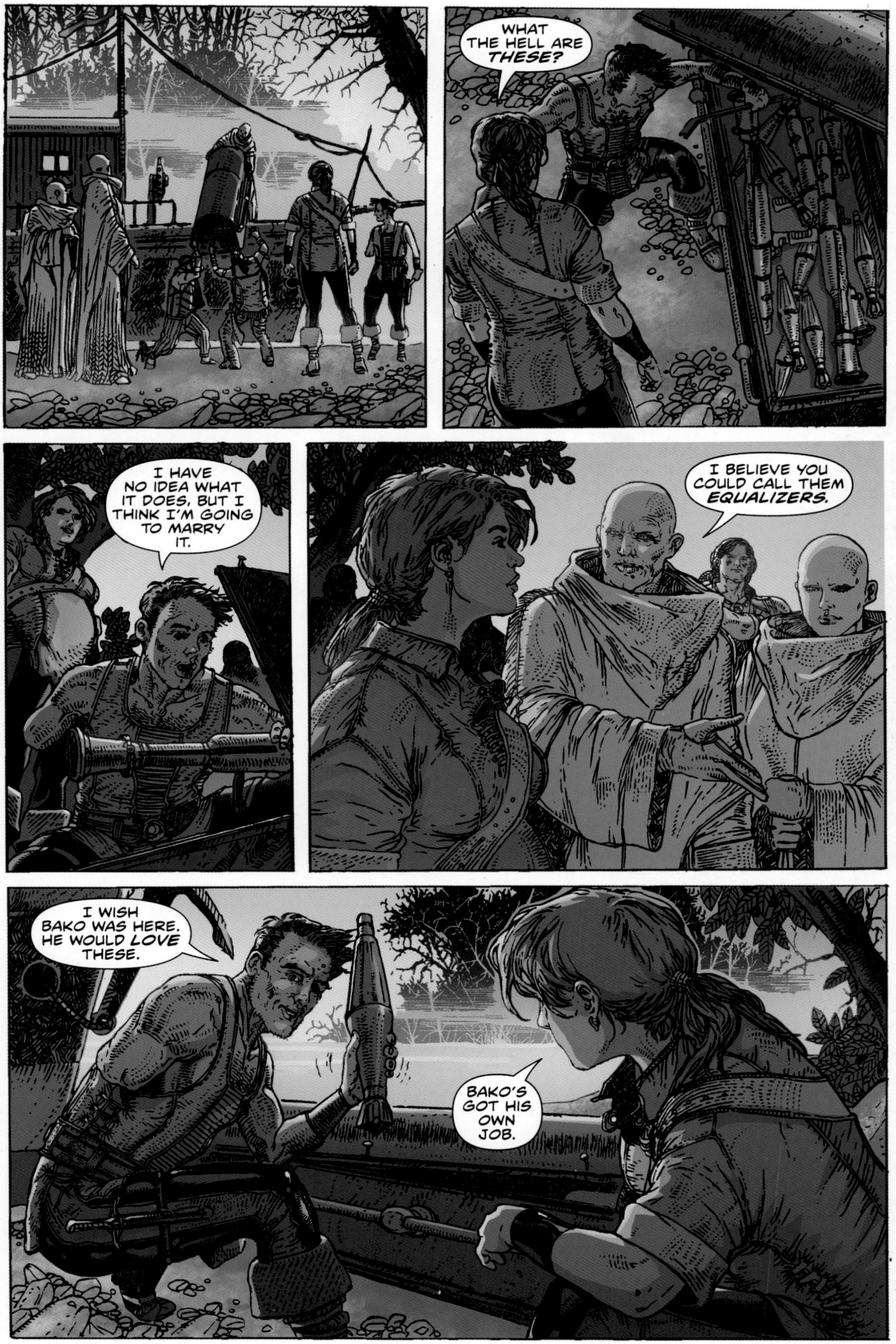
WHAT THE HELL ARE *THESE?*
I HAVE NO IDEA WHAT IT DOES, BUT I THINK I'M GOING TO MARRY IT.
I BELIEVE YOU COULD CALL THEM *EQUALIZERS.*
I WISH BAKO WAS HERE. HE WOULD *LOVE* THESE.
BAKO'S GOT HIS OWN JOB.

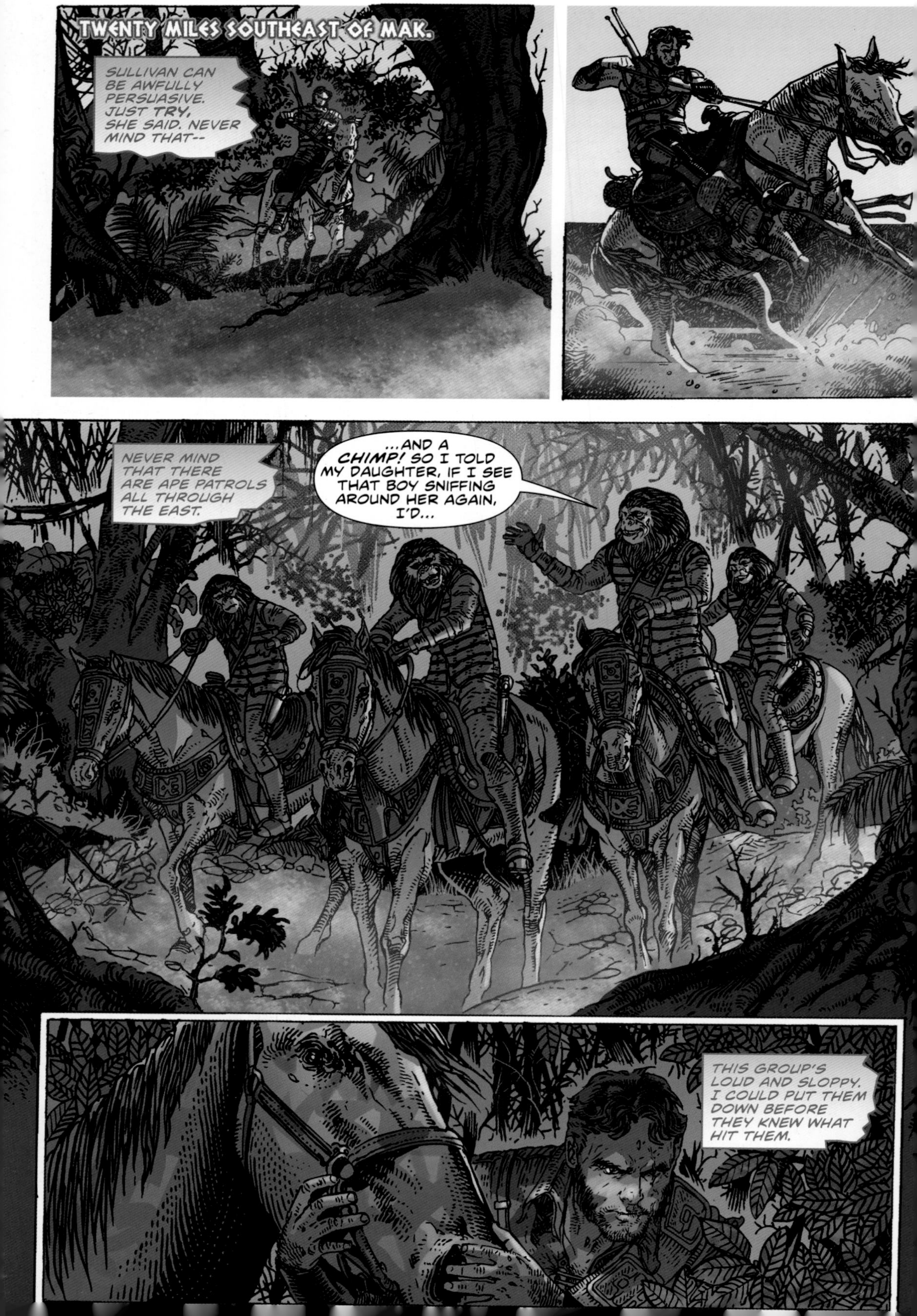
TWENTY MILES SOUTHEAST OF MAK.
SULLIVAN CAN BE AWFULLY PERSUASIVE. JUST TRY, SHE SAID. NEVER MIND THAT--
NEVER MIND THAT THERE ARE APE PATROLS ALL THROUGH THE EAST.
...AND A CHIMP! SO I TOLD MY DAUGHTER, IF I SEE THAT BOY SNIFFING AROUND HER AGAIN, I'D...
THIS GROUP'S LOUD AND SLOPPY. I COULD PUT THEM DOWN BEFORE THEY KNEW WHAT HIT THEM.

BUT THERE IS A TIME TO ATTACK. AND A TIME TO HIDE.

DELPHI. 18 YEARS EARLIER.

YOU CAN'T MAKE ME LEAVE YOU, BAKO.

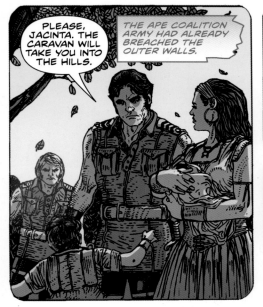

PLEASE, JACINTA. THE CARAVAN WILL TAKE YOU INTO THE HILLS.

THE APE COALITION ARMY HAD ALREADY BREACHED THE OUTER WALLS.

BAKO, WE GOT TO GO. APES DON'T KILL THEMSELVES.

CHIMA, TAKE CARE OF LITTLE CHAIKA WHILE I'M GONE, OKAY?

UH HUH.

I'LL FIND YOU AS SOON AS THIS IS OVER-- ONE WAY OR ANOTHER.

OR I WILL FIND YOU, MY HUSBAND.

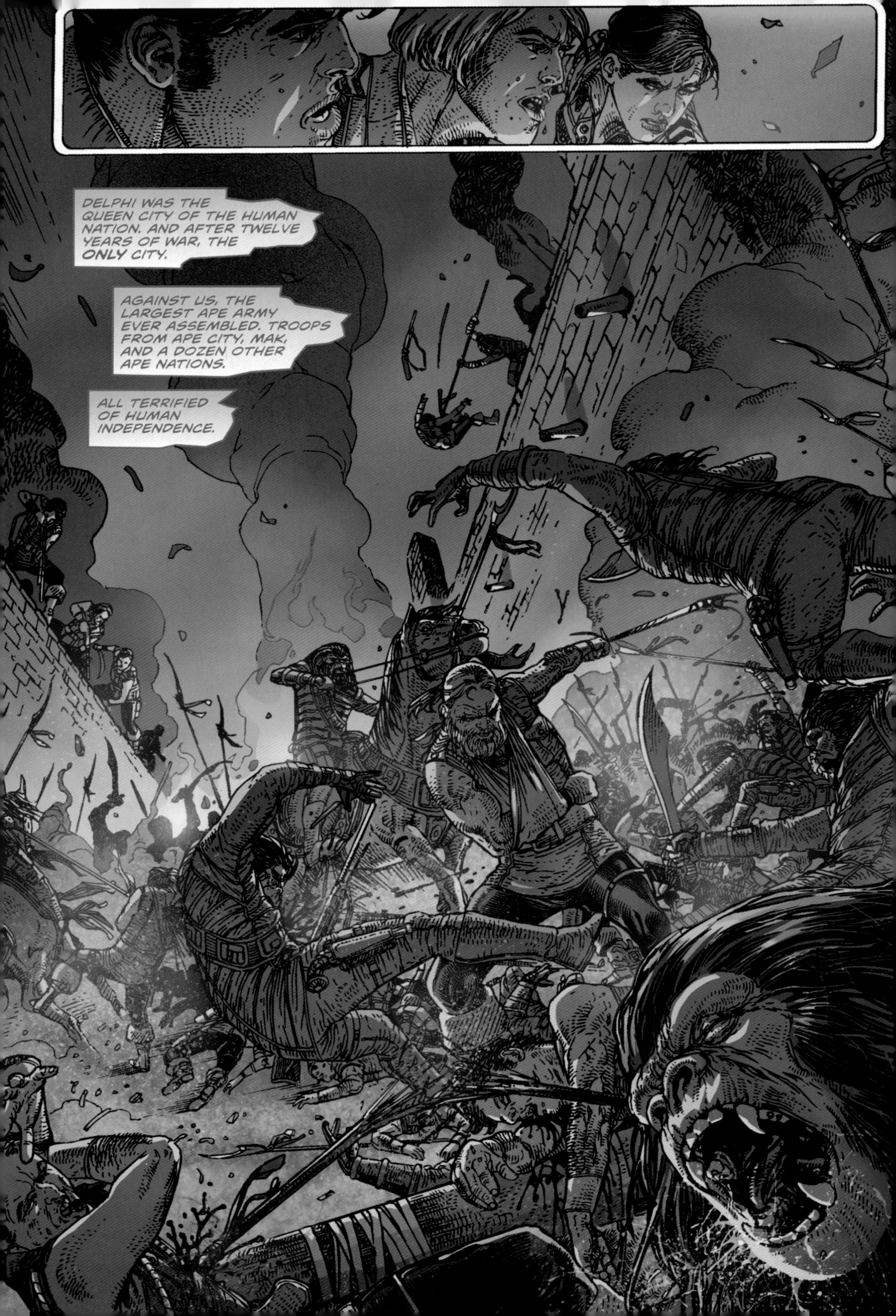
DELPHI WAS THE QUEEN CITY OF THE HUMAN NATION. AND AFTER TWELVE YEARS OF WAR, THE ONLY CITY.
AGAINST US, THE LARGEST APE ARMY EVER ASSEMBLED. TROOPS FROM APE CITY, MAK, AND A DOZEN OTHER APE NATIONS.
ALL TERRIFIED OF HUMAN INDEPENDENCE.

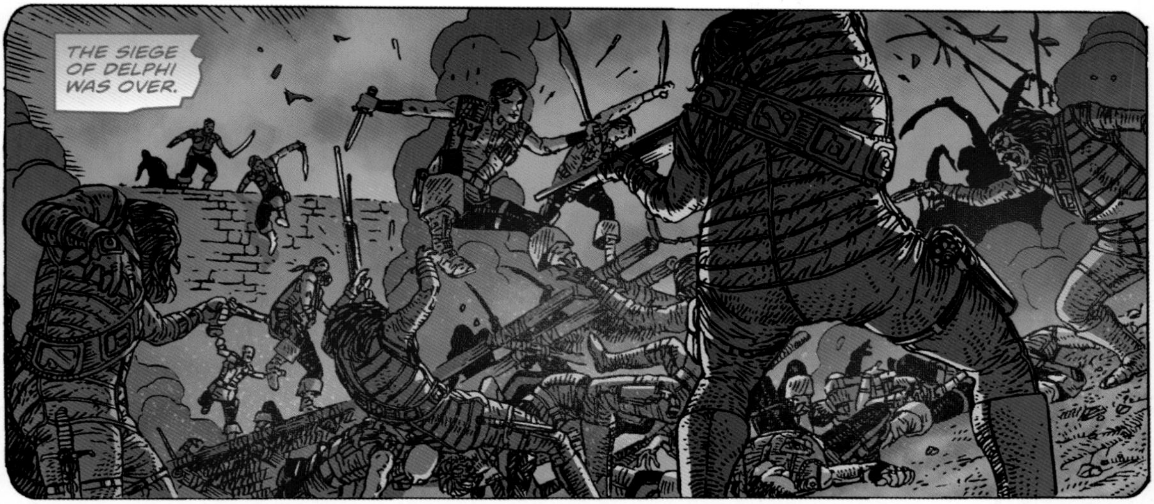
THE SIEGE OF DELPHI WAS OVER.

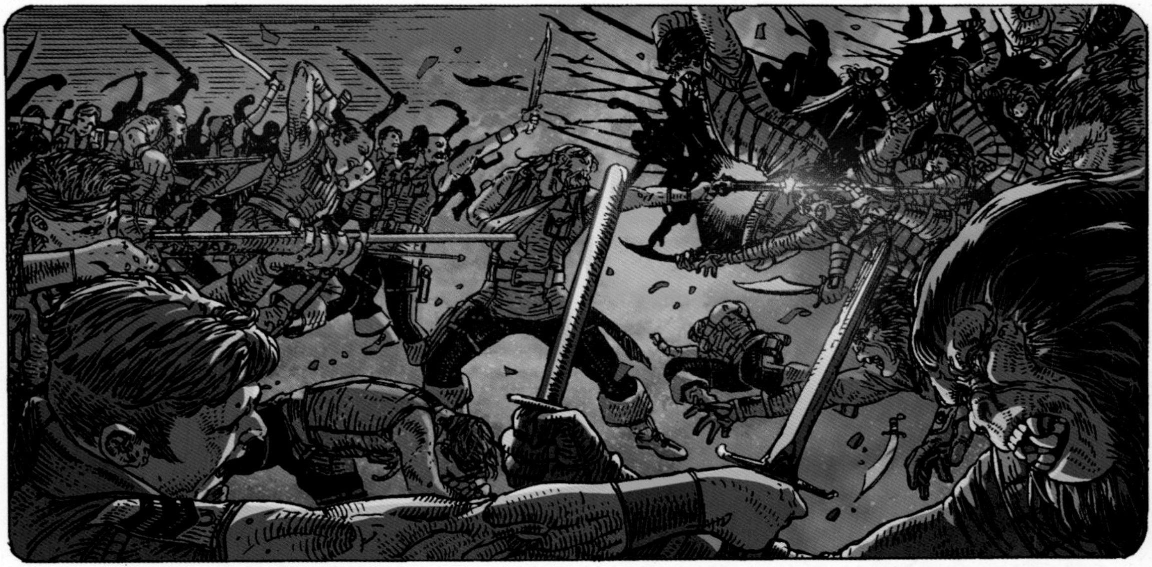

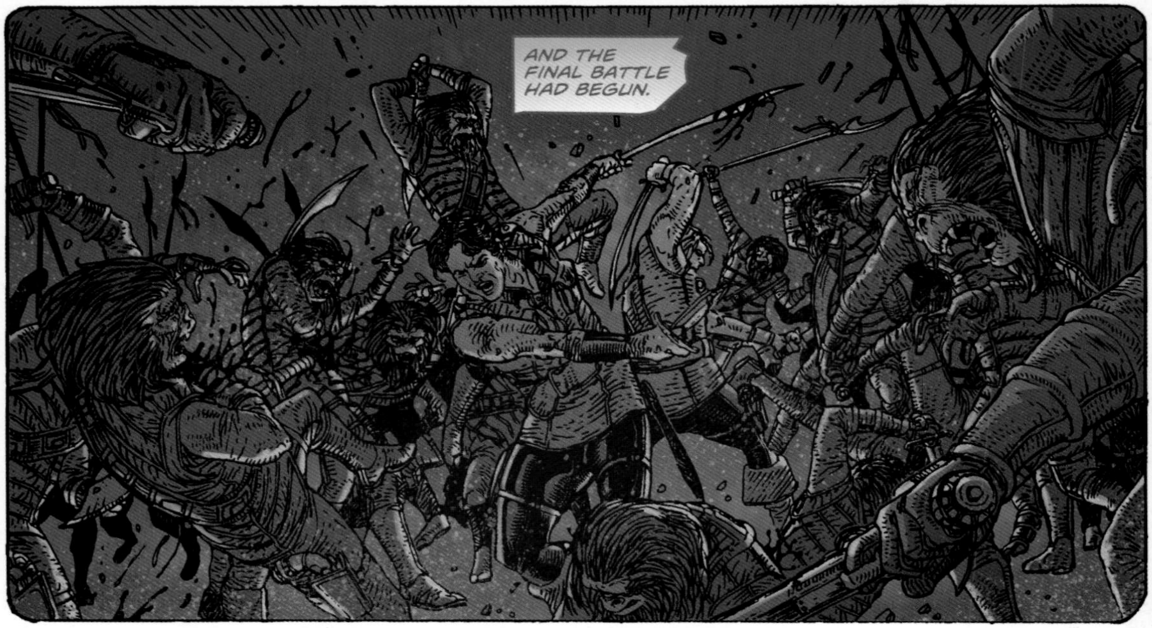
AND THE FINAL BATTLE HAD BEGUN.

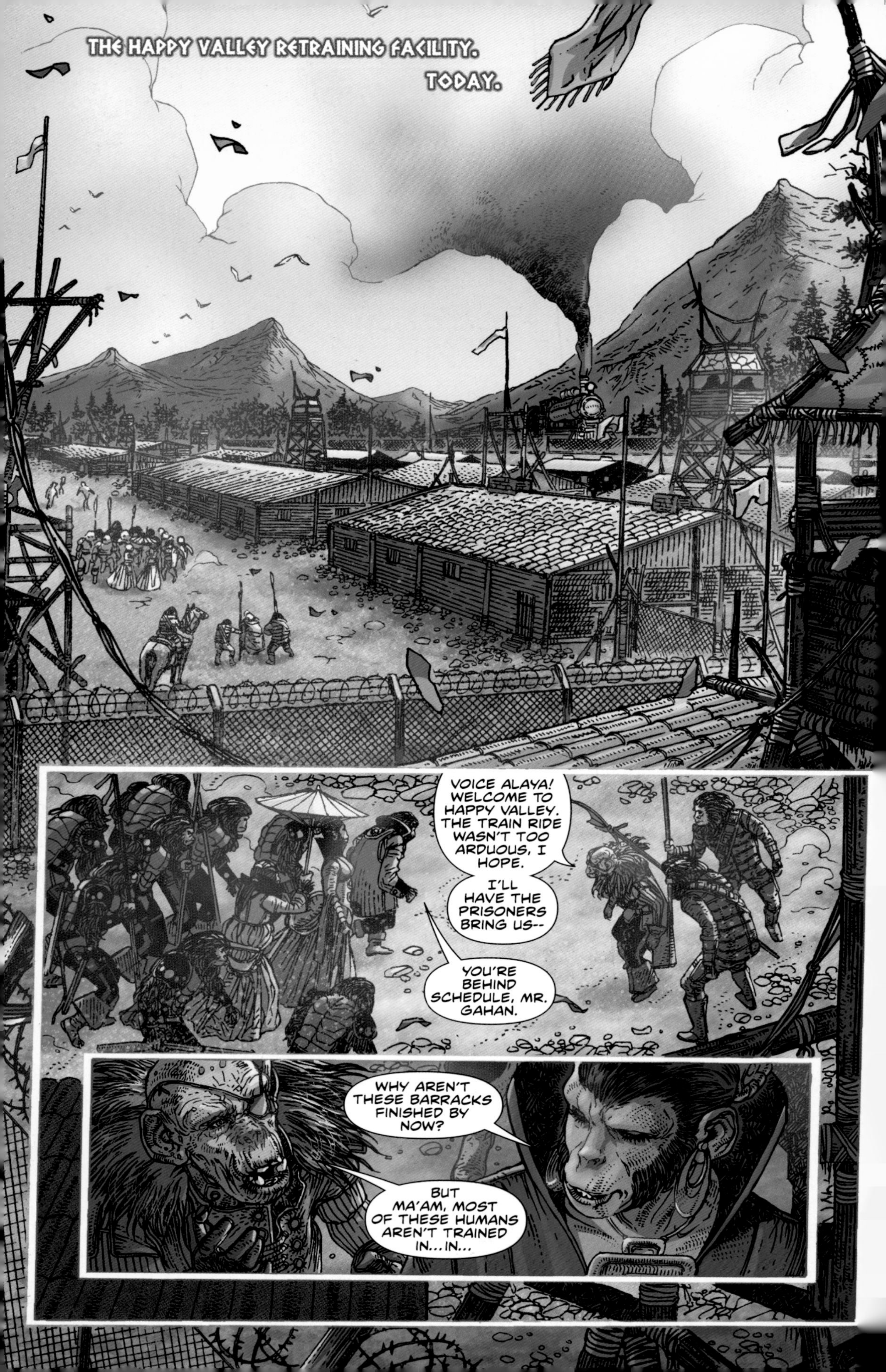
THE HAPPY VALLEY RETRAINING FACILITY.
TODAY.
VOICE ALAYA! WELCOME TO HAPPY VALLEY. THE TRAIN RIDE WASN'T TOO ARDUOUS, I HOPE.
I'LL HAVE THE PRISONERS BRING US--
YOU'RE BEHIND SCHEDULE, MR. GAHAN.
WHY AREN'T THESE BARRACKS FINISHED BY NOW?
BUT MA'AM, MOST OF THESE HUMANS AREN'T TRAINED IN... IN...

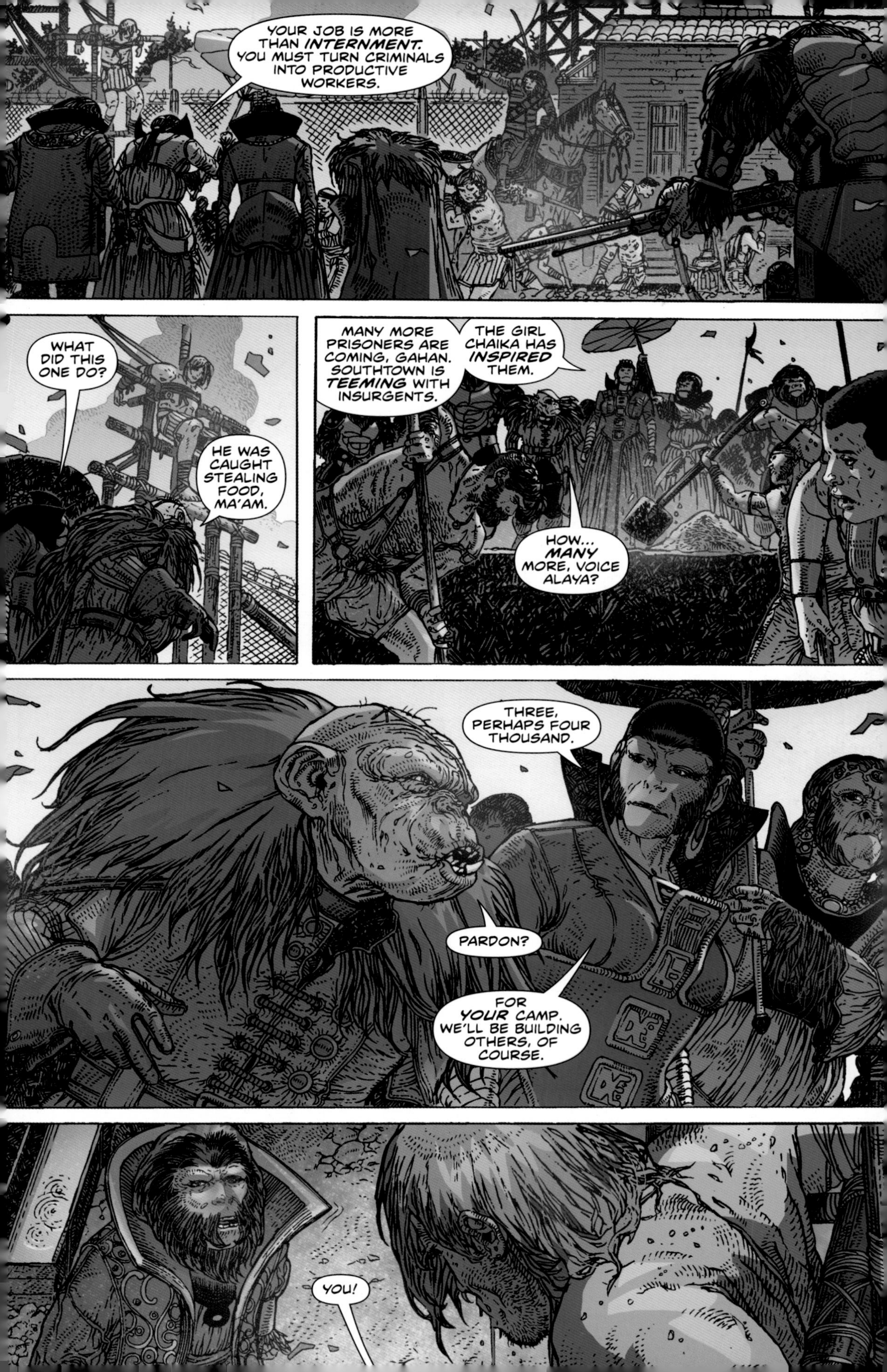
YOUR JOB IS MORE THAN INTERNMENT. YOU MUST TURN CRIMINALS INTO PRODUCTIVE WORKERS.
WHAT DID THIS ONE DO?
HE WAS CAUGHT STEALING FOOD, MA'AM.
MANY MORE PRISONERS ARE COMING, GAHAN. SOUTHTOWN IS TEEMING WITH INSURGENTS.
THE GIRL CHAIKA HAS INSPIRED THEM.
HOW... MANY MORE, VOICE ALAYA?
THREE, PERHAPS FOUR THOUSAND.
PARDON?
FOR YOUR CAMP. WE'LL BE BUILDING OTHERS, OF COURSE.
YOU!

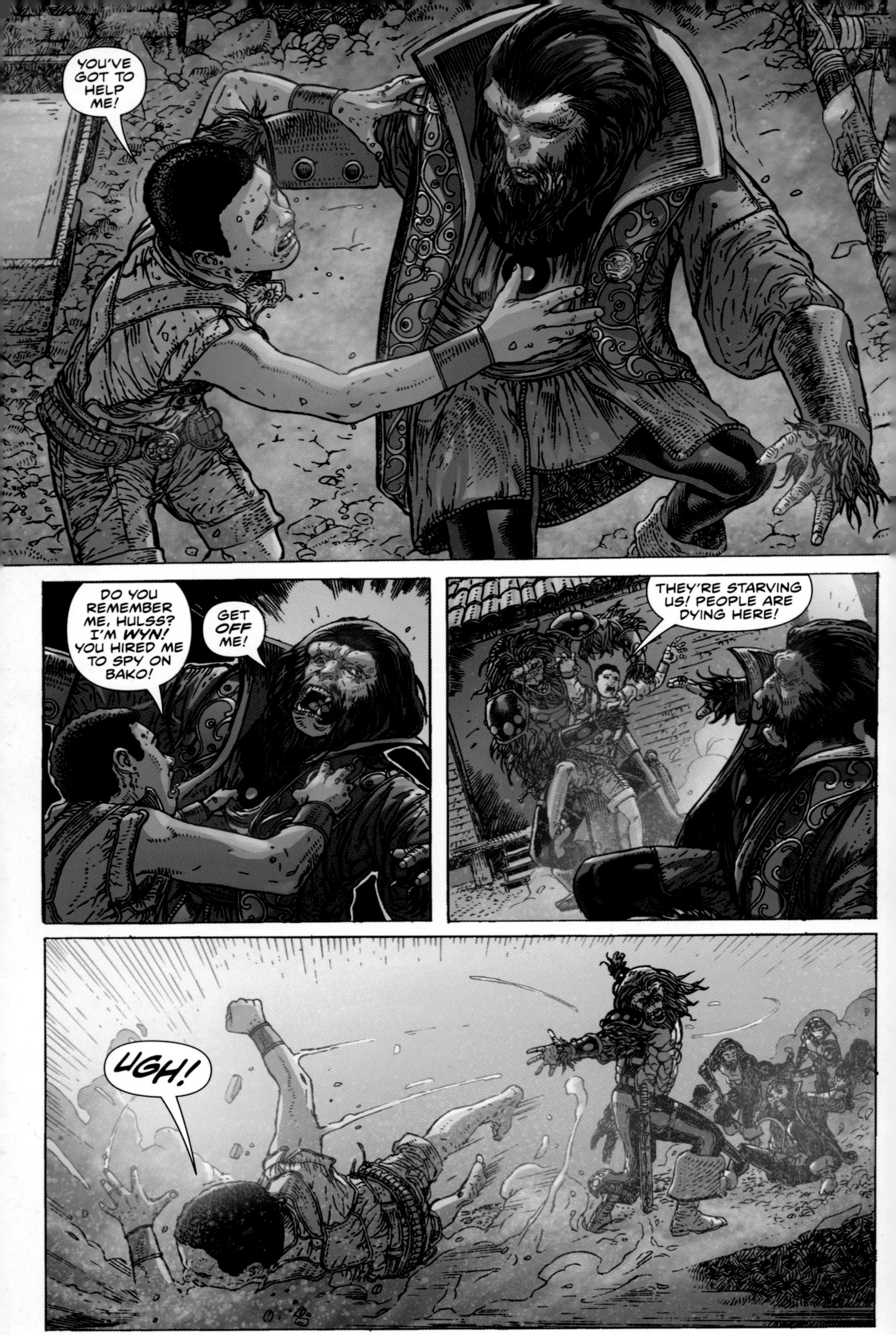
YOU'VE GOT TO HELP ME!
DO YOU REMEMBER ME, HULSS? I'M WYN! YOU HIRED ME TO SPY ON BAKO!
GET OFF ME!
THEY'RE STARVING US! PEOPLE ARE DYING HERE!
UGH!

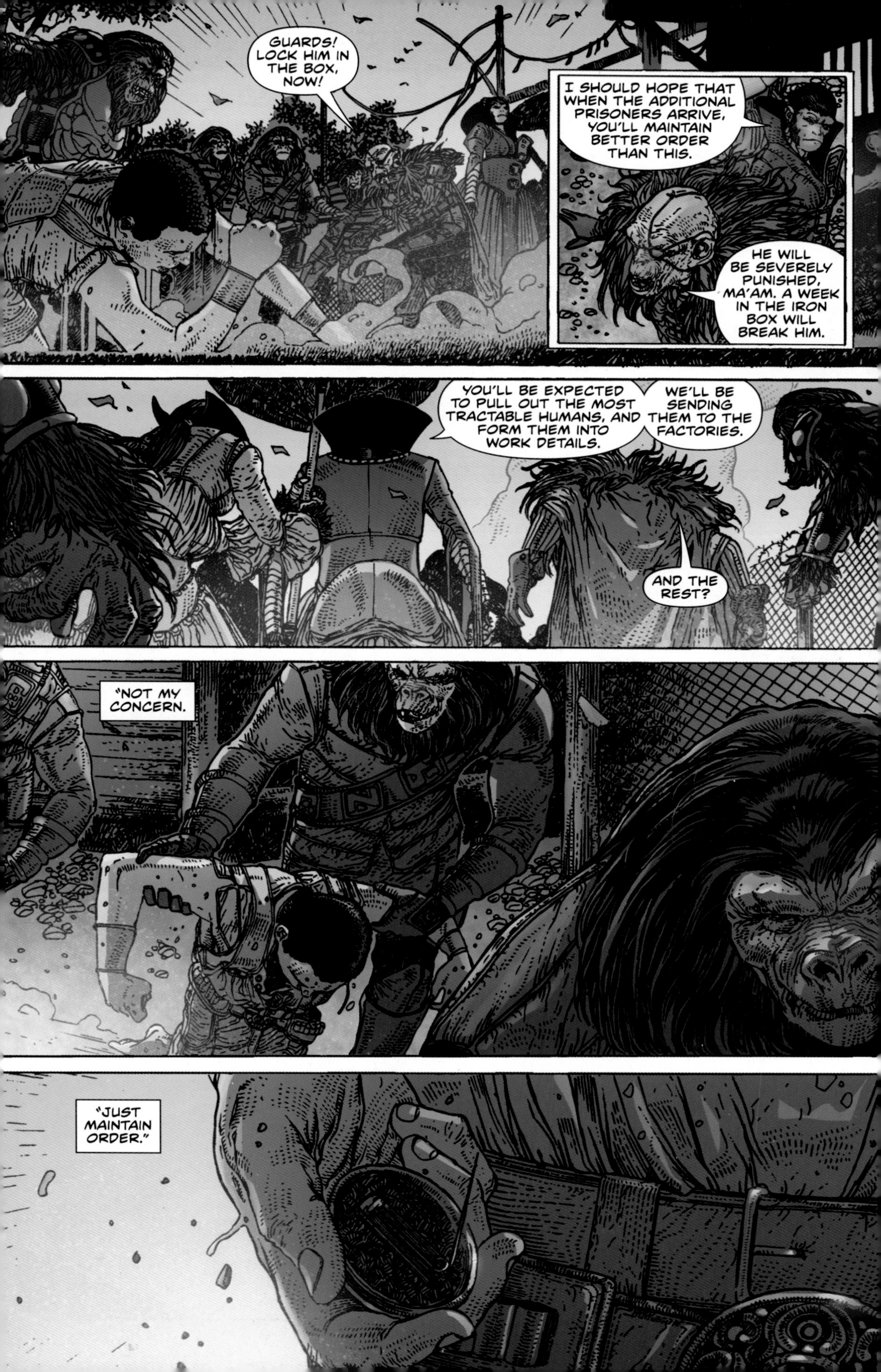
GUARDS! LOCK HIM IN THE BOX, NOW!
I SHOULD HOPE THAT WHEN THE ADDITIONAL PRISONERS ARRIVE, YOU'LL MAINTAIN BETTER ORDER THAN THIS.
HE WILL BE SEVERELY PUNISHED, MA'AM. A WEEK IN THE IRON BOX WILL BREAK HIM.
YOU'LL BE EXPECTED TO PULL OUT THE MOST TRACTABLE HUMANS, AND FORM THEM INTO WORK DETAILS.
WE'LL BE SENDING THEM TO THE FACTORIES.
AND THE REST?
"NOT MY CONCERN.
"JUST MAINTAIN ORDER."

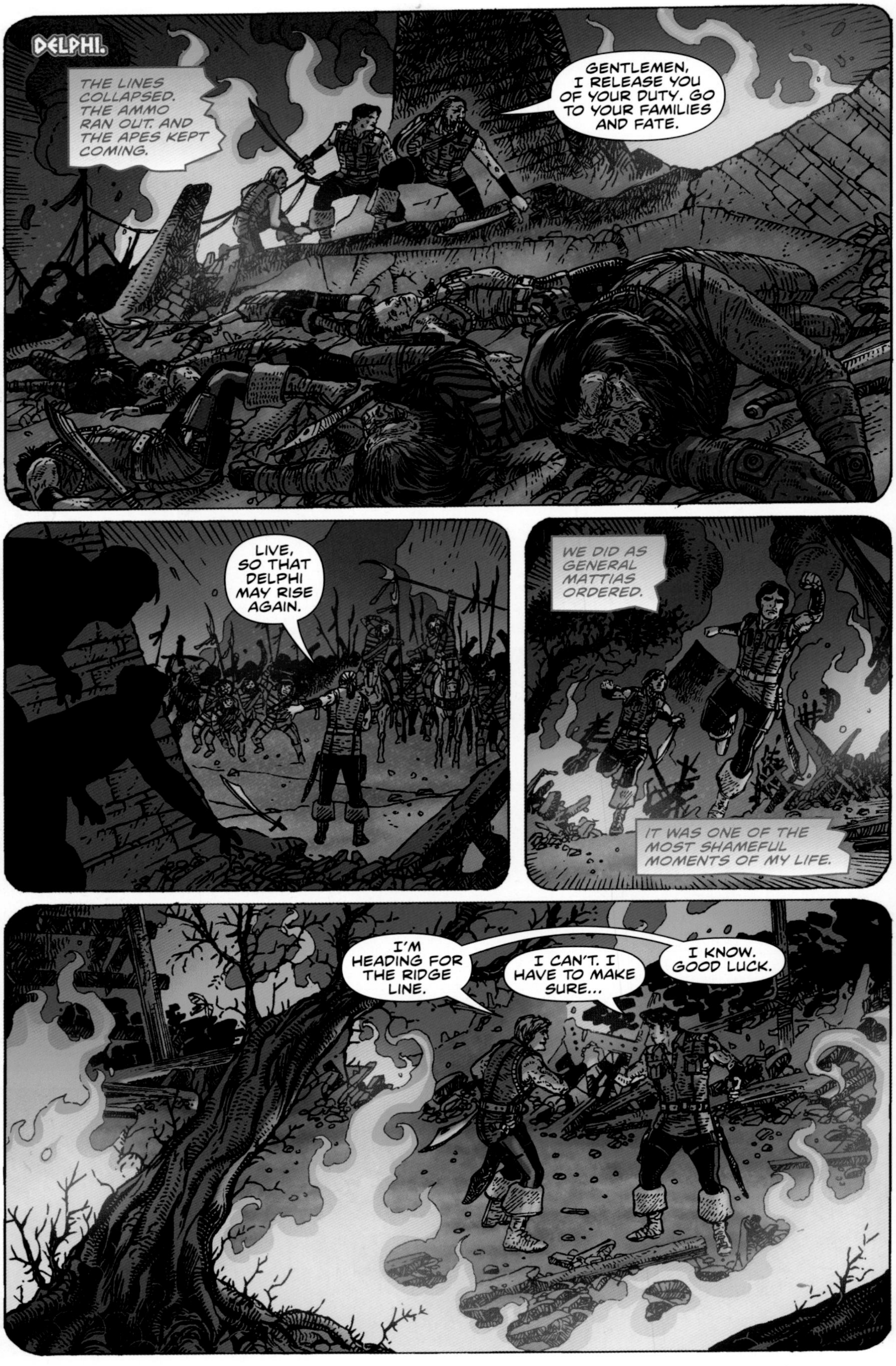
DELPHI.
THE LINES COLLAPSED. THE AMMO RAN OUT. AND THE APES KEPT COMING.
GENTLEMEN, I RELEASE YOU OF YOUR DUTY. GO TO YOUR FAMILIES AND FATE.
LIVE, SO THAT DELPHI MAY RISE AGAIN.
WE DID AS GENERAL MATTIAS ORDERED.
IT WAS ONE OF THE MOST SHAMEFUL MOMENTS OF MY LIFE.
I'M HEADING FOR THE RIDGE LINE.
I CAN'T. I HAVE TO MAKE SURE...
I KNOW. GOOD LUCK.

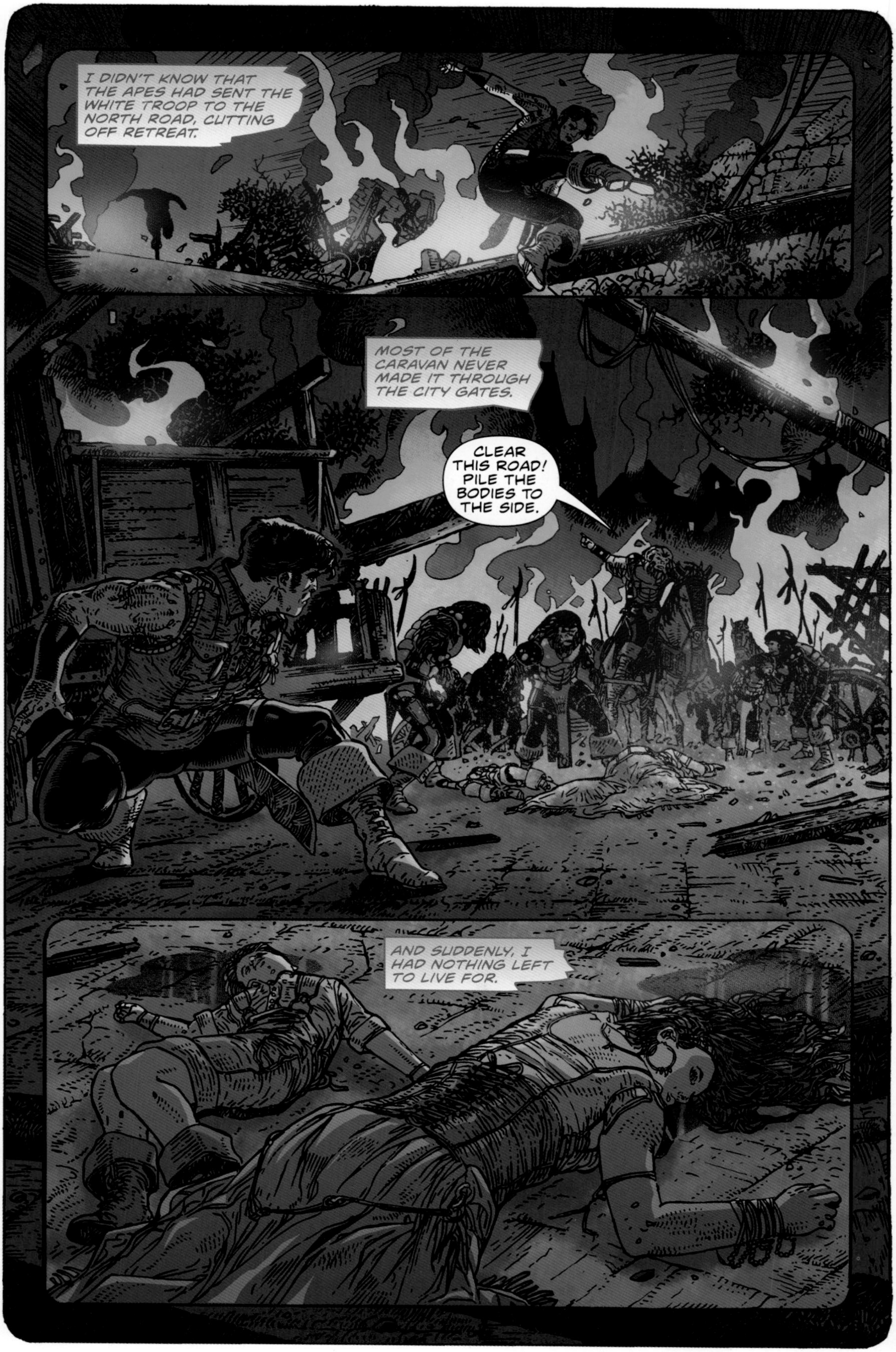
I DIDN'T KNOW THAT THE APES HAD SENT THE WHITE TROOP TO THE NORTH ROAD, CUTTING OFF RETREAT.
MOST OF THE CARAVAN NEVER MADE IT THROUGH THE CITY GATES.
CLEAR THIS ROAD! PILE THE BODIES TO THE SIDE.
AND SUDDENLY, I HAD NOTHING LEFT TO LIVE FOR.

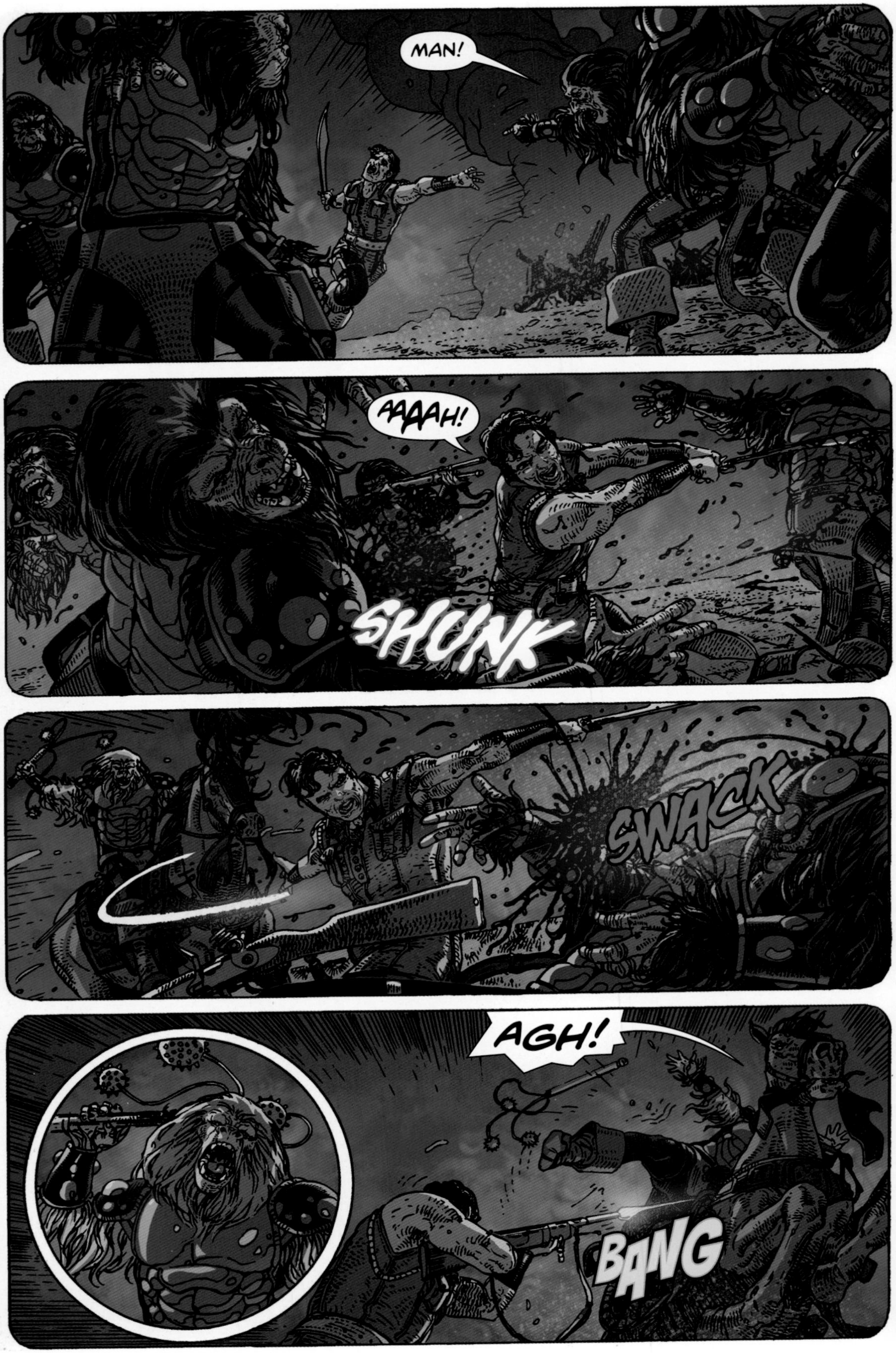
MAN!
AAAAH!
SHUNK
SWACK
AGH!
BANG

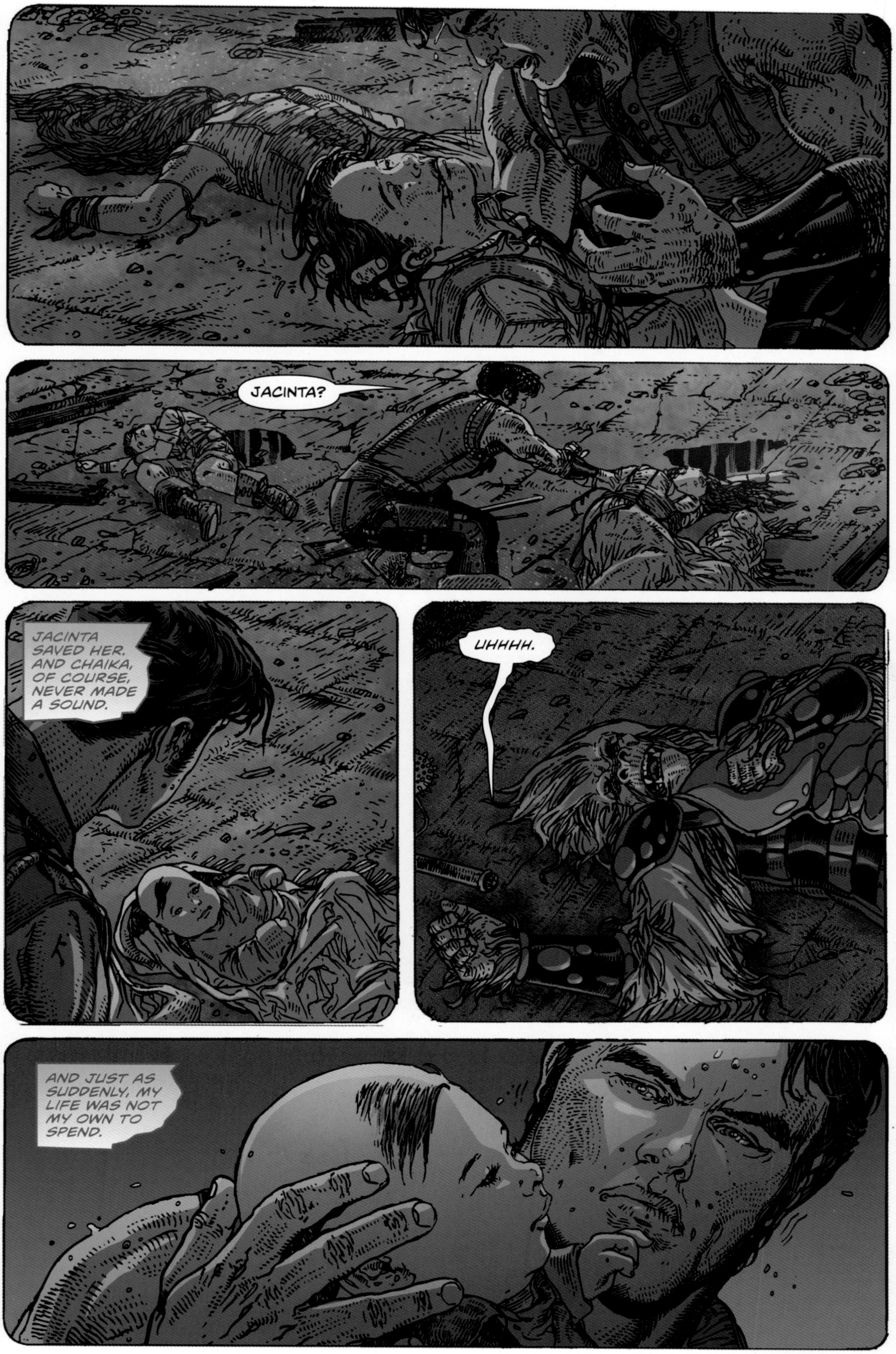
JACINTA?
JACINTA SAVED HER. AND CHAIKA, OF COURSE, NEVER MADE A SOUND.
UHHHH.
AND JUST AS SUDDENLY, MY LIFE WAS NOT MY OWN TO SPEND.

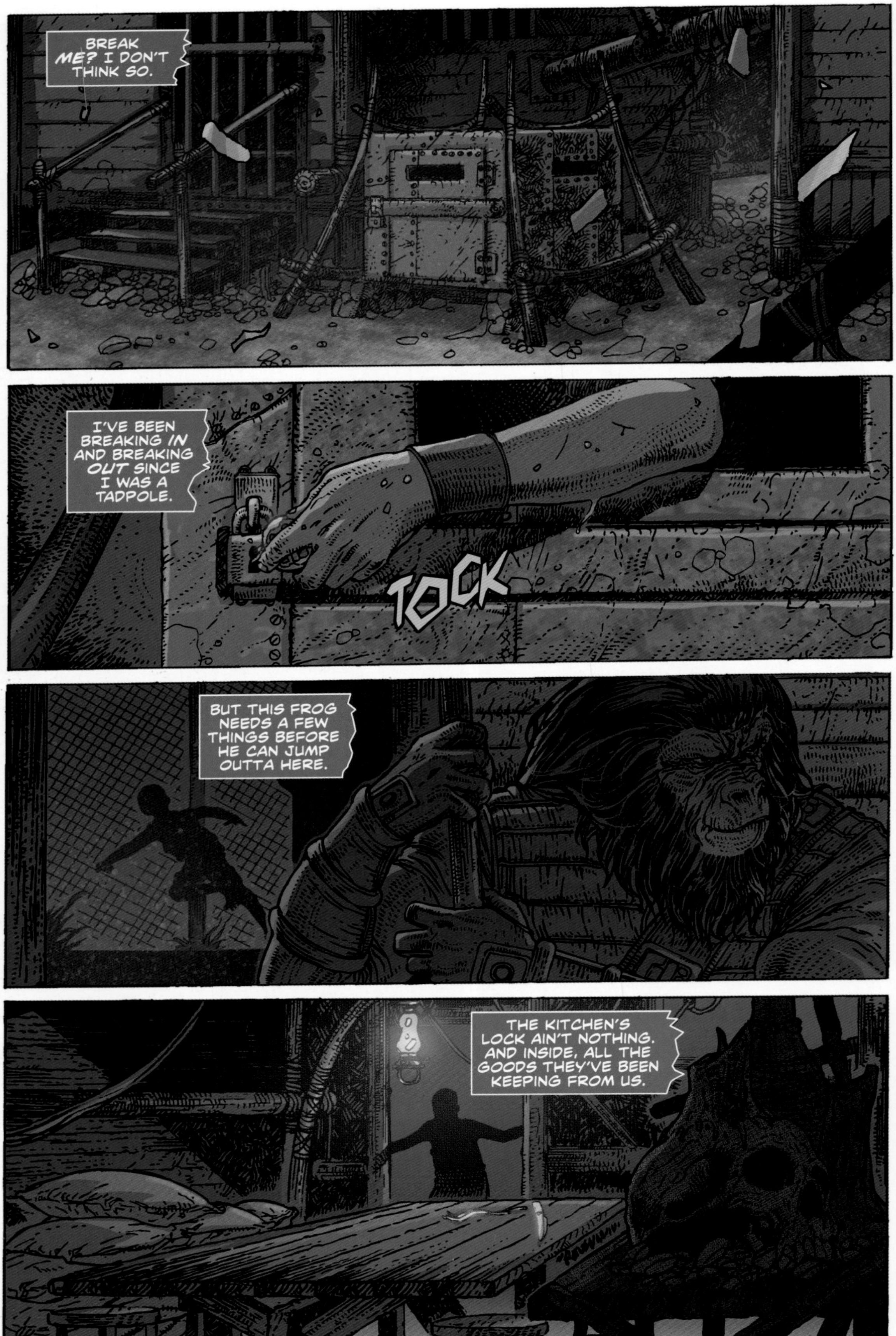
BREAK *ME*? I DON'T THINK SO.
I'VE BEEN BREAKING *IN* AND BREAKING *OUT* SINCE I WAS A TADPOLE.
TOCK
BUT THIS FROG NEEDS A FEW THINGS BEFORE HE CAN JUMP OUTTA HERE.
THE KITCHEN'S LOCK AIN'T NOTHING. AND INSIDE, ALL THE GOODS THEY'VE BEEN KEEPING FROM US.

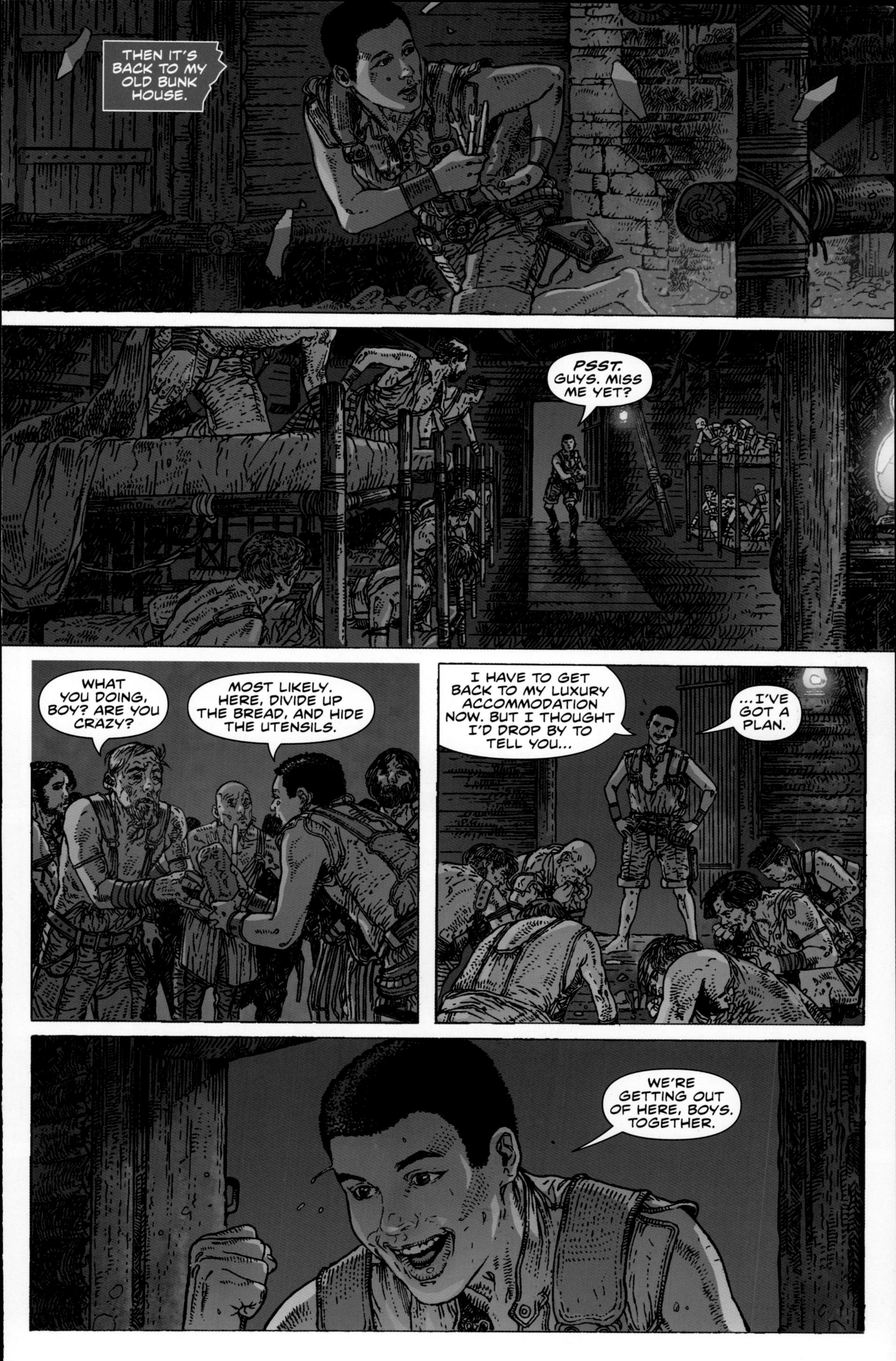
THEN IT'S BACK TO MY OLD BUNK HOUSE.
PSST. GUYS. MISS ME YET?
WHAT YOU DOING, BOY? ARE YOU CRAZY?
MOST LIKELY. HERE, DIVIDE UP THE BREAD, AND HIDE THE UTENSILS.
I HAVE TO GET BACK TO MY LUXURY ACCOMMODATION NOW. BUT I THOUGHT I'D DROP BY TO TELL YOU...
...I'VE GOT A PLAN.
WE'RE GETTING OUT OF HERE, BOYS. TOGETHER.

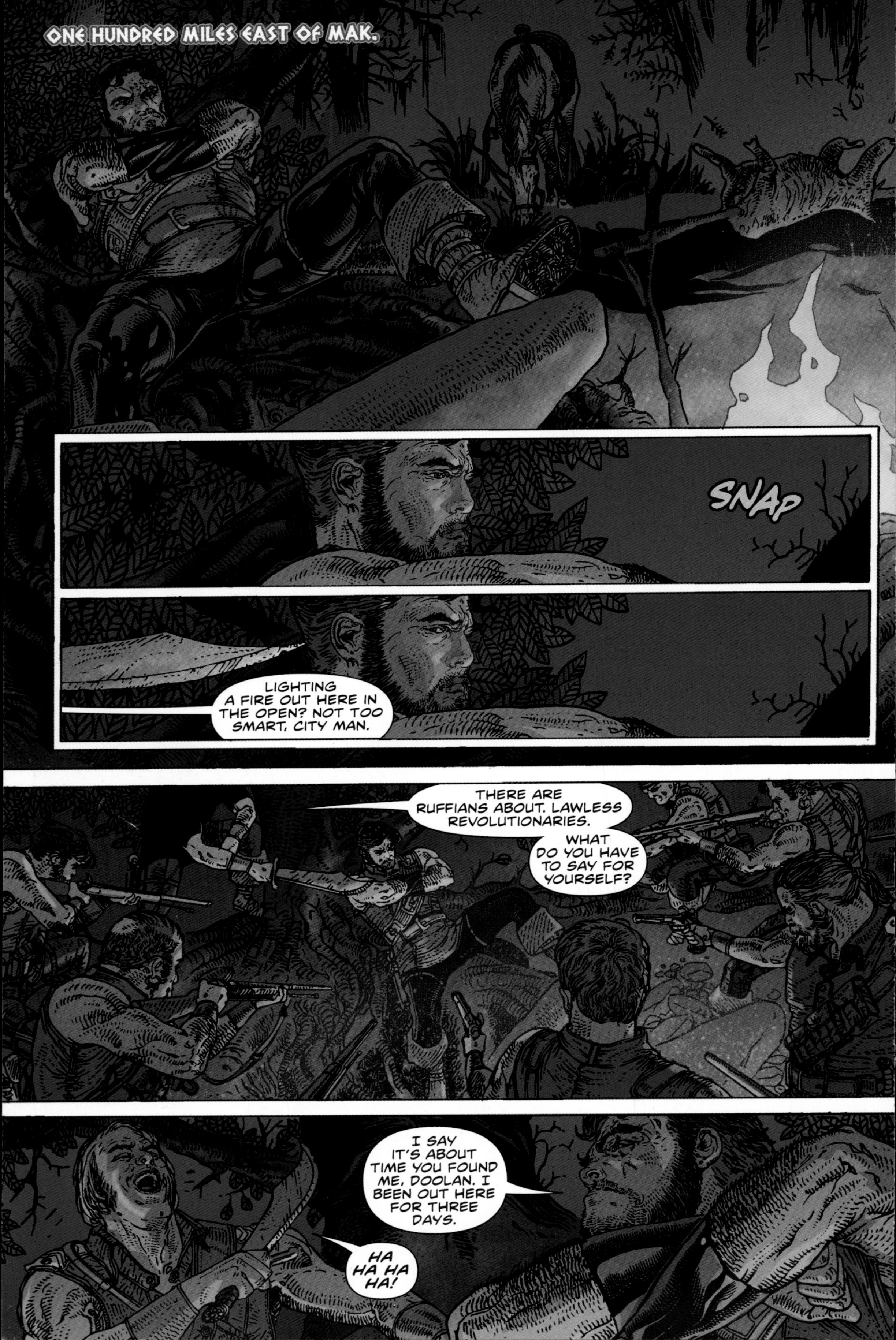
ONE HUNDRED MILES EAST OF MAK.
SNAP
LIGHTING A FIRE OUT HERE IN THE OPEN? NOT TOO SMART, CITY MAN.
THERE ARE RUFFIANS ABOUT. LAWLESS REVOLUTIONARIES.
WHAT DO YOU HAVE TO SAY FOR YOURSELF?
I SAY IT'S ABOUT TIME YOU FOUND ME, DOOLAN. I BEEN OUT HERE FOR THREE DAYS.
HA HA HA HA HA!

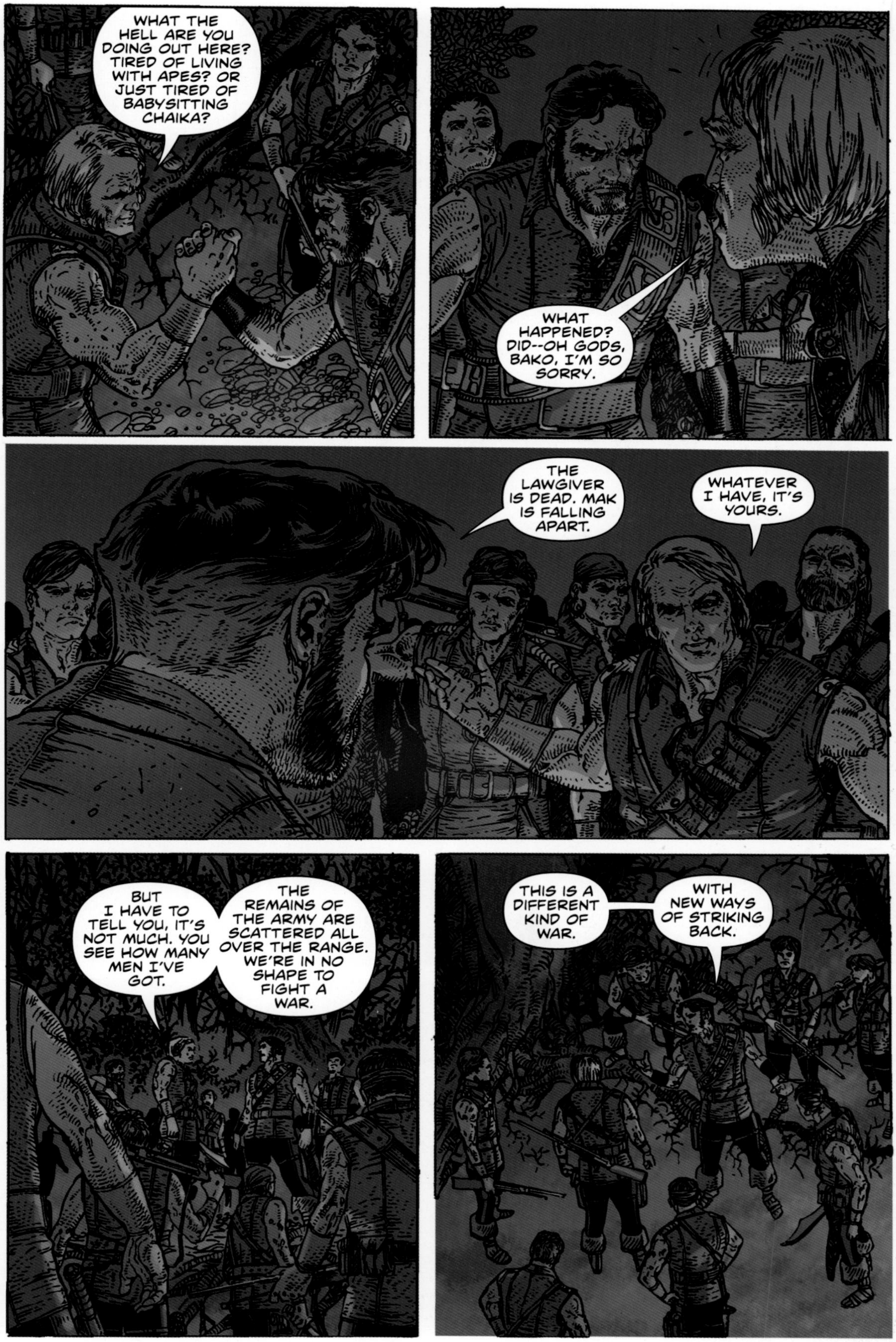
WHAT THE HELL ARE YOU DOING OUT HERE? TIRED OF LIVING WITH APES? OR JUST TIRED OF BABYSITTING CHAIKA?
WHAT HAPPENED? DID--OH GODS, BAKO, I'M SO SORRY.
THE LAWGIVER IS DEAD. MAK IS FALLING APART.
WHATEVER I HAVE, IT'S YOURS.
BUT I HAVE TO TELL YOU, IT'S NOT MUCH. YOU SEE HOW MANY MEN I'VE GOT.
THE REMAINS OF THE ARMY ARE SCATTERED ALL OVER THE RANGE. WE'RE IN NO SHAPE TO FIGHT A WAR.
THIS IS A DIFFERENT KIND OF WAR.
WITH NEW WAYS OF STRIKING BACK.

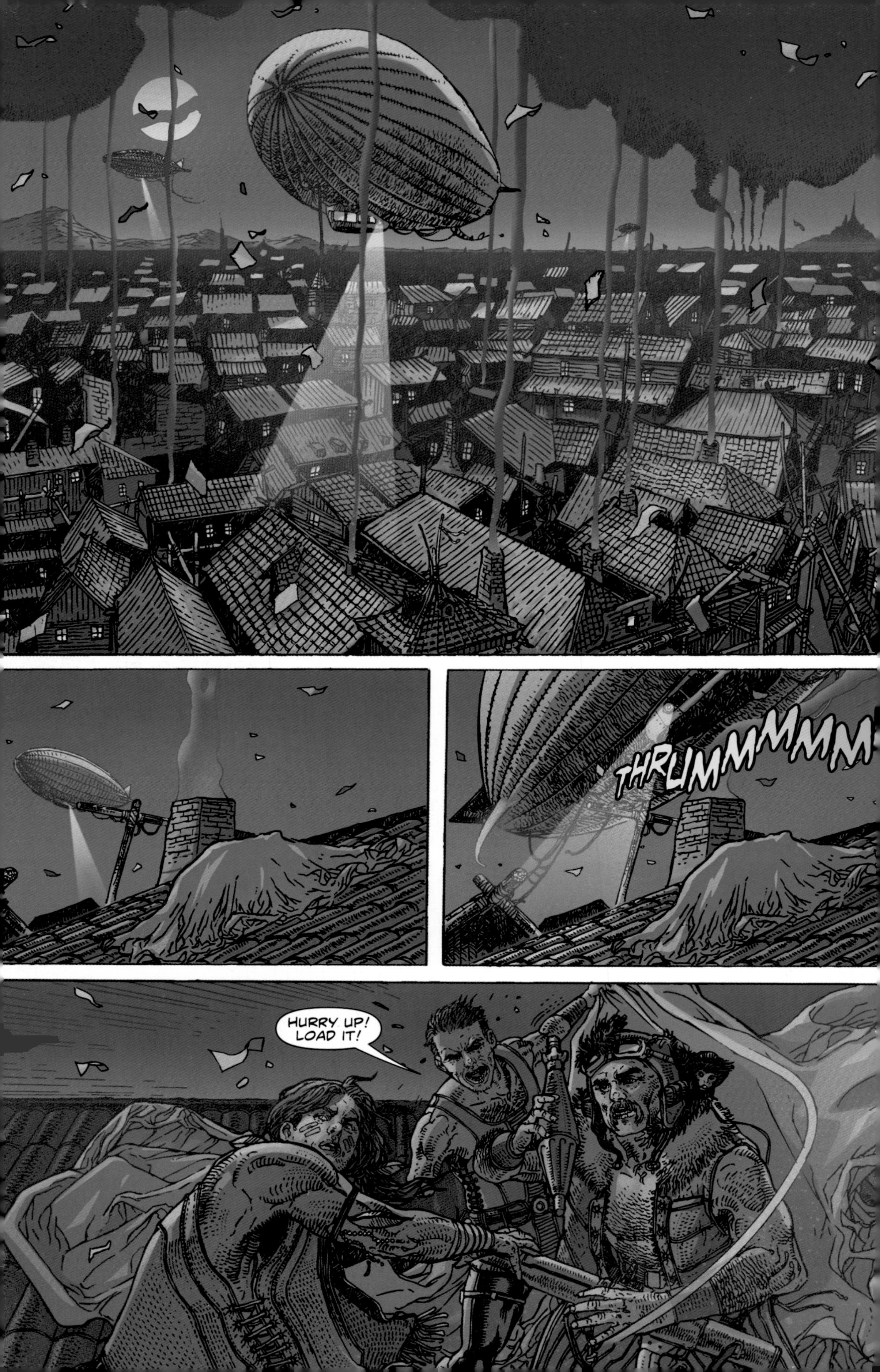
THRUMMMMMM
HURRY UP! LOAD IT!

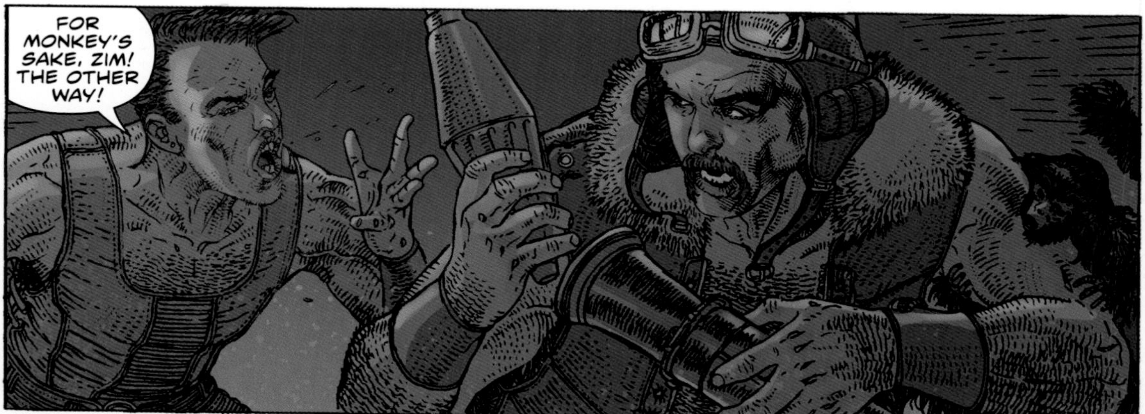
FOR MONKEY'S SAKE, ZIM! THE OTHER WAY!

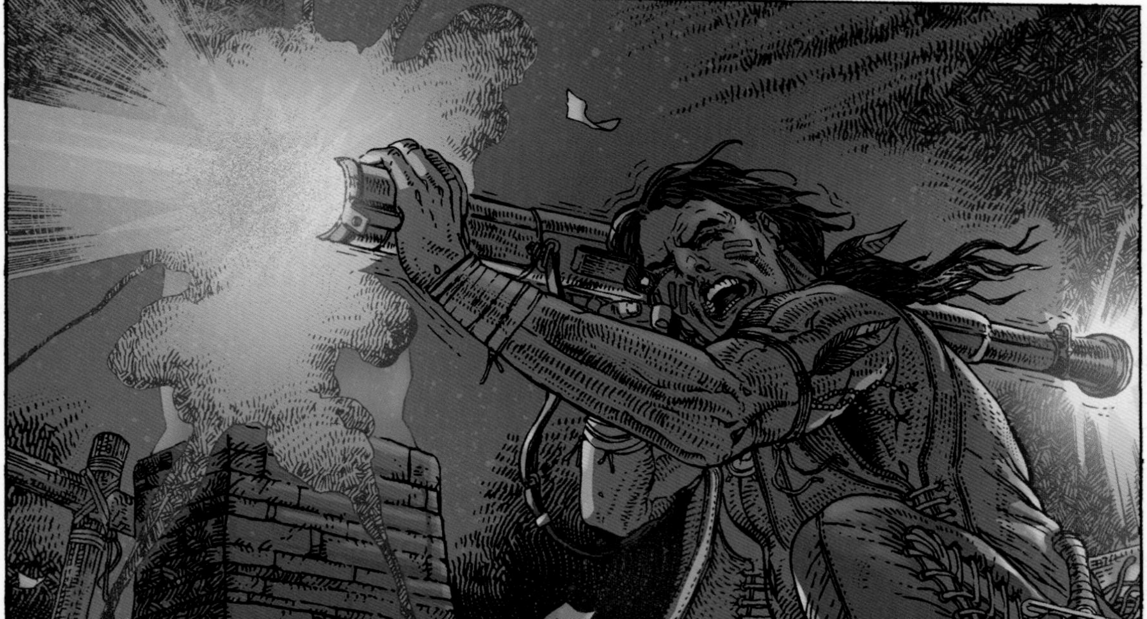

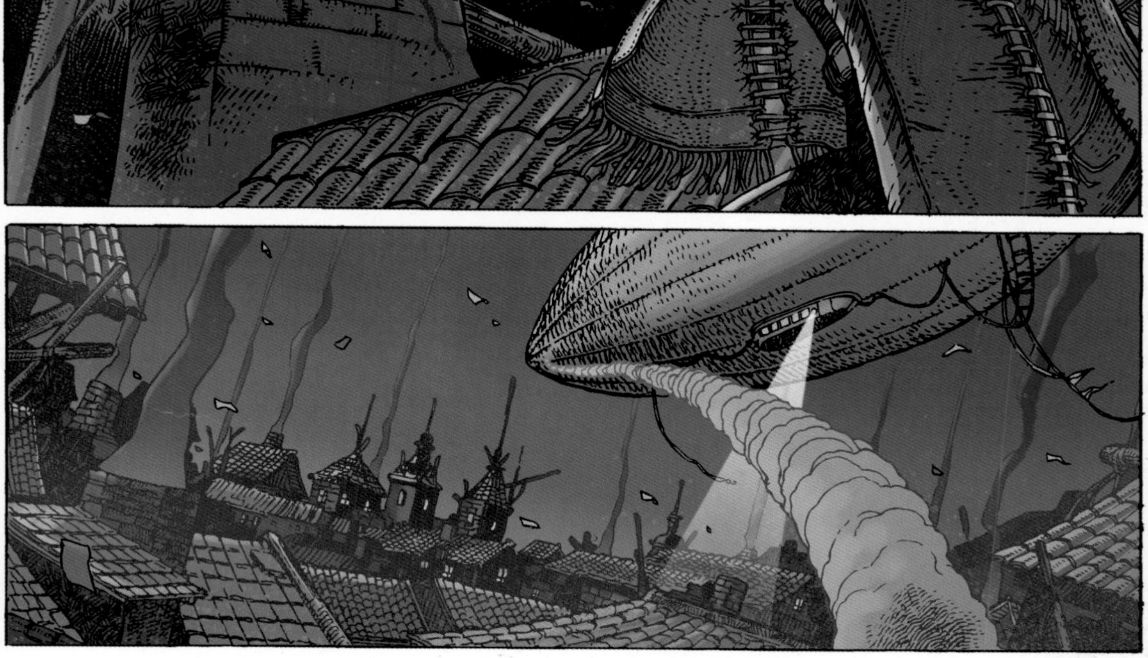

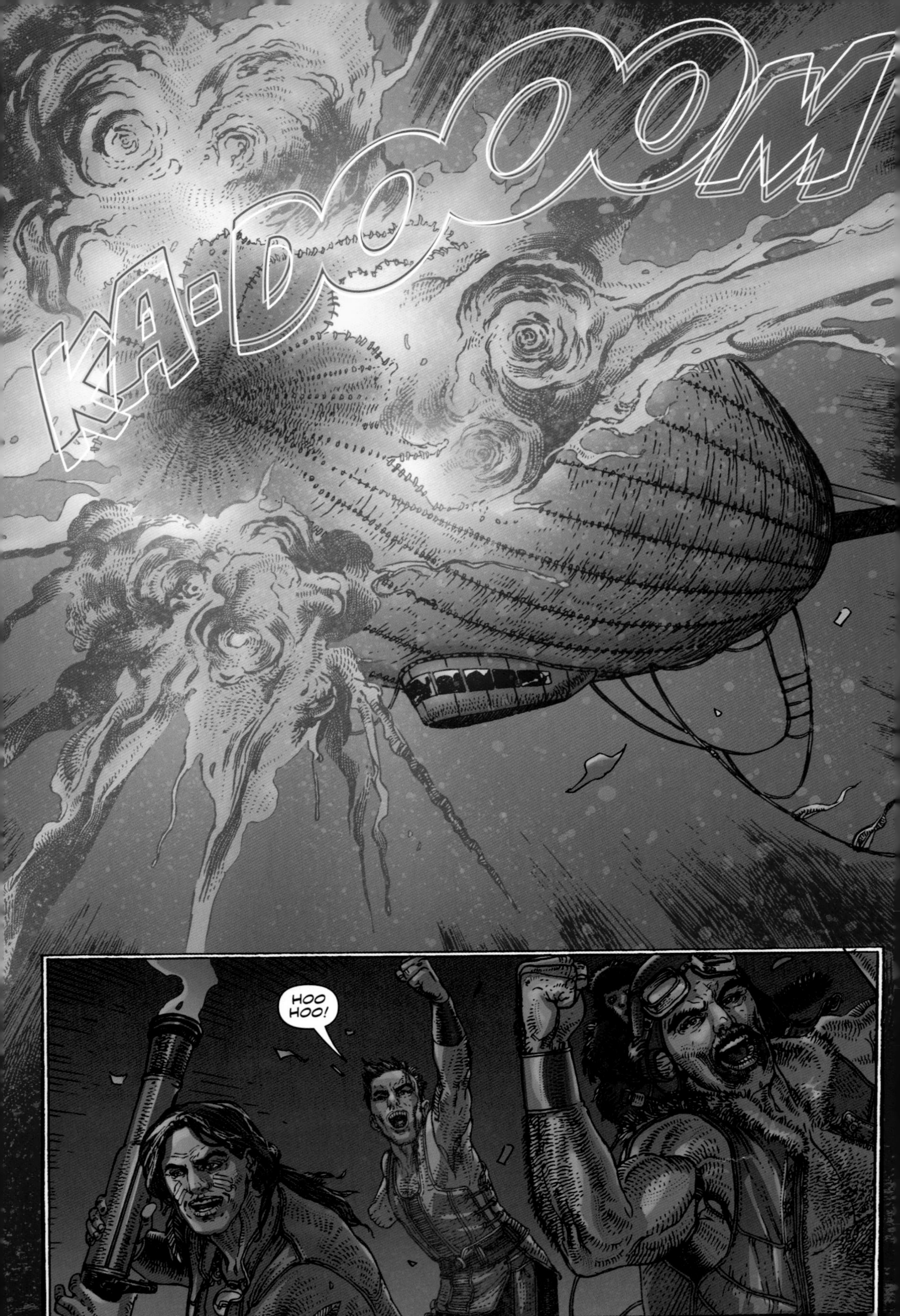
KA-DOOOM
HOO HOO!

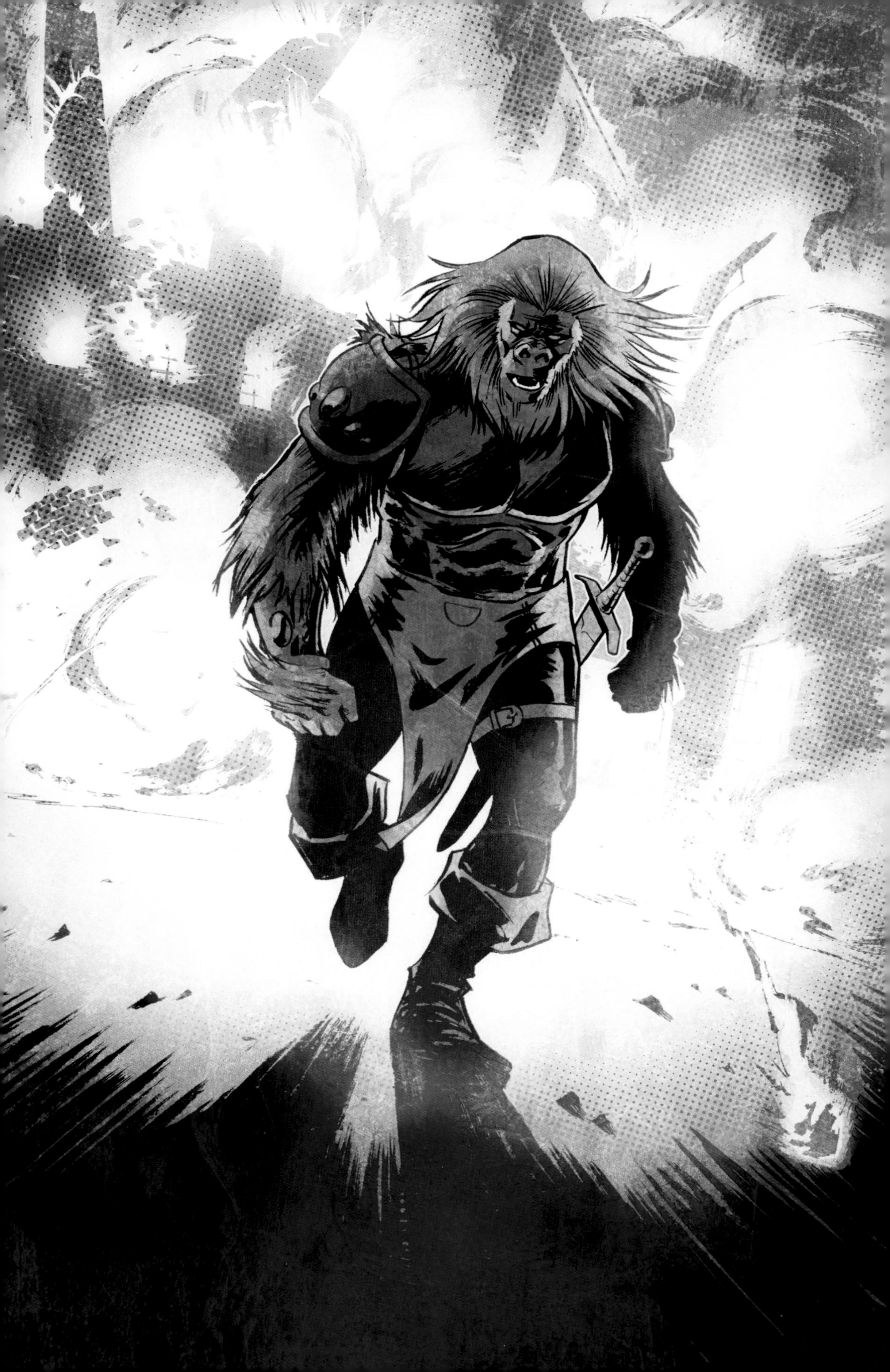

# CHAPTER SEVEN

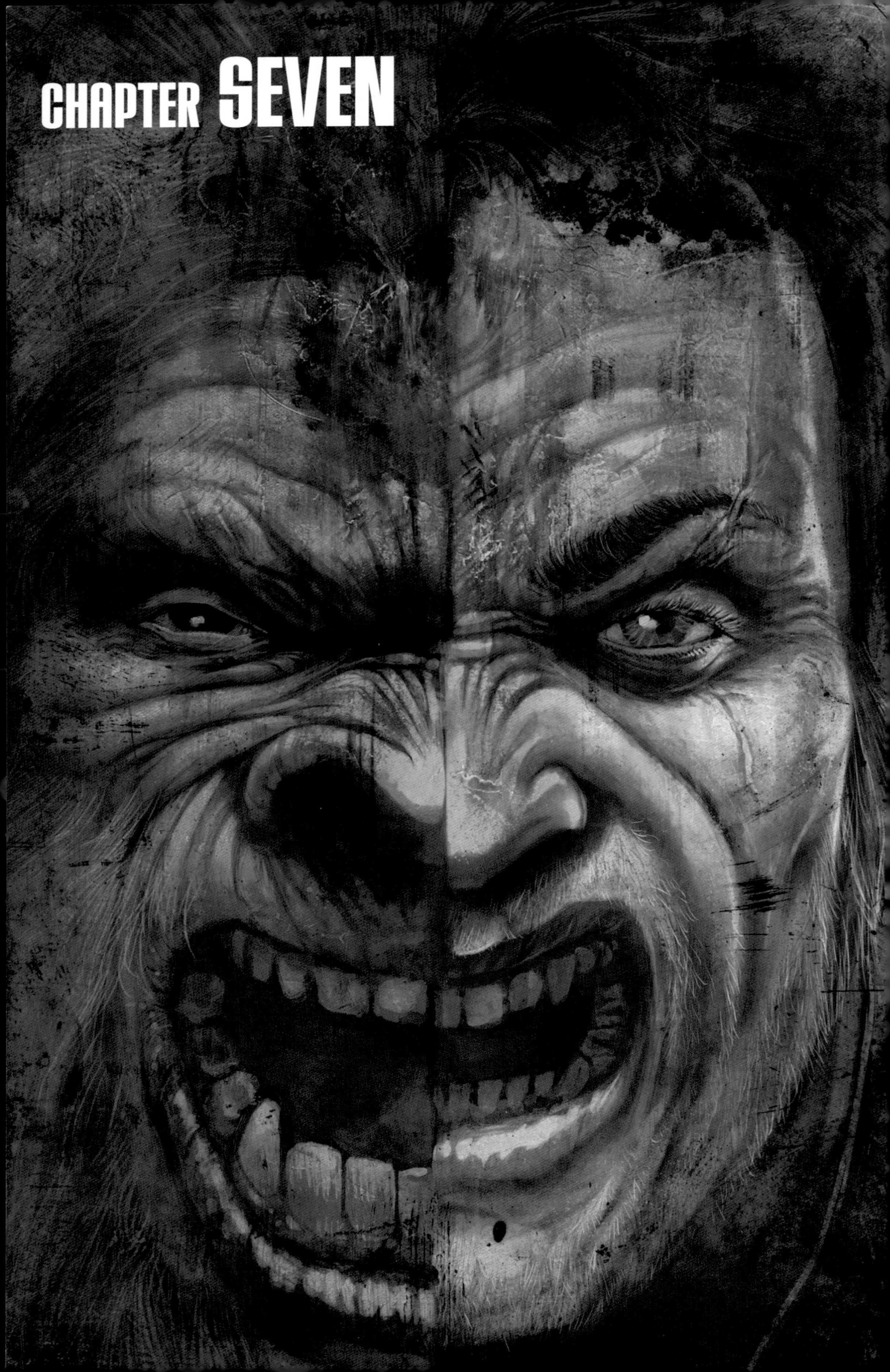

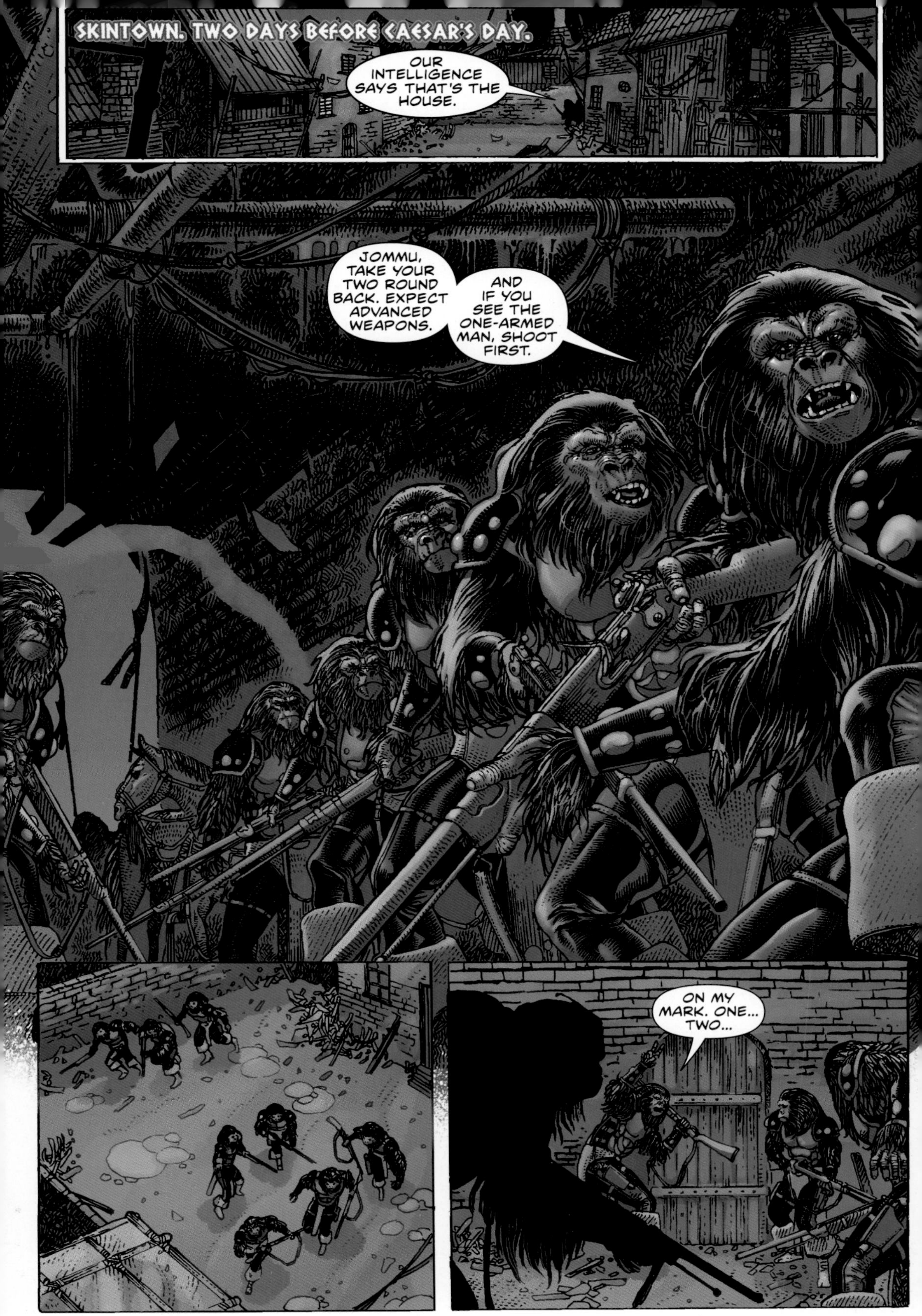
SKINTOWN. TWO DAYS BEFORE CAESAR'S DAY.
OUR INTELLIGENCE SAYS THAT'S THE HOUSE.
JOMMU, TAKE YOUR TWO ROUND BACK. EXPECT ADVANCED WEAPONS.
AND IF YOU SEE THE ONE-ARMED MAN, SHOOT FIRST.
ON MY MARK. ONE... TWO...

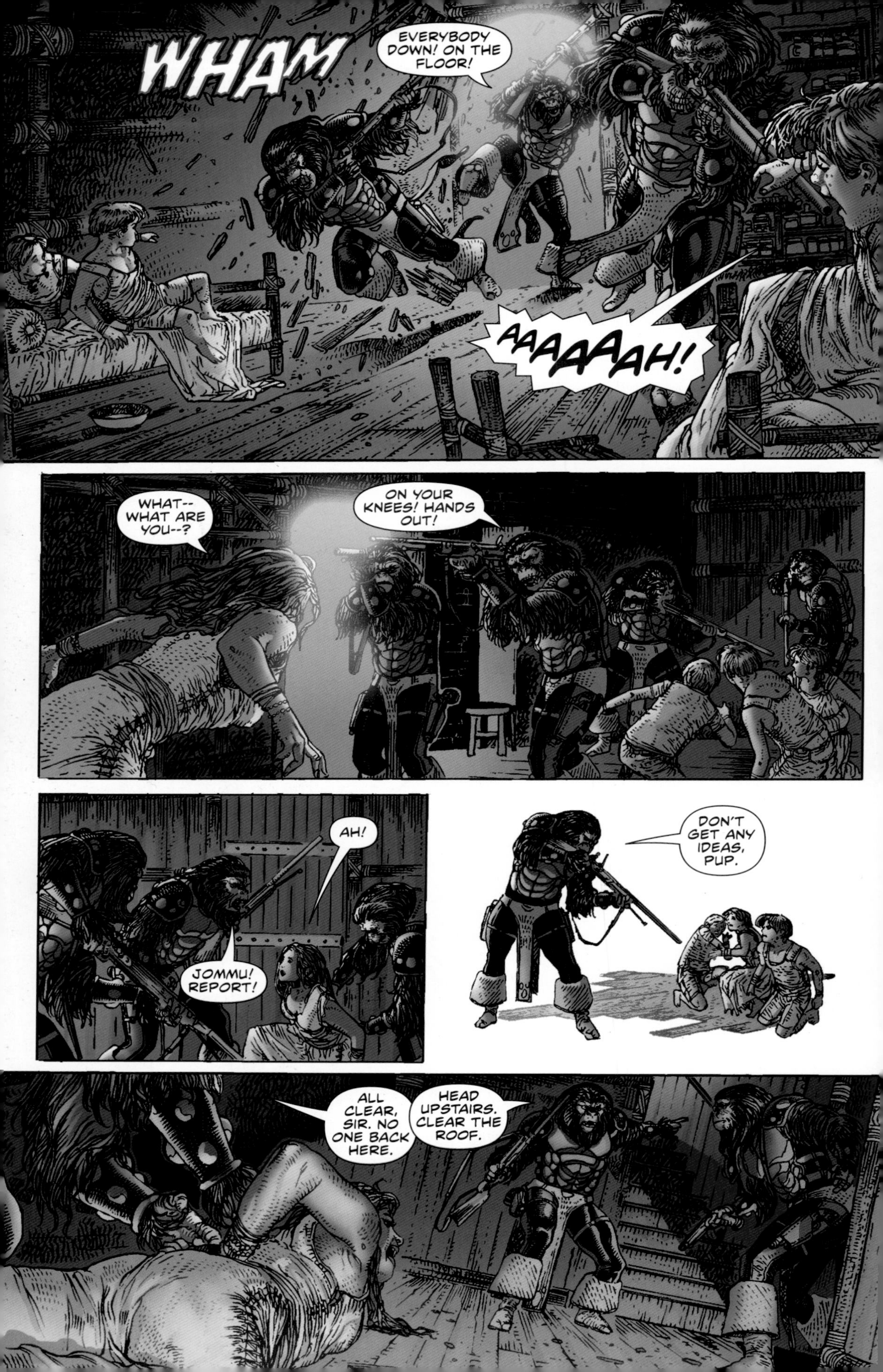
WHAM
EVERYBODY DOWN! ON THE FLOOR!
AAAAAAH!
WHAT-- WHAT ARE YOU--?
ON YOUR KNEES! HANDS OUT!
AH!
JOMMU! REPORT!
DON'T GET ANY IDEAS, PUP.
ALL CLEAR, SIR. NO ONE BACK HERE.
HEAD UPSTAIRS. CLEAR THE ROOF.

CASIMIR! WHERE IS HE?

WHO?

CASIMIR! CASIMIR!

I DON'T KNOW WHO THAT IS!

I TOLD YOU HE WOULDN'T BE HERE, JOMMU. THE INTELLIGENCE IS ALWAYS WRONG.

SHUT THE HELL UP.

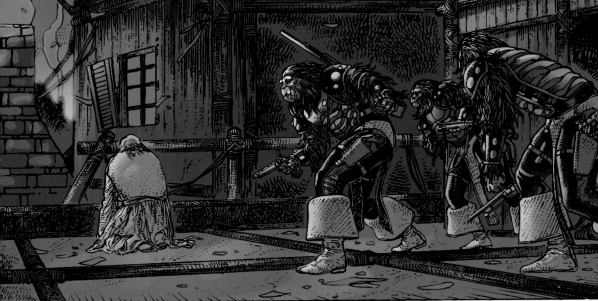

YOU! SKINNY! SHOW US YOUR HANDS!

GIVE ME STRENGTH.

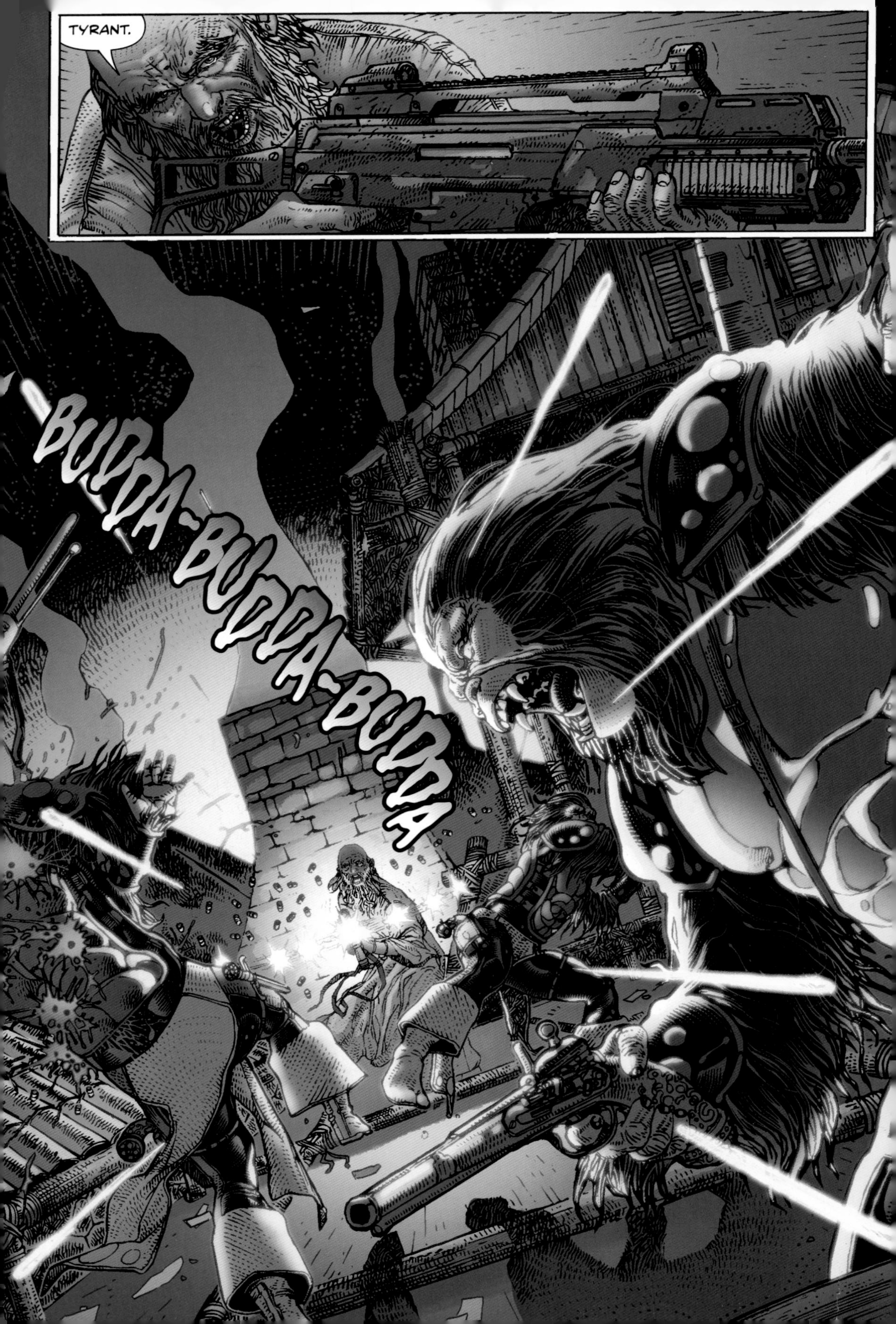
TYRANT.
BUDDA-BUDDA-BUDDA-BUDDA

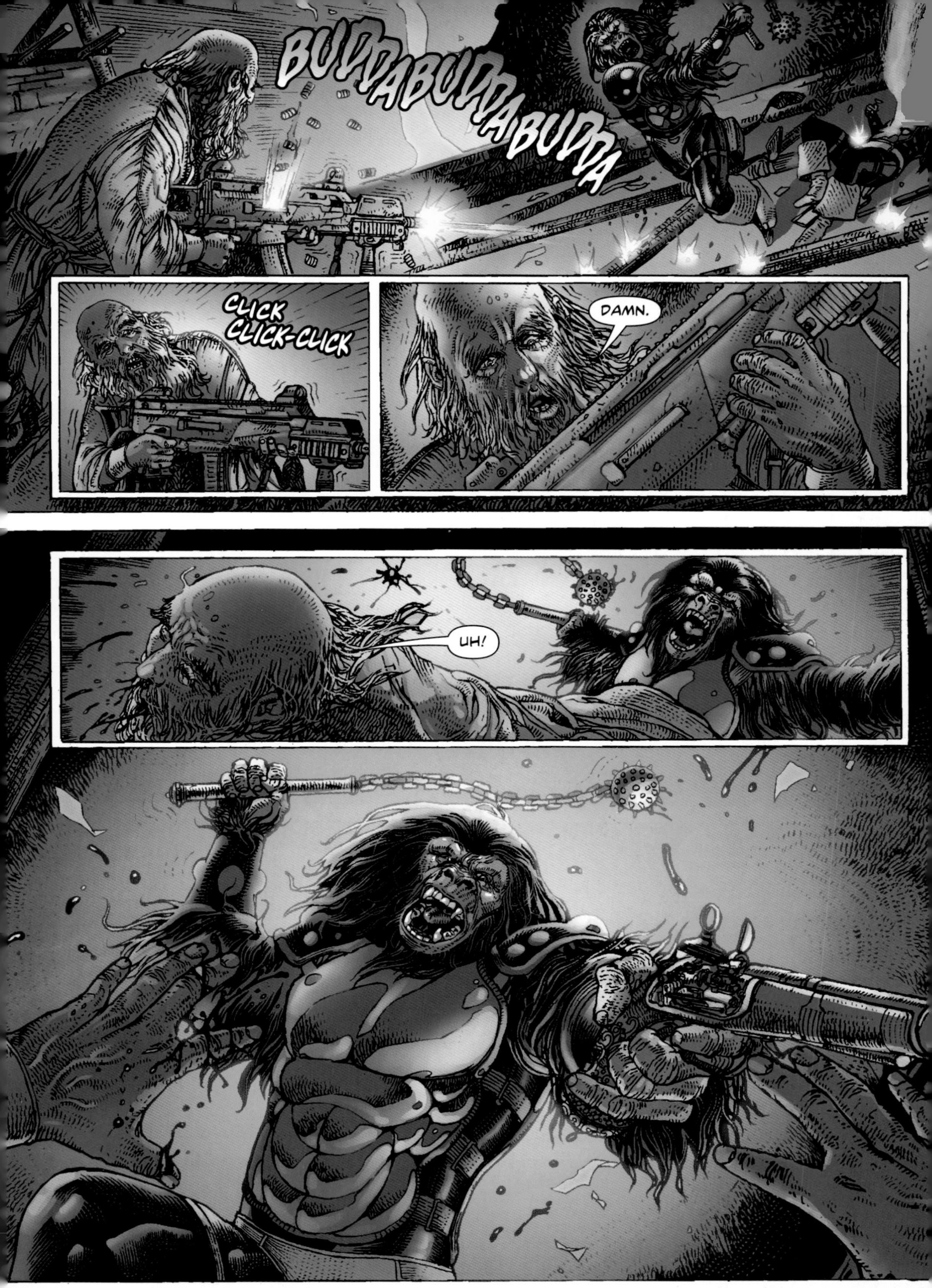
BUDDABUDDABUDDA
CLICK CLICK-CLICK
DAMN.
UH!

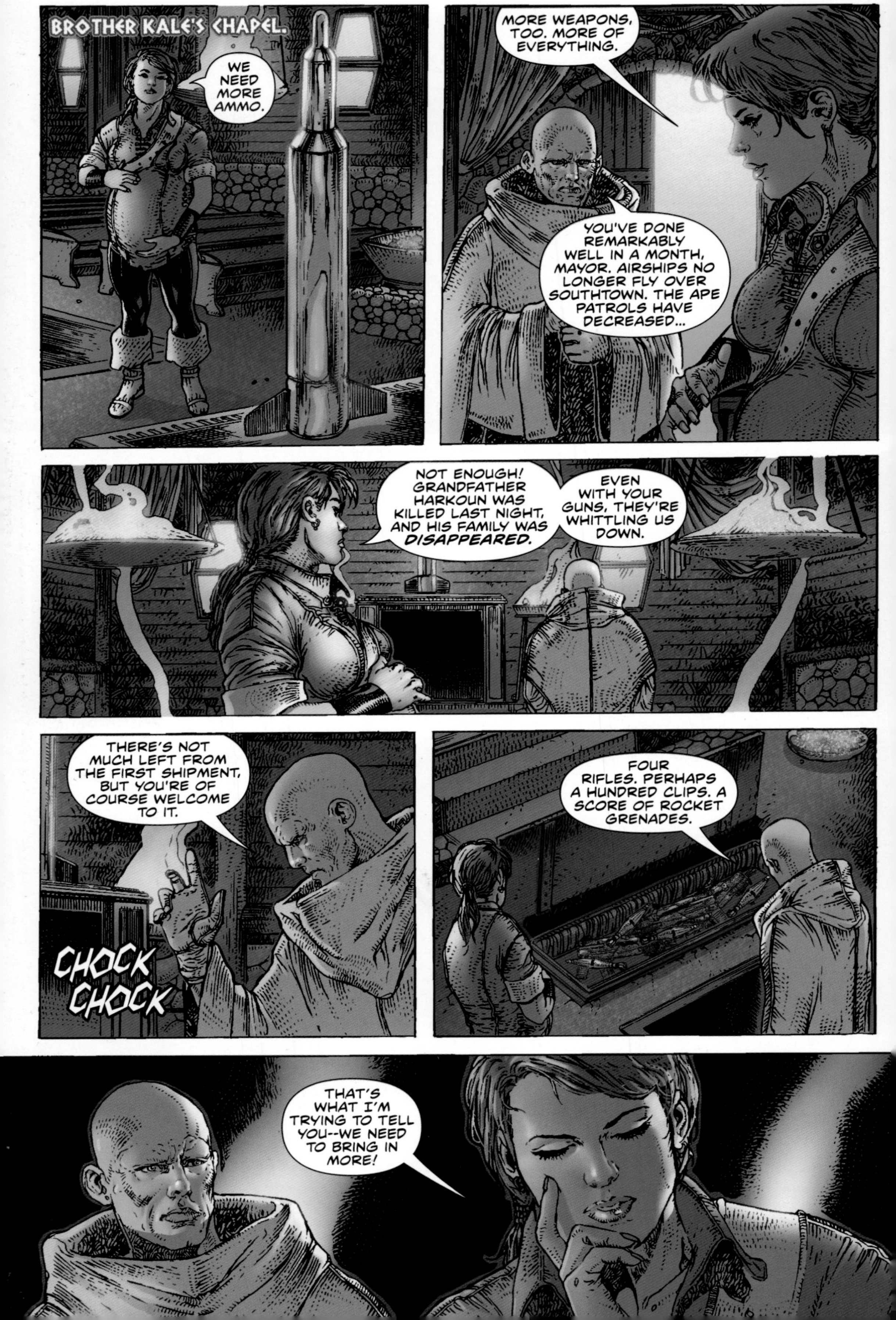
BROTHER KALE'S CHAPEL.
WE NEED MORE AMMO.
MORE WEAPONS, TOO. MORE OF EVERYTHING.
YOU'VE DONE REMARKABLY WELL IN A MONTH, MAYOR. AIRSHIPS NO LONGER FLY OVER SOUTHTOWN. THE APE PATROLS HAVE DECREASED...
NOT ENOUGH! GRANDFATHER HARKOUN WAS KILLED LAST NIGHT, AND HIS FAMILY WAS *DISAPPEARED.*
EVEN WITH YOUR GUNS, THEY'RE WHITTLING US DOWN.
THERE'S NOT MUCH LEFT FROM THE FIRST SHIPMENT, BUT YOU'RE OF COURSE WELCOME TO IT.
CHOCK CHOCK
FOUR RIFLES. PERHAPS A HUNDRED CLIPS. A SCORE OF ROCKET GRENADES.
THAT'S WHAT I'M TRYING TO TELL YOU--WE NEED TO BRING IN MORE!

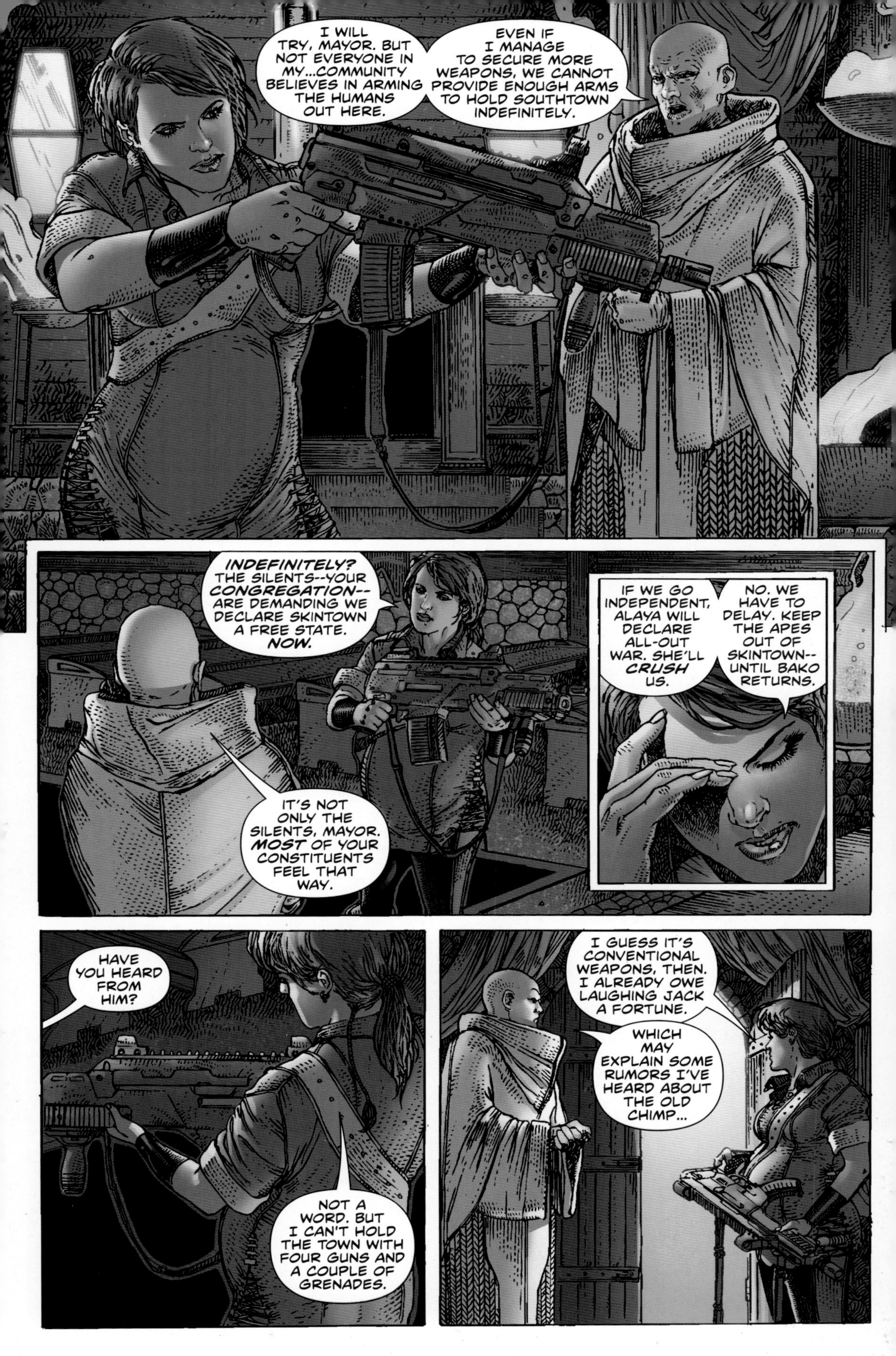
I WILL TRY, MAYOR. BUT NOT EVERYONE IN MY...COMMUNITY BELIEVES IN ARMING THE HUMANS OUT HERE.
EVEN IF I MANAGE TO SECURE MORE WEAPONS, WE CANNOT PROVIDE ENOUGH ARMS TO HOLD SOUTHTOWN INDEFINITELY.
INDEFINITELY? THE SILENTS--YOUR CONGREGATION--ARE DEMANDING WE DECLARE SKINTOWN A FREE STATE. NOW.
IT'S NOT ONLY THE SILENTS, MAYOR. MOST OF YOUR CONSTITUENTS FEEL THAT WAY.
IF WE GO INDEPENDENT, ALAYA WILL DECLARE ALL-OUT WAR. SHE'LL CRUSH US.
NO. WE HAVE TO DELAY. KEEP THE APES OUT OF SKINTOWN--UNTIL BAKO RETURNS.
HAVE YOU HEARD FROM HIM?
NOT A WORD. BUT I CAN'T HOLD THE TOWN WITH FOUR GUNS AND A COUPLE OF GRENADES.
I GUESS IT'S CONVENTIONAL WEAPONS, THEN. I ALREADY OWE LAUGHING JACK A FORTUNE.
WHICH MAY EXPLAIN SOME RUMORS I'VE HEARD ABOUT THE OLD CHIMP...

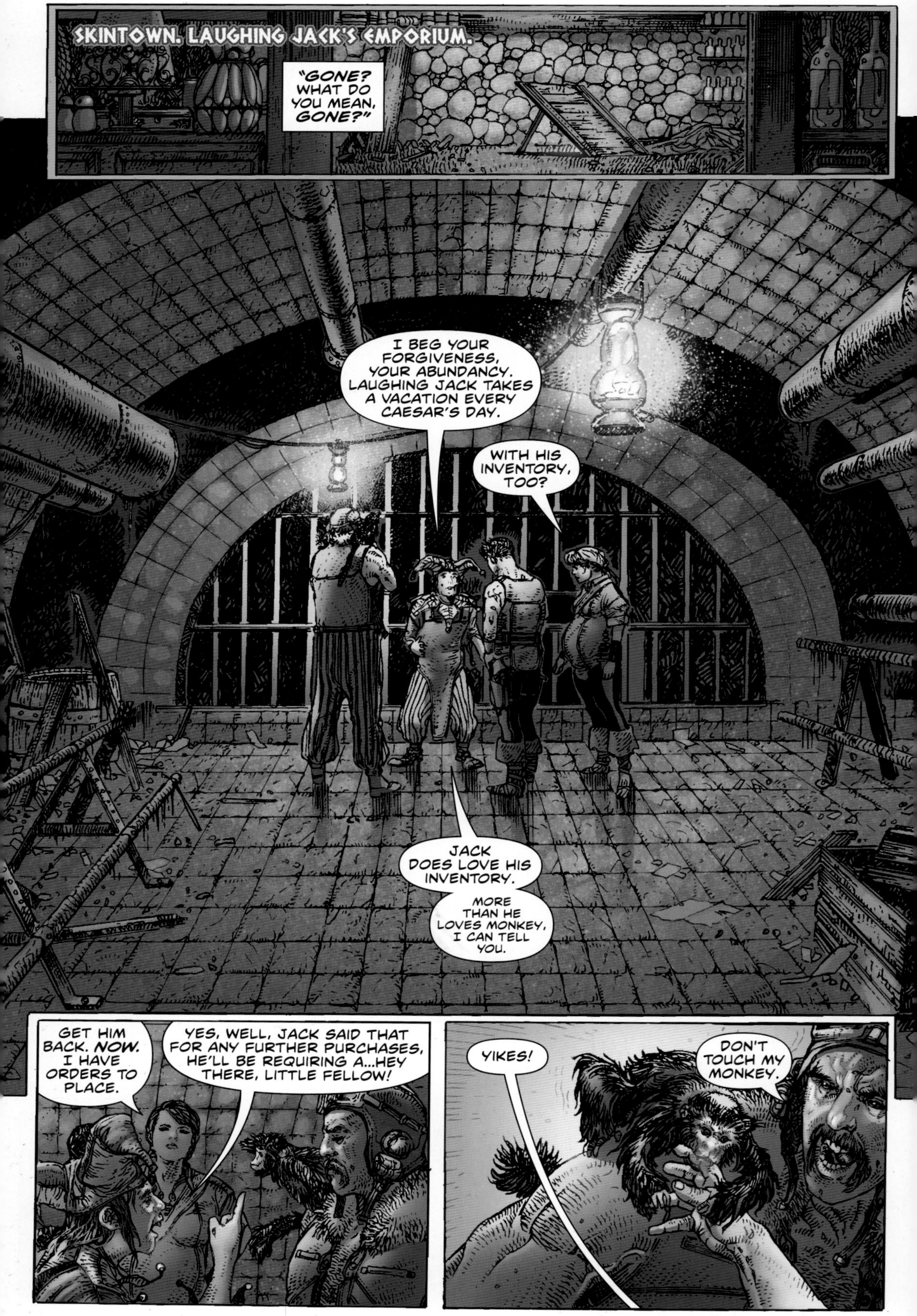
SKINTOWN. LAUGHING JACK'S EMPORIUM.
"GONE? WHAT DO YOU MEAN, GONE?"
I BEG YOUR FORGIVENESS, YOUR ABUNDANCY. LAUGHING JACK TAKES A VACATION EVERY CAESAR'S DAY.
WITH HIS INVENTORY, TOO?
JACK DOES LOVE HIS INVENTORY.
MORE THAN HE LOVES MONKEY, I CAN TELL YOU.
GET HIM BACK. NOW. I HAVE ORDERS TO PLACE.
YES, WELL, JACK SAID THAT FOR ANY FURTHER PURCHASES, HE'LL BE REQUIRING A...HEY THERE, LITTLE FELLOW!
YIKES!
DON'T TOUCH MY MONKEY.

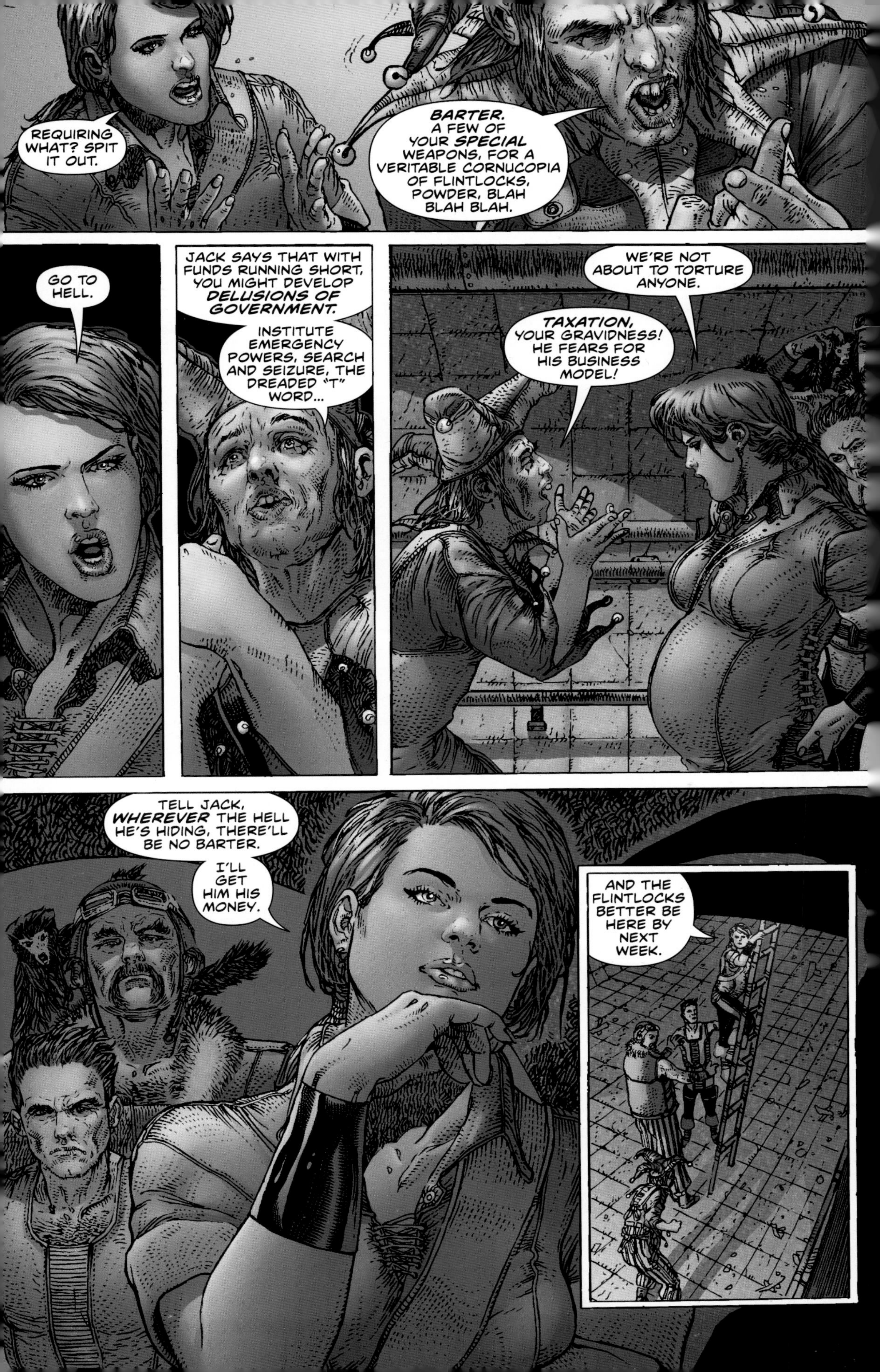
REQUIRING WHAT? SPIT IT OUT.
BARTER. A FEW OF YOUR SPECIAL WEAPONS, FOR A VERITABLE CORNUCOPIA OF FLINTLOCKS, POWDER, BLAH BLAH BLAH.
GO TO HELL.
JACK SAYS THAT WITH FUNDS RUNNING SHORT, YOU MIGHT DEVELOP DELUSIONS OF GOVERNMENT.
INSTITUTE EMERGENCY POWERS, SEARCH AND SEIZURE, THE DREADED "T" WORD...
WE'RE NOT ABOUT TO TORTURE ANYONE.
TAXATION, YOUR GRAVIDNESS! HE FEARS FOR HIS BUSINESS MODEL!
TELL JACK, WHEREVER THE HELL HE'S HIDING, THERE'LL BE NO BARTER.
I'LL GET HIM HIS MONEY.
AND THE FLINTLOCKS BETTER BE HERE BY NEXT WEEK.

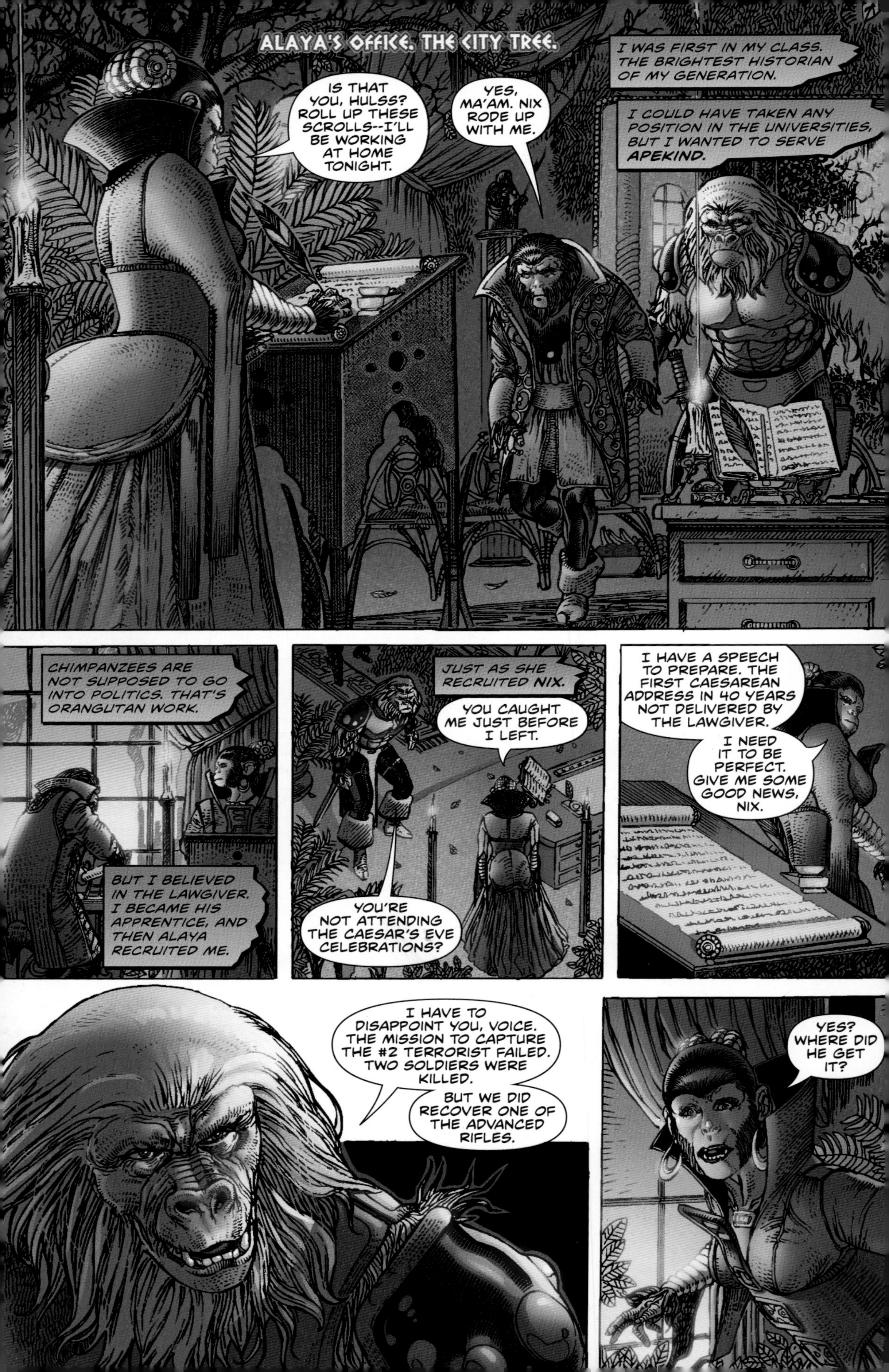
ALAYA'S OFFICE. THE CITY TREE.
I WAS FIRST IN MY CLASS. THE BRIGHTEST HISTORIAN OF MY GENERATION.
IS THAT YOU, HULSS? ROLL UP THESE SCROLLS--I'LL BE WORKING AT HOME TONIGHT.
YES, MA'AM. NIX RODE UP WITH ME.
I COULD HAVE TAKEN ANY POSITION IN THE UNIVERSITIES, BUT I WANTED TO SERVE APEKIND.
CHIMPANZEES ARE NOT SUPPOSED TO GO INTO POLITICS. THAT'S ORANGUTAN WORK.
BUT I BELIEVED IN THE LAWGIVER. I BECAME HIS APPRENTICE, AND THEN ALAYA RECRUITED ME.
JUST AS SHE RECRUITED NIX.
YOU CAUGHT ME JUST BEFORE I LEFT.
YOU'RE NOT ATTENDING THE CAESAR'S EVE CELEBRATIONS?
I HAVE A SPEECH TO PREPARE. THE FIRST CAESAREAN ADDRESS IN 40 YEARS NOT DELIVERED BY THE LAWGIVER.
I NEED IT TO BE PERFECT. GIVE ME SOME GOOD NEWS, NIX.
I HAVE TO DISAPPOINT YOU, VOICE. THE MISSION TO CAPTURE THE #2 TERRORIST FAILED. TWO SOLDIERS WERE KILLED.
BUT WE DID RECOVER ONE OF THE ADVANCED RIFLES.
YES? WHERE DID HE GET IT?

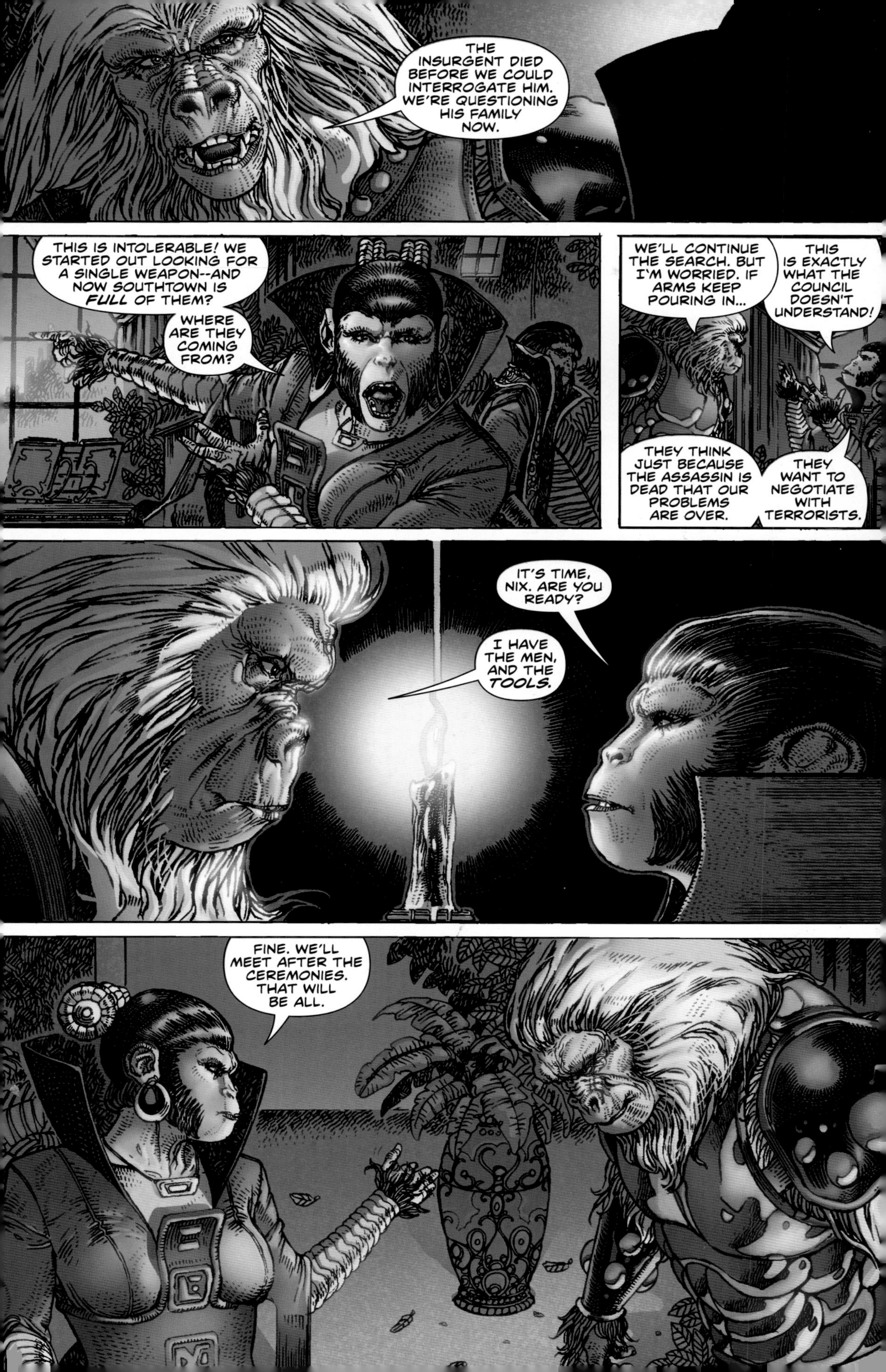
THE INSURGENT DIED BEFORE WE COULD INTERROGATE HIM. WE'RE QUESTIONING HIS FAMILY NOW.
THIS IS INTOLERABLE! WE STARTED OUT LOOKING FOR A SINGLE WEAPON--AND NOW SOUTHTOWN IS *FULL* OF THEM?
WHERE ARE THEY COMING FROM?
WE'LL CONTINUE THE SEARCH. BUT I'M WORRIED. IF ARMS KEEP POURING IN...
THIS IS EXACTLY WHAT THE COUNCIL DOESN'T UNDERSTAND!
THEY THINK JUST BECAUSE THE ASSASSIN IS DEAD THAT OUR PROBLEMS ARE OVER.
THEY WANT TO NEGOTIATE WITH TERRORISTS.
IT'S TIME, NIX. ARE YOU READY?
I HAVE THE MEN, AND THE *TOOLS*.
FINE. WE'LL MEET AFTER THE CEREMONIES. THAT WILL BE ALL.

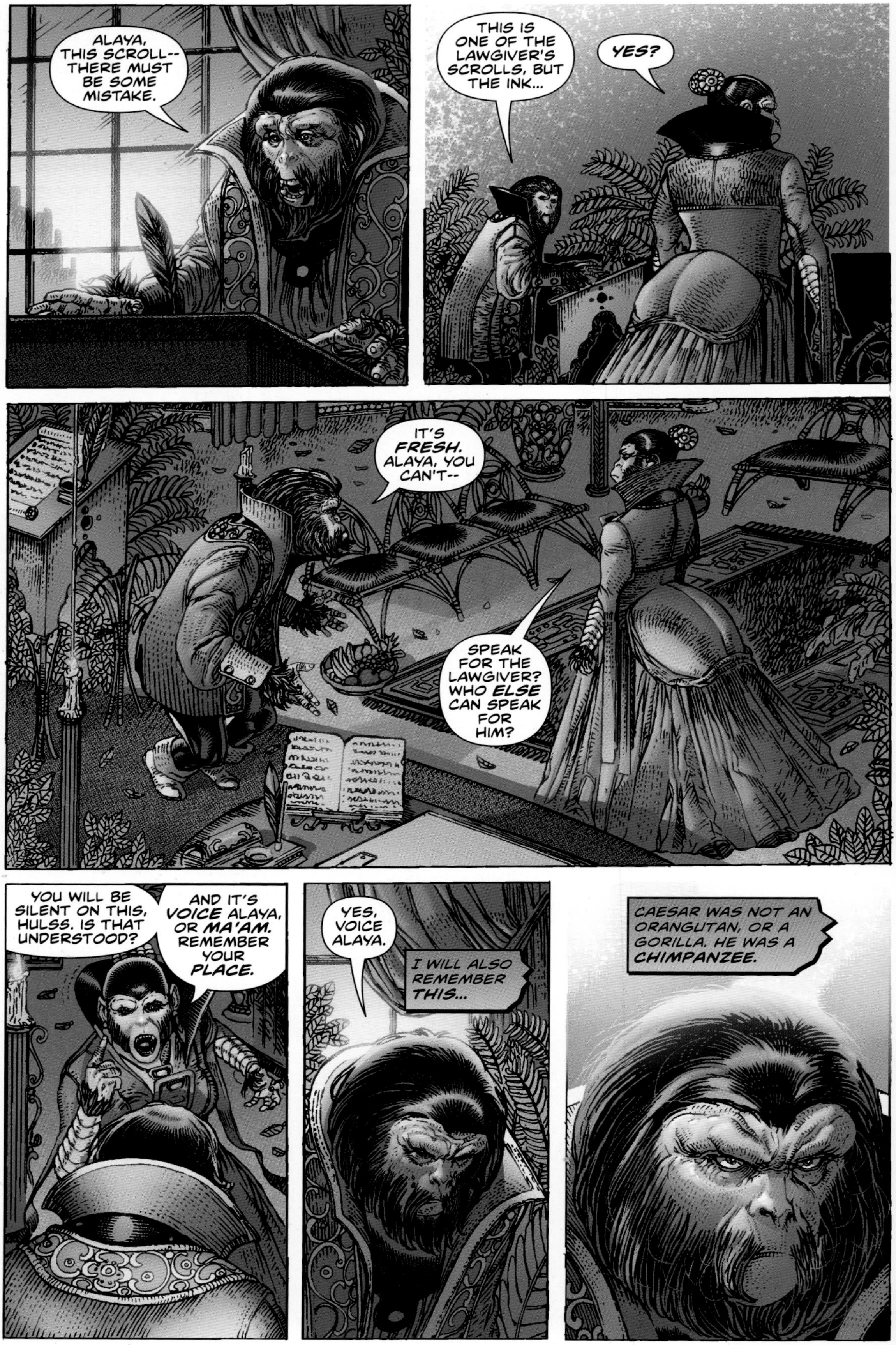
ALAYA, THIS SCROLL-- THERE MUST BE SOME MISTAKE.
THIS IS ONE OF THE LAWGIVER'S SCROLLS, BUT THE INK...
YES?
IT'S FRESH. ALAYA, YOU CAN'T--
SPEAK FOR THE LAWGIVER? WHO ELSE CAN SPEAK FOR HIM?
YOU WILL BE SILENT ON THIS, HULSS. IS THAT UNDERSTOOD?
AND IT'S VOICE ALAYA, OR MA'AM. REMEMBER YOUR PLACE.
YES, VOICE ALAYA.
I WILL ALSO REMEMBER THIS...
CAESAR WAS NOT AN ORANGUTAN, OR A GORILLA. HE WAS A CHIMPANZEE.

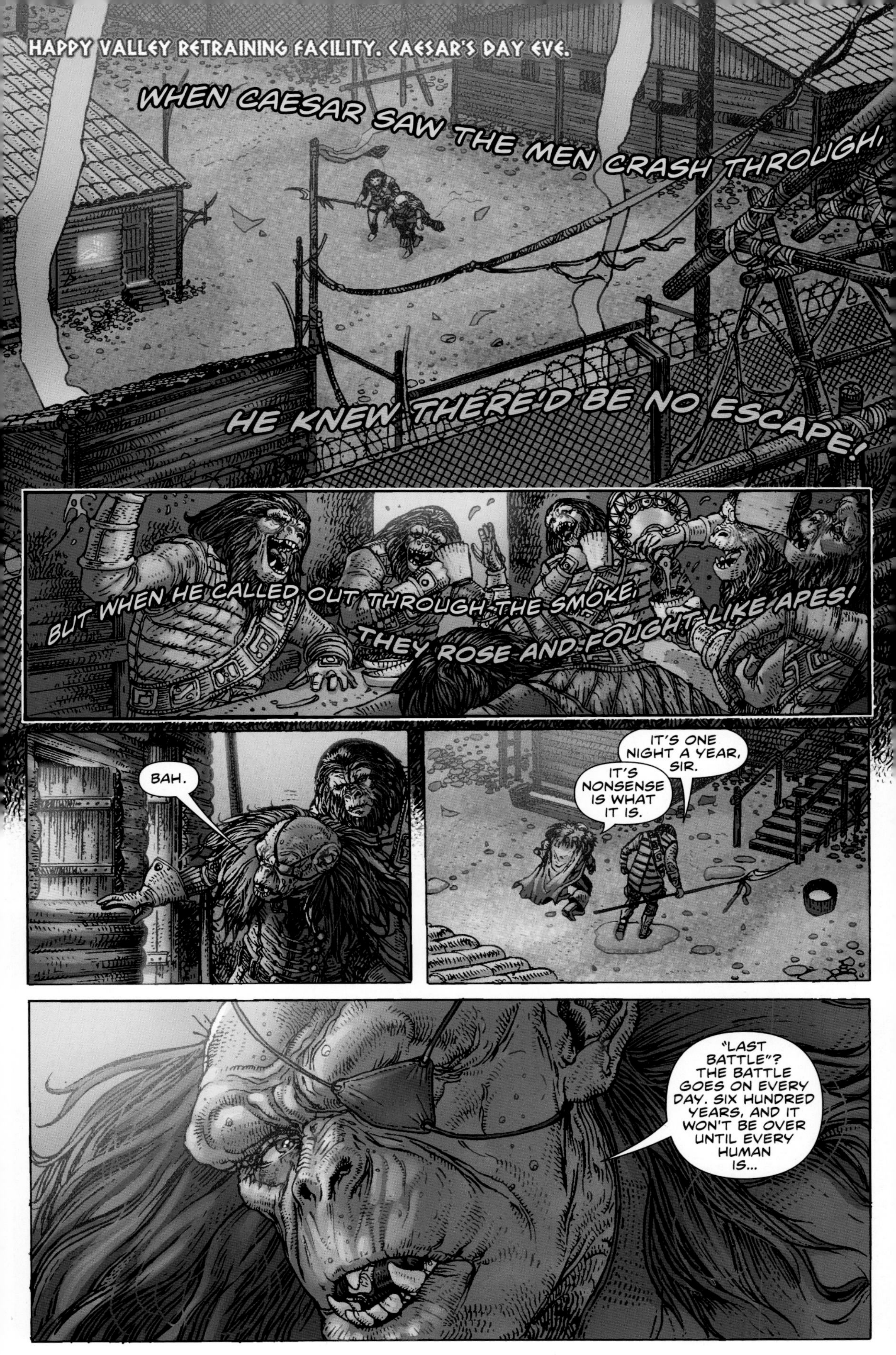
HAPPY VALLEY RETRAINING FACILITY. CAESAR'S DAY EVE.
WHEN CAESAR SAW THE MEN CRASH THROUGH,
HE KNEW THERE'D BE NO ESCAPE!
BUT WHEN HE CALLED OUT THROUGH THE SMOKE,
THEY ROSE AND FOUGHT LIKE APES!
BAH.
IT'S ONE NIGHT A YEAR, SIR.
IT'S NONSENSE IS WHAT IT IS.
"LAST BATTLE"? THE BATTLE GOES ON EVERY DAY. SIX HUNDRED YEARS, AND IT WON'T BE OVER UNTIL EVERY HUMAN IS...

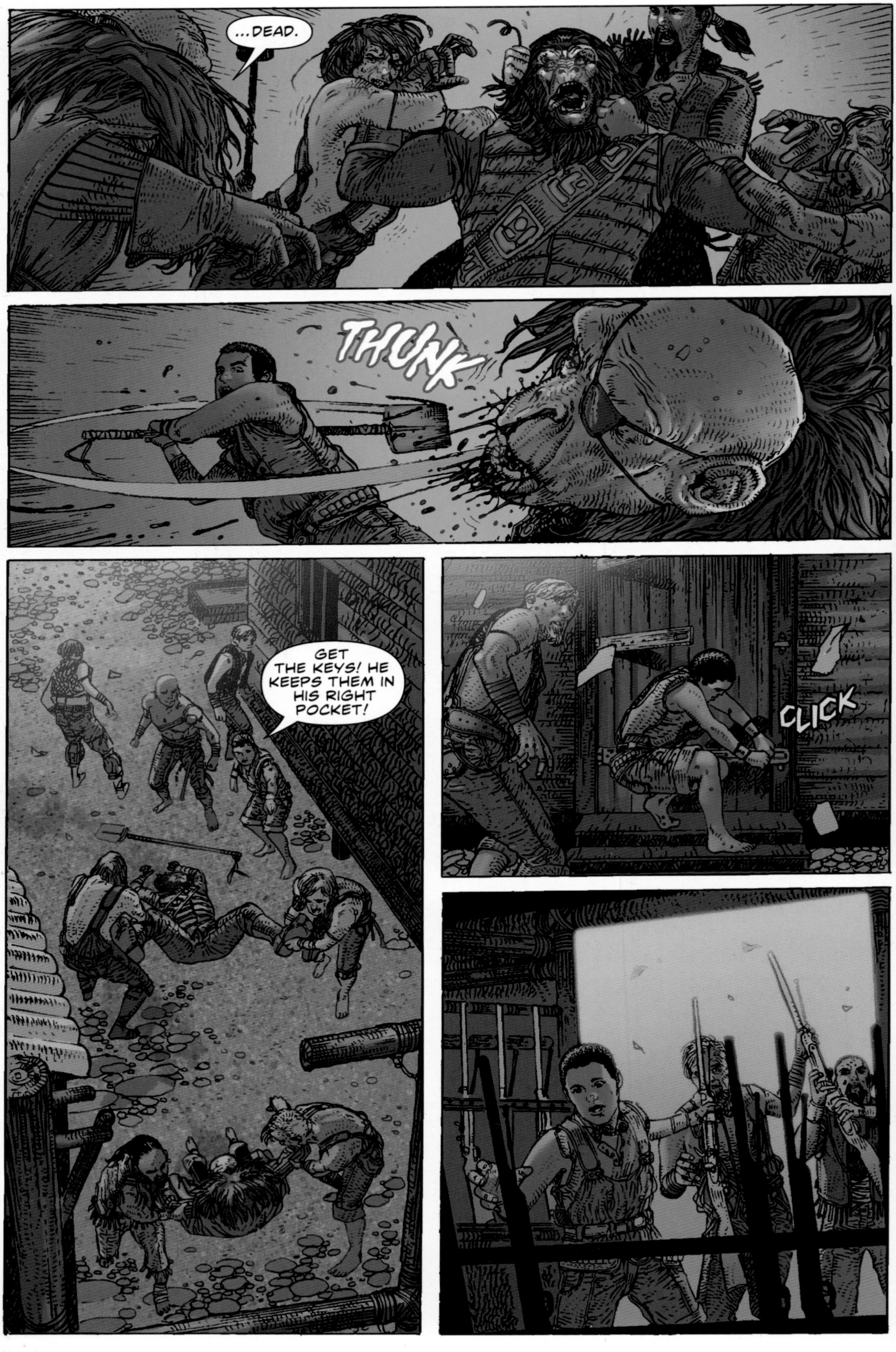
...DEAD.
THUNK
GET THE KEYS! HE KEEPS THEM IN HIS RIGHT POCKET!
CLICK

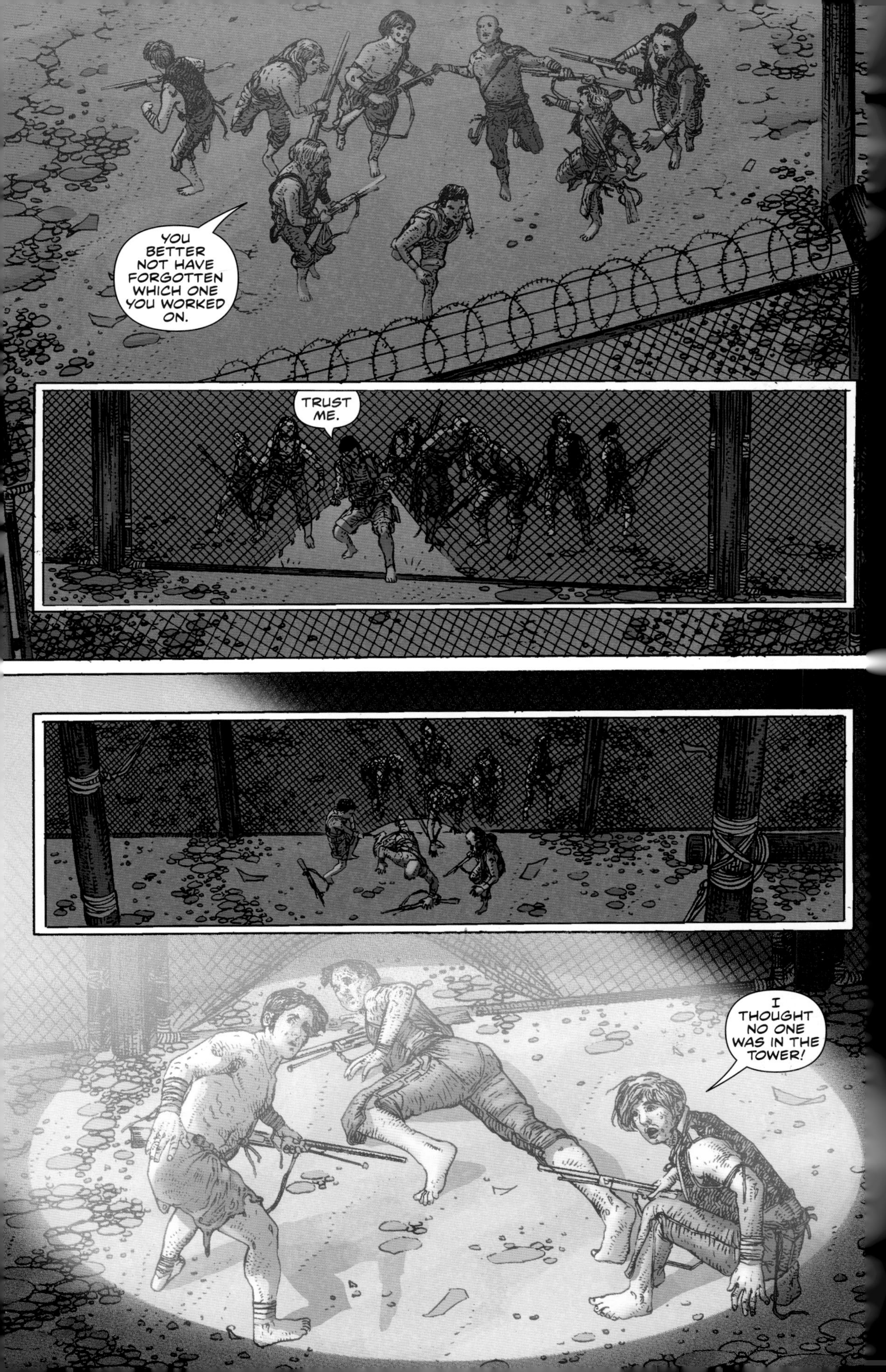
YOU BETTER NOT HAVE FORGOTTEN WHICH ONE YOU WORKED ON.
TRUST ME.
I THOUGHT NO ONE WAS IN THE TOWER!

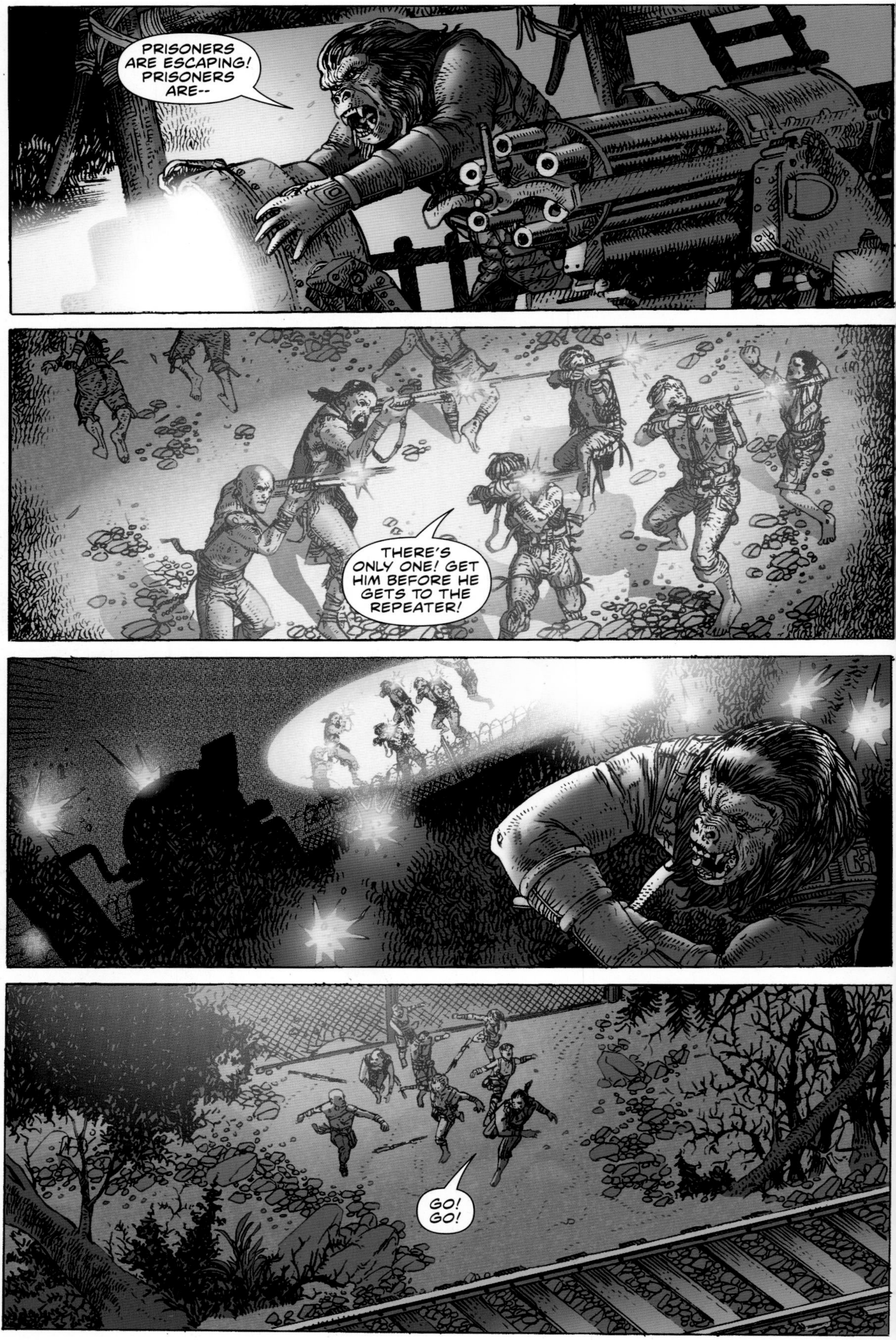
PRISONERS ARE ESCAPING! PRISONERS ARE--
THERE'S ONLY ONE! GET HIM BEFORE HE GETS TO THE REPEATER!
GO! GO!

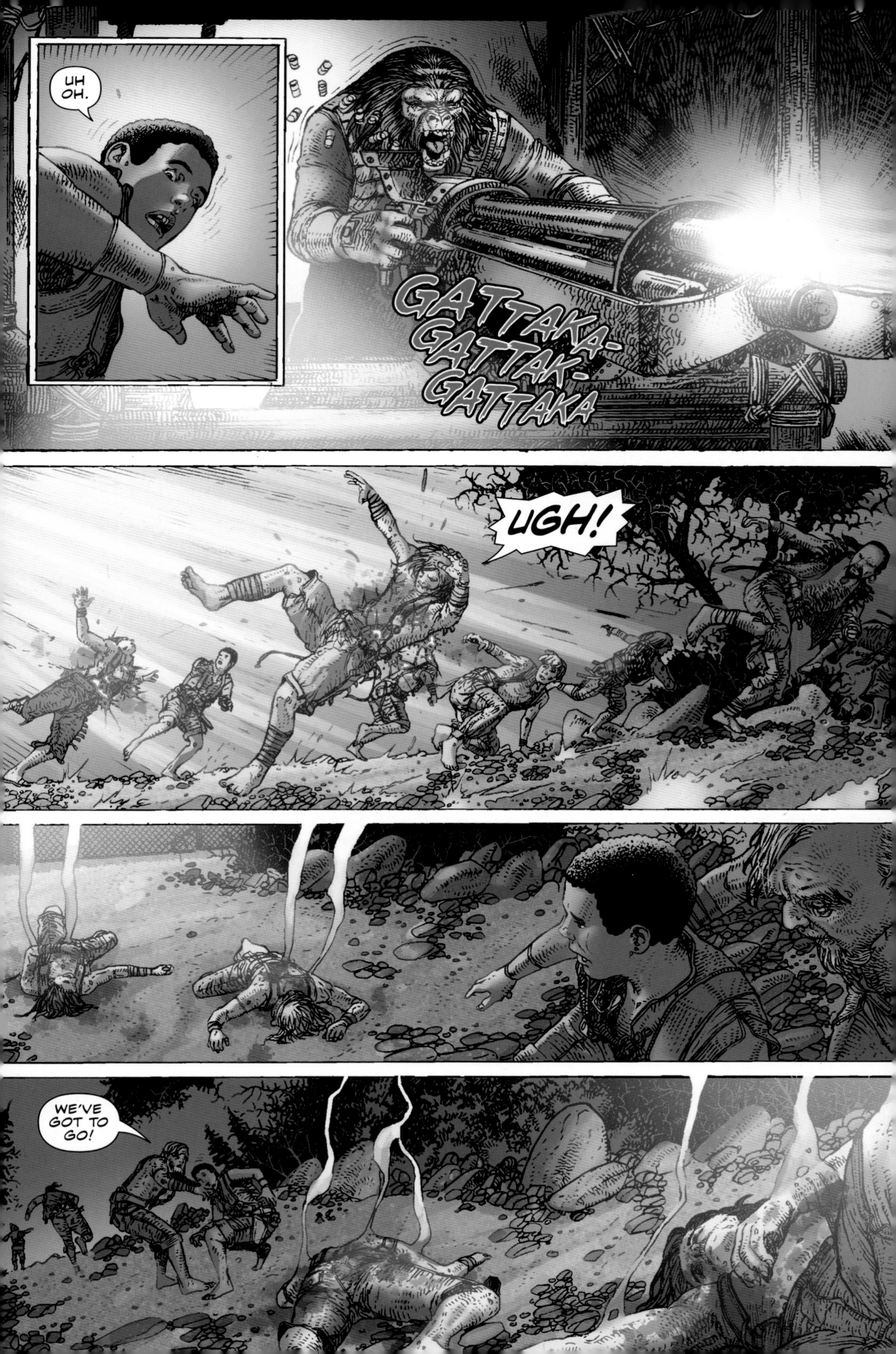
UH OH.
GATTAKA-GATTAK-GATTAKA
UGH!
WE'VE GOT TO GO!

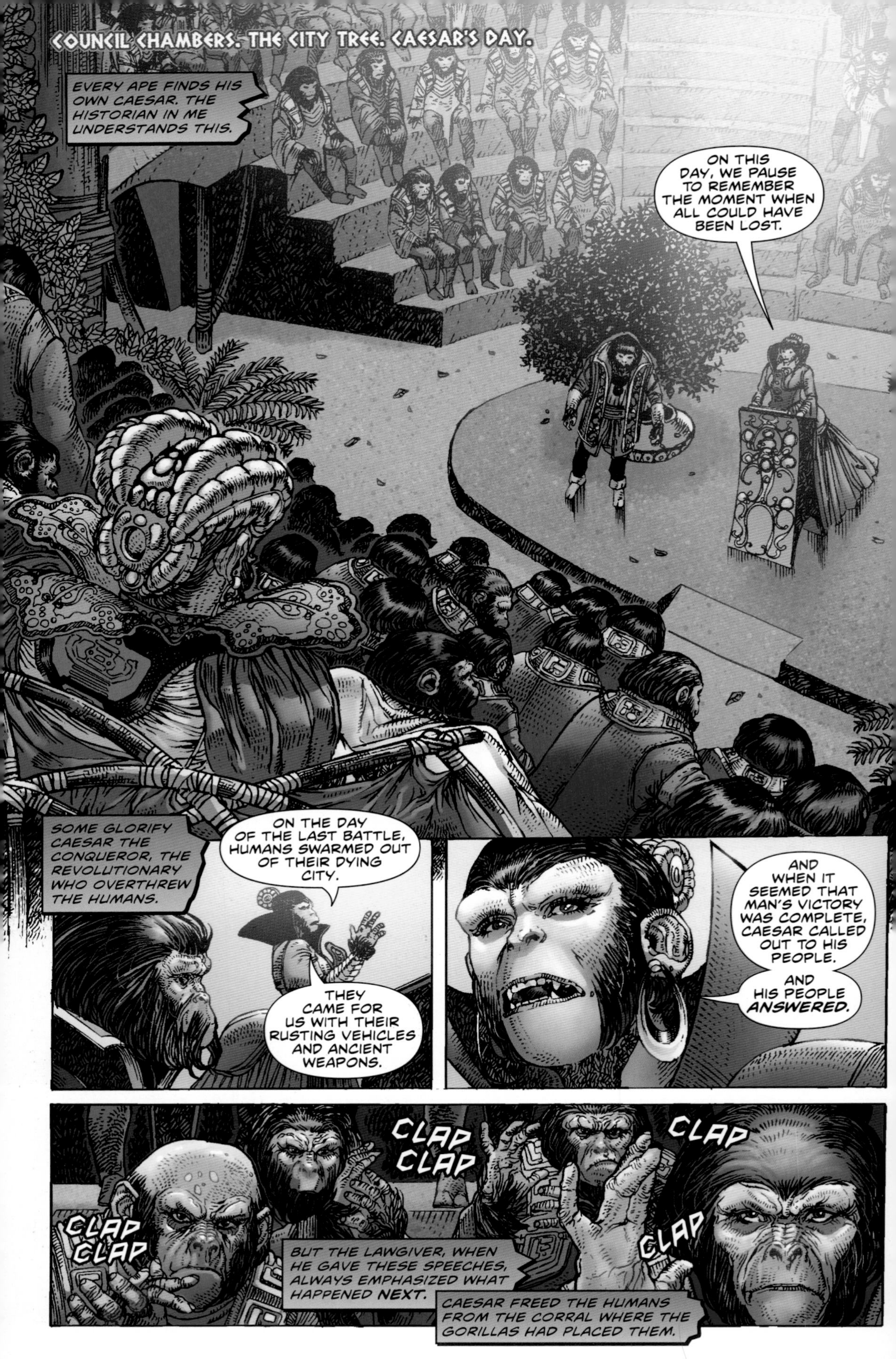
COUNCIL CHAMBERS. THE CITY TREE. CAESAR'S DAY.
EVERY APE FINDS HIS OWN CAESAR. THE HISTORIAN IN ME UNDERSTANDS THIS.
ON THIS DAY, WE PAUSE TO REMEMBER THE MOMENT WHEN ALL COULD HAVE BEEN LOST.
SOME GLORIFY CAESAR THE CONQUEROR, THE REVOLUTIONARY WHO OVERTHREW THE HUMANS.
ON THE DAY OF THE LAST BATTLE, HUMANS SWARMED OUT OF THEIR DYING CITY.
THEY CAME FOR US WITH THEIR RUSTING VEHICLES AND ANCIENT WEAPONS.
AND WHEN IT SEEMED THAT MAN'S VICTORY WAS COMPLETE, CAESAR CALLED OUT TO HIS PEOPLE.
AND HIS PEOPLE ANSWERED.
CLAP CLAP
CLAP
CLAP CLAP
CLAP
BUT THE LAWGIVER, WHEN HE GAVE THESE SPEECHES, ALWAYS EMPHASIZED WHAT HAPPENED NEXT.
CAESAR FREED THE HUMANS FROM THE CORRAL WHERE THE GORILLAS HAD PLACED THEM.

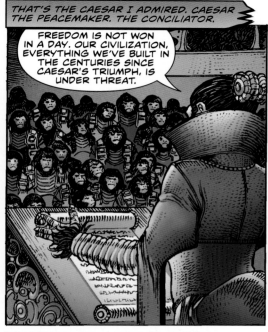

THAT'S THE CAESAR I ADMIRED. CAESAR THE PEACEMAKER. THE CONCILIATOR.

FREEDOM IS NOT WON IN A DAY. OUR CIVILIZATION, EVERYTHING WE'VE BUILT IN THE CENTURIES SINCE CAESAR'S TRIUMPH, IS UNDER THREAT.

ALAYA IS THE MOST GIFTED SPEAKER I'VE EVER HEARD. IT'S NOT MERELY THE WORDS SHE USES.

MY GRANDFATHER, THE LAWGIVER, FORESAW THIS THREAT.

HE WORKED TO SAVE THE HUMANS FROM THEMSELVES, EVEN AS HE KNEW IT MIGHT BE IMPOSSIBLE.

IT IS THE EMOTION WITH WHICH SHE IMBUES EACH SYLLABLE. WHEN SHE SPEAKS, YOU BELIEVE.

BEFORE HE WAS MURDERED, HE WAS WORKING ON A FINAL SCROLL.

HE FEARED THAT IF HE SPOKE THE UNVARNISHED TRUTH, THAT THE HUMANS WOULD REVOLT.

BUT THAT DAY IS ALREADY UPON US.

I READ NOW FROM THE TWENTY-THIRD SCROLL, THE NINTH VERSE.

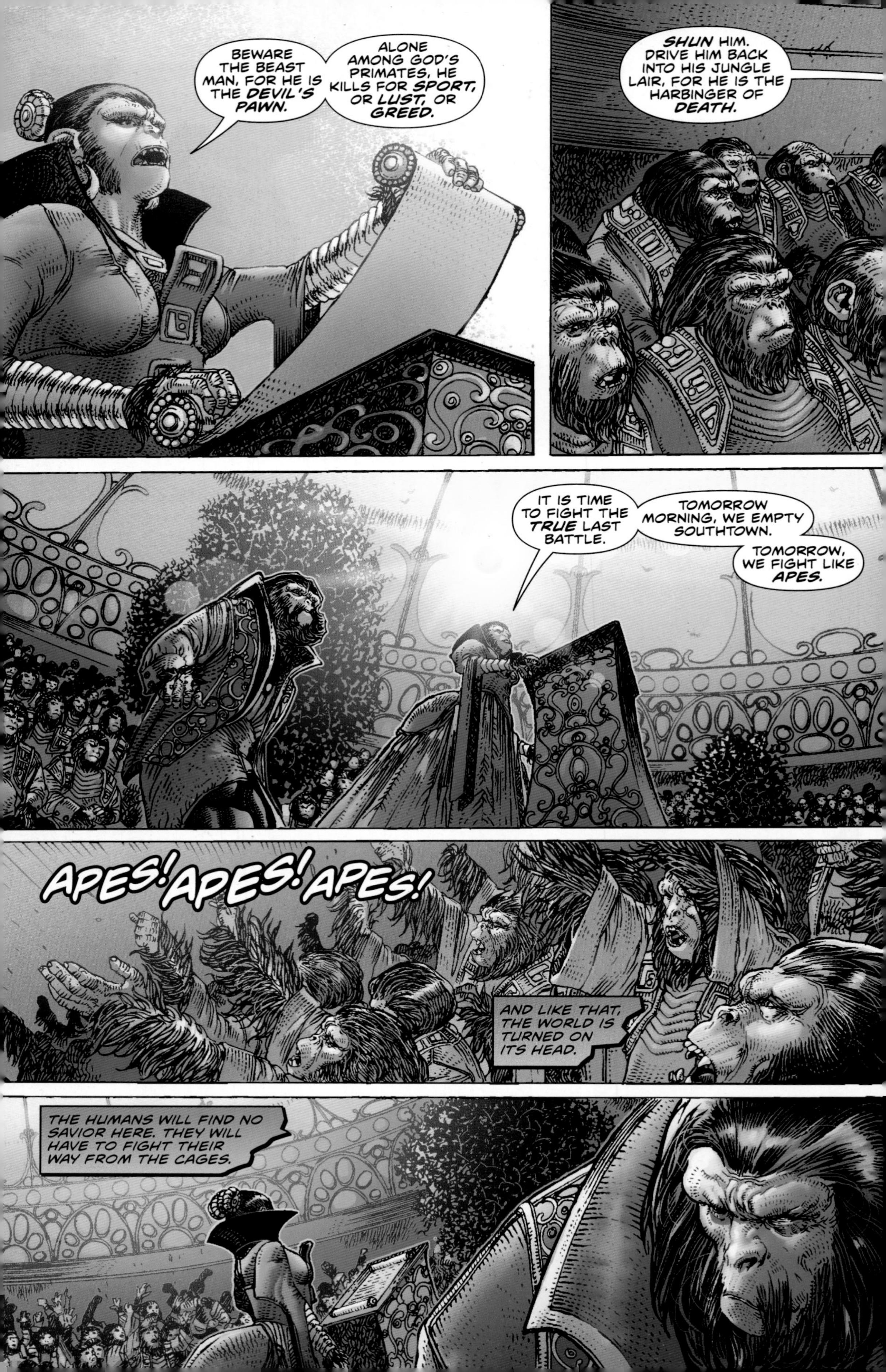
BEWARE THE BEAST MAN, FOR HE IS THE DEVIL'S PAWN.
ALONE AMONG GOD'S PRIMATES, HE KILLS FOR SPORT, OR LUST, OR GREED.
SHUN HIM. DRIVE HIM BACK INTO HIS JUNGLE LAIR, FOR HE IS THE HARBINGER OF DEATH.
IT IS TIME TO FIGHT THE TRUE LAST BATTLE.
TOMORROW MORNING, WE EMPTY SOUTHTOWN.
TOMORROW, WE FIGHT LIKE APES.
APES! APES! APES!
AND LIKE THAT, THE WORLD IS TURNED ON ITS HEAD.
THE HUMANS WILL FIND NO SAVIOR HERE. THEY WILL HAVE TO FIGHT THEIR WAY FROM THE CAGES.

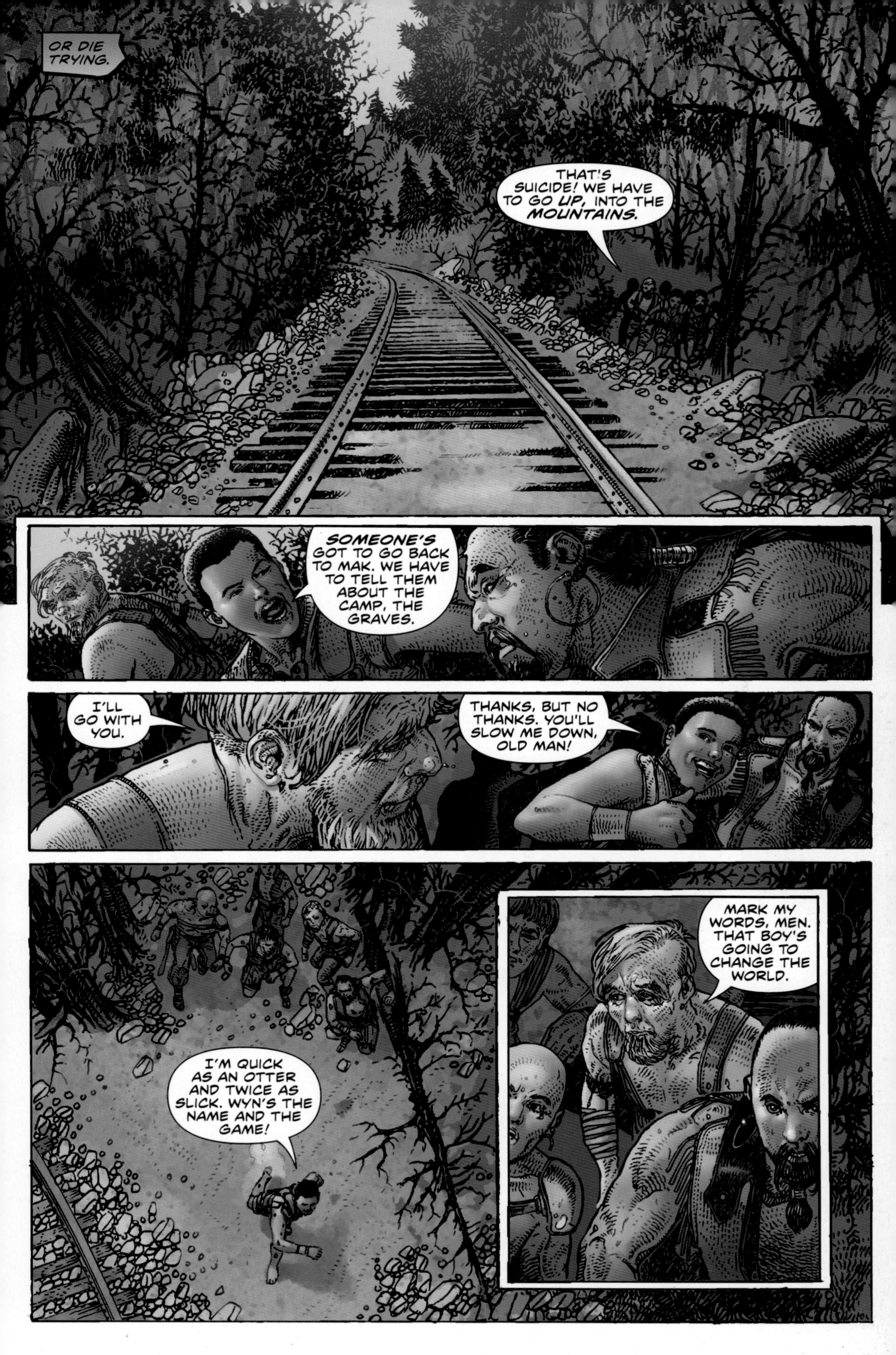
OR DIE TRYING.
THAT'S SUICIDE! WE HAVE TO GO *UP*, INTO THE *MOUNTAINS*.
*SOMEONE'S* GOT TO GO BACK TO MAK. WE HAVE TO TELL THEM ABOUT THE CAMP, THE GRAVES.
I'LL GO WITH YOU.
THANKS, BUT NO THANKS. YOU'LL SLOW ME DOWN, OLD MAN!
I'M QUICK AS AN OTTER AND TWICE AS SLICK. WYN'S THE NAME AND THE GAME!
MARK MY WORDS, MEN. THAT BOY'S GOING TO CHANGE THE WORLD.

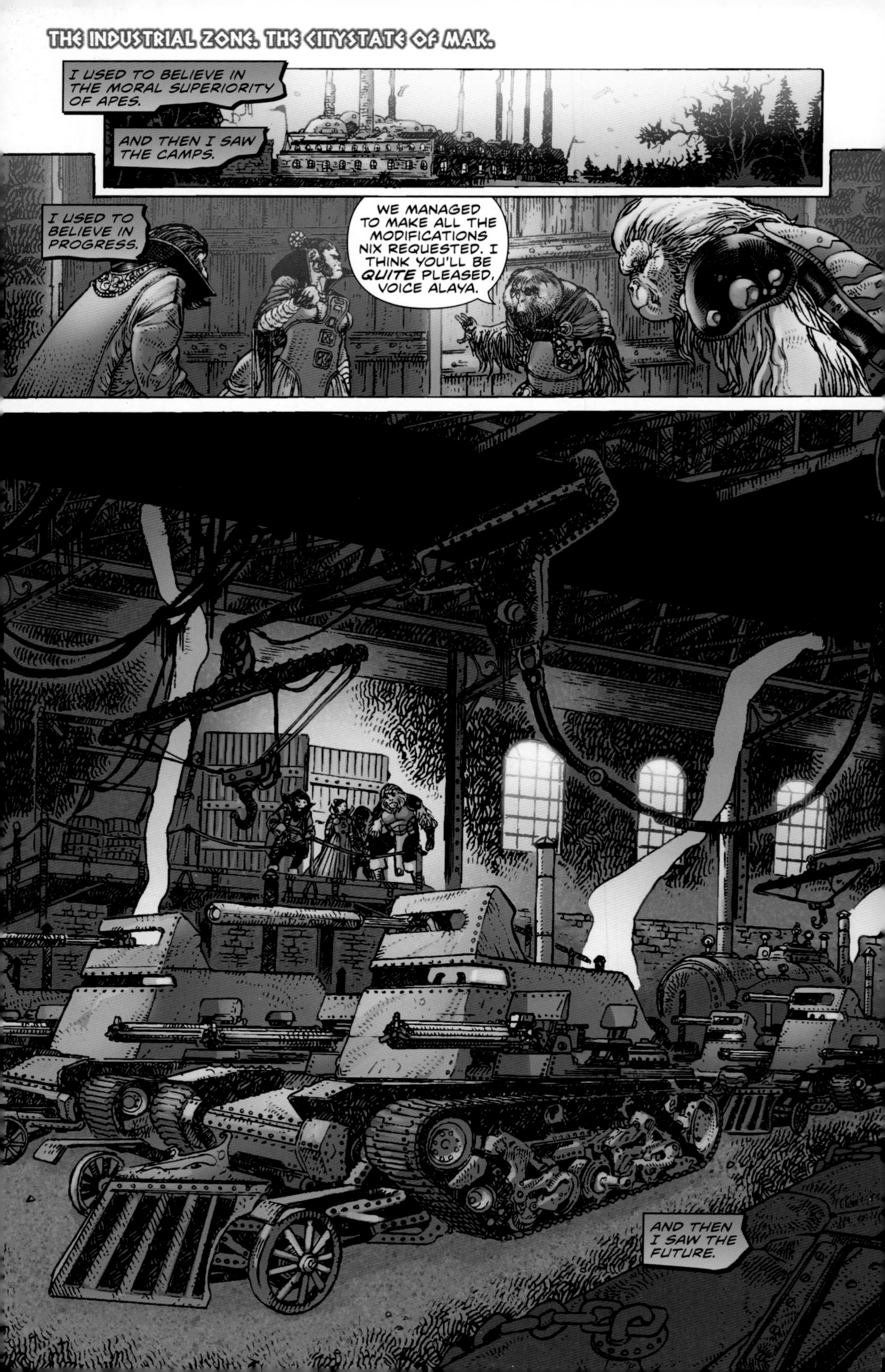
THE INDUSTRIAL ZONE. THE CITYSTATE OF MAK.
I USED TO BELIEVE IN THE MORAL SUPERIORITY OF APES.
AND THEN I SAW THE CAMPS.
I USED TO BELIEVE IN PROGRESS.
WE MANAGED TO MAKE ALL THE MODIFICATIONS NIX REQUESTED. I THINK YOU'LL BE QUITE PLEASED, VOICE ALAYA.
AND THEN I SAW THE FUTURE.

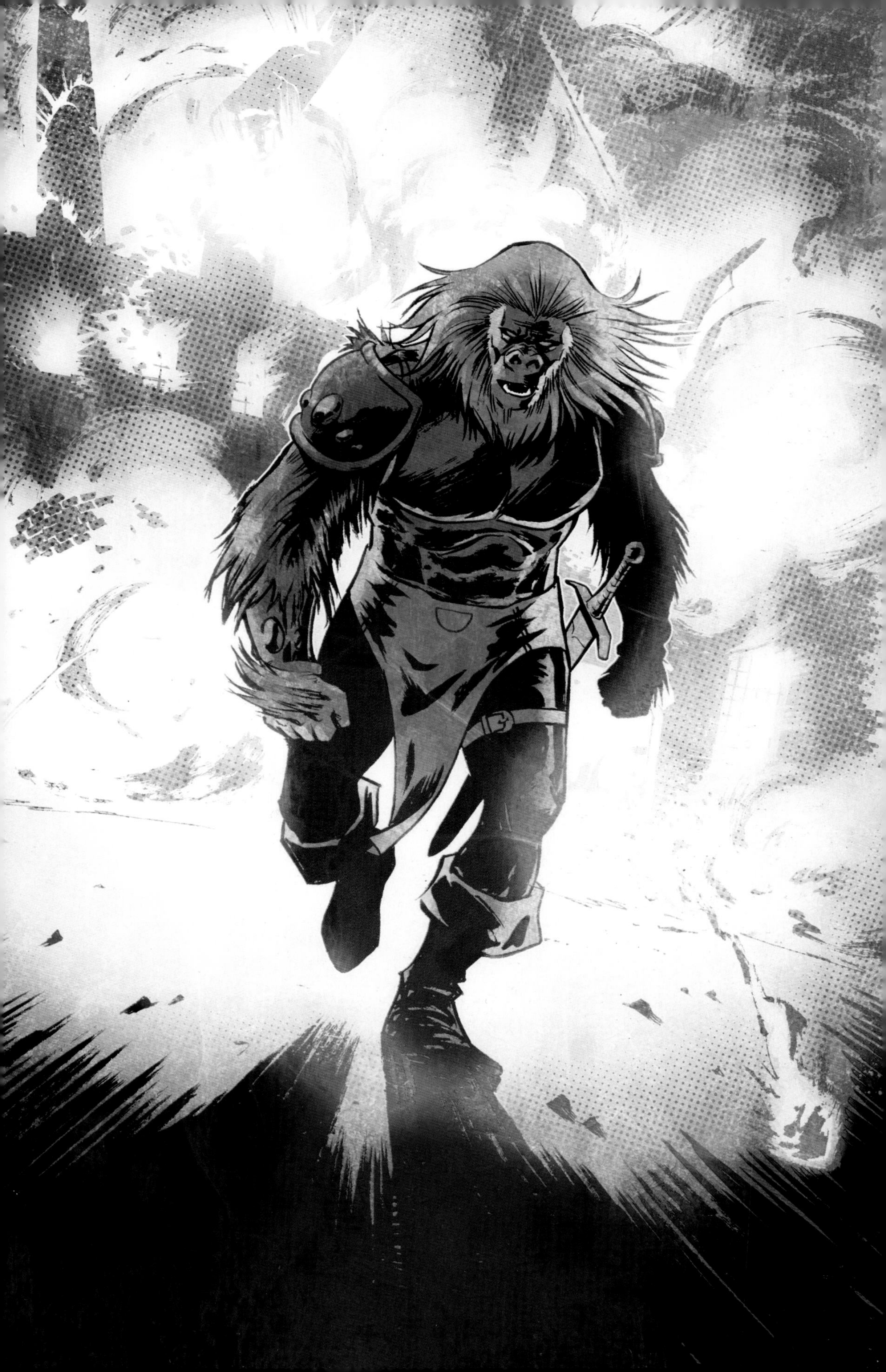

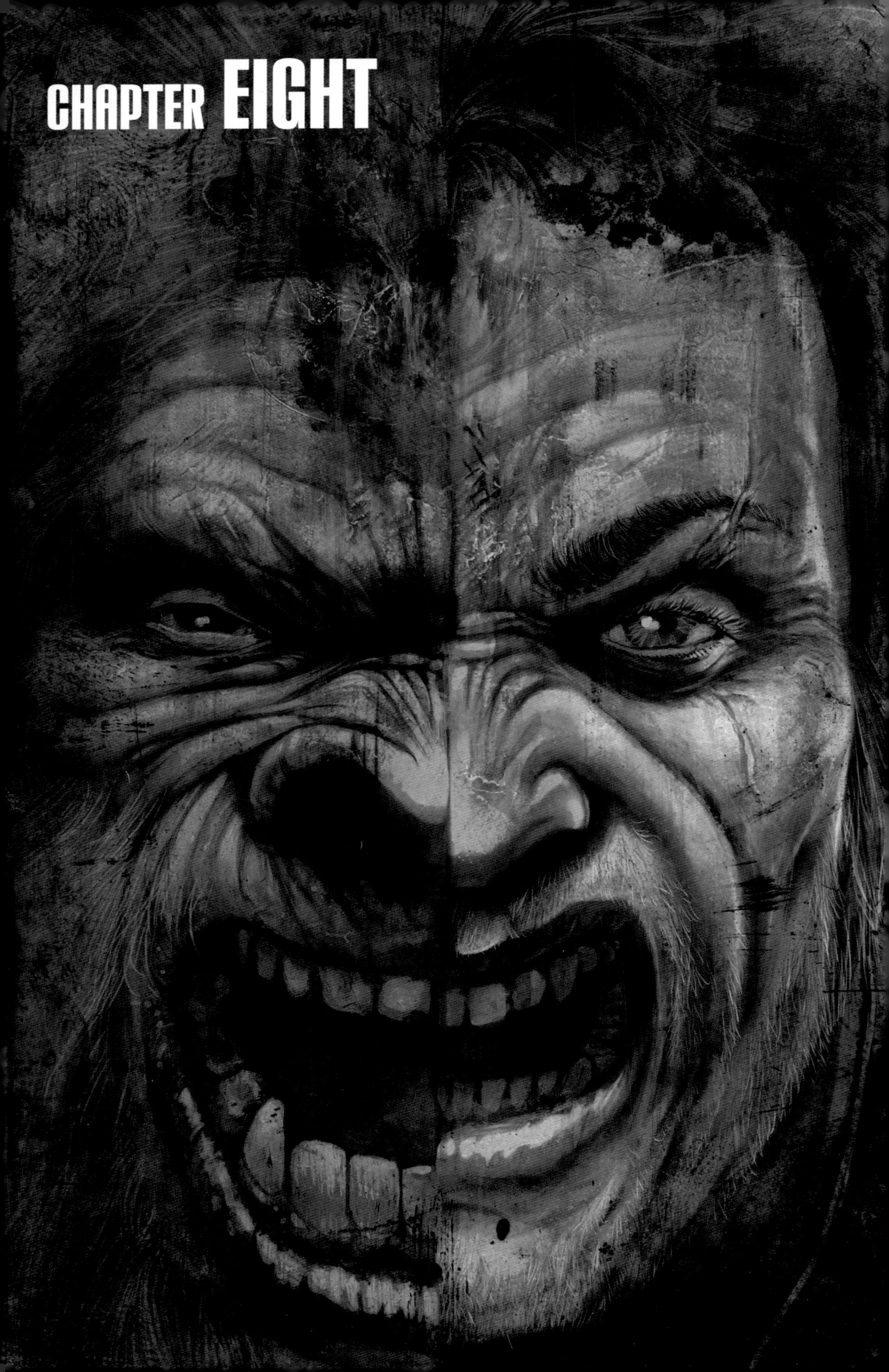
CHAPTER EIGHT

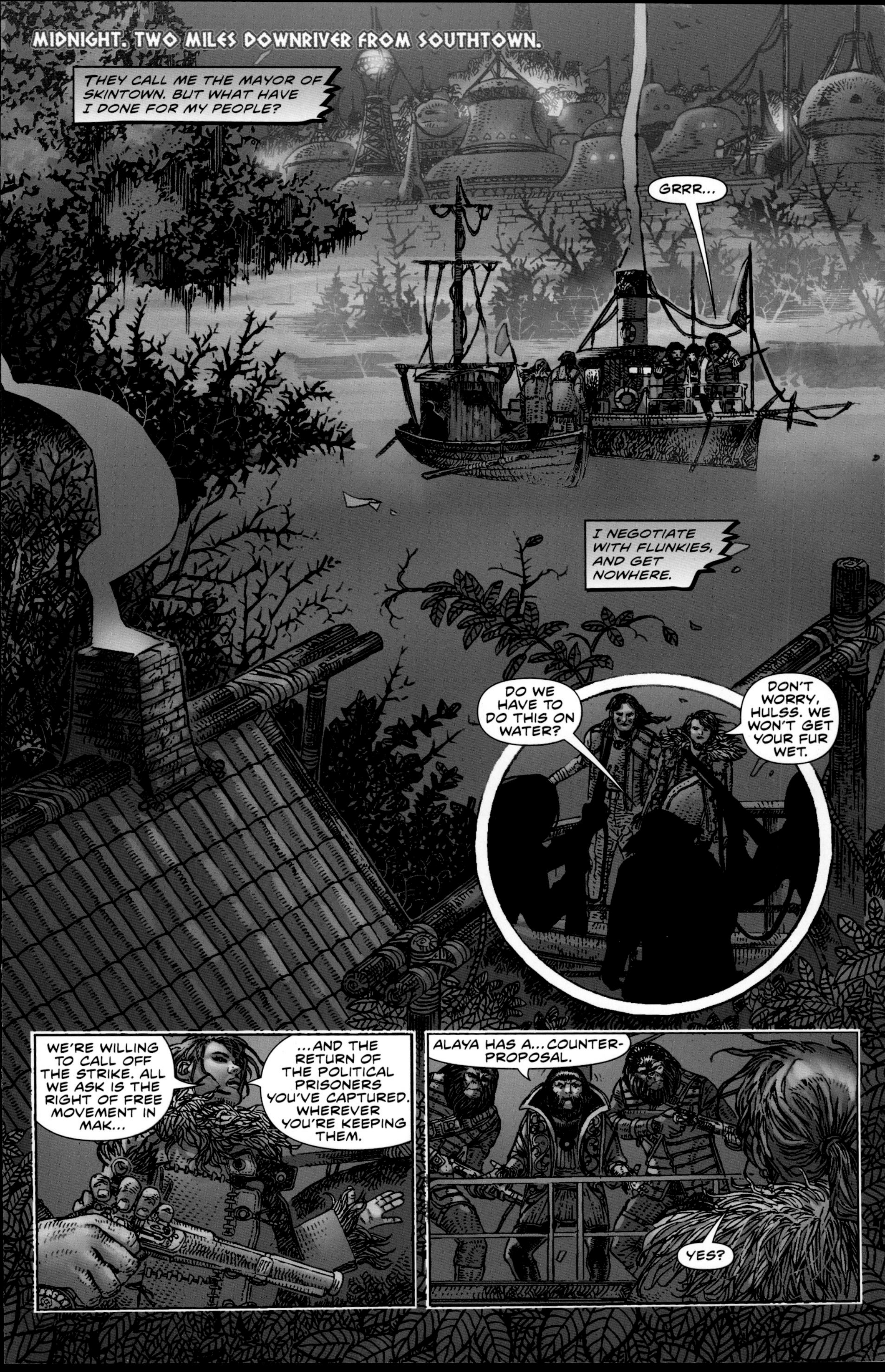
MIDNIGHT. TWO MILES DOWNRIVER FROM SOUTHTOWN.
THEY CALL ME THE MAYOR OF SKINTOWN. BUT WHAT HAVE I DONE FOR MY PEOPLE?
GRRR...
I NEGOTIATE WITH FLUNKIES, AND GET NOWHERE.
DO WE HAVE TO DO THIS ON WATER?
DON'T WORRY, HULSS. WE WON'T GET YOUR FUR WET.
WE'RE WILLING TO CALL OFF THE STRIKE. ALL WE ASK IS THE RIGHT OF FREE MOVEMENT IN MAK...
...AND THE RETURN OF THE POLITICAL PRISONERS YOU'VE CAPTURED. WHEREVER YOU'RE KEEPING THEM.
ALAYA HAS A...COUNTER-PROPOSAL.
YES?

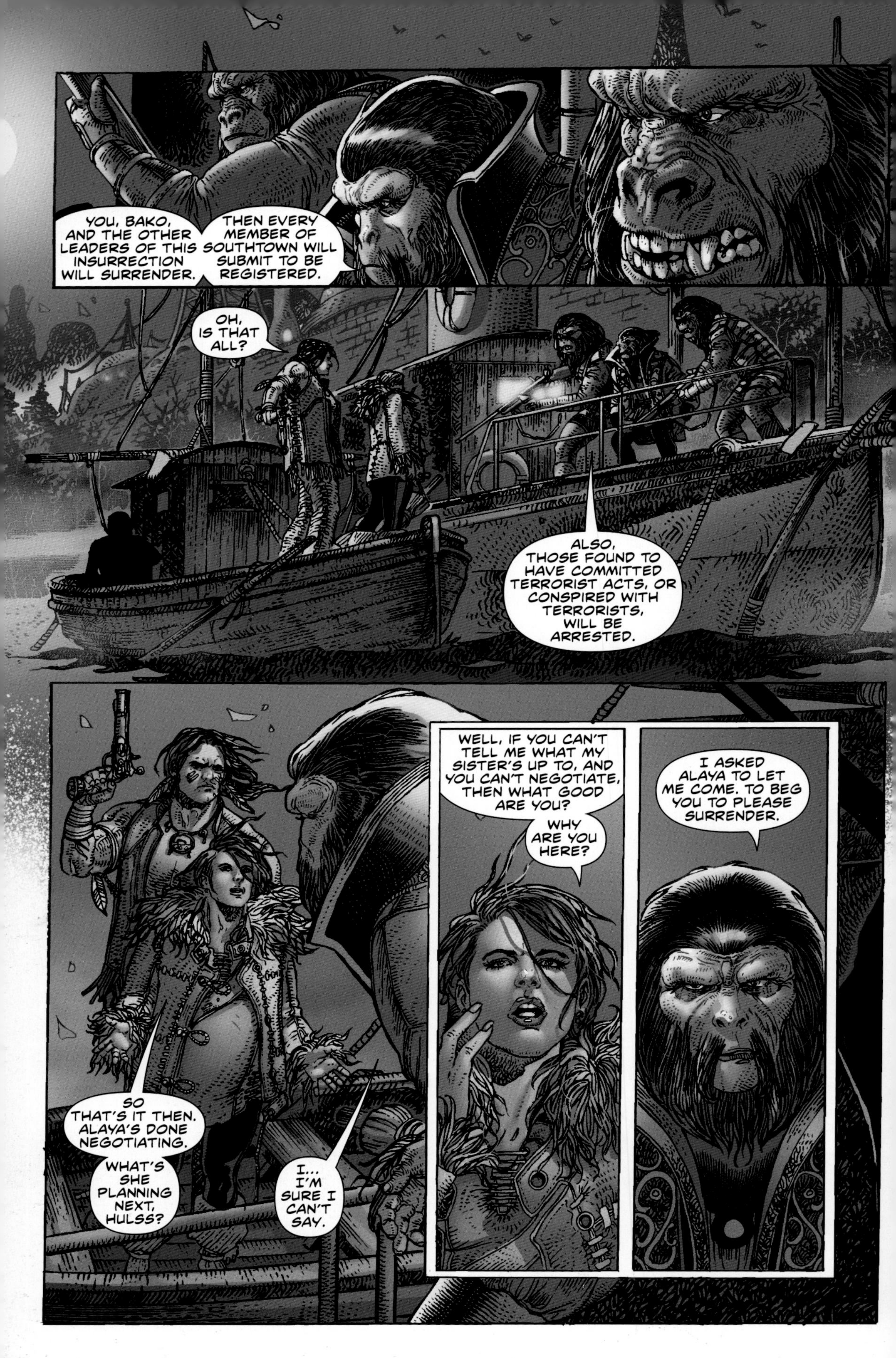
YOU, BAKO, AND THE OTHER LEADERS OF THIS INSURRECTION WILL SURRENDER.
THEN EVERY MEMBER OF SOUTHTOWN WILL SUBMIT TO BE REGISTERED.
OH, IS THAT ALL?
ALSO, THOSE FOUND TO HAVE COMMITTED TERRORIST ACTS, OR CONSPIRED WITH TERRORISTS, WILL BE ARRESTED.
SO THAT'S IT THEN. ALAYA'S DONE NEGOTIATING.
WHAT'S SHE PLANNING NEXT, HULSS?
I... I'M SURE I CAN'T SAY.
WELL, IF YOU CAN'T TELL ME WHAT MY SISTER'S UP TO, AND YOU CAN'T NEGOTIATE, THEN WHAT GOOD ARE YOU?
WHY ARE YOU HERE?
I ASKED ALAYA TO LET ME COME. TO BEG YOU TO PLEASE SURRENDER.

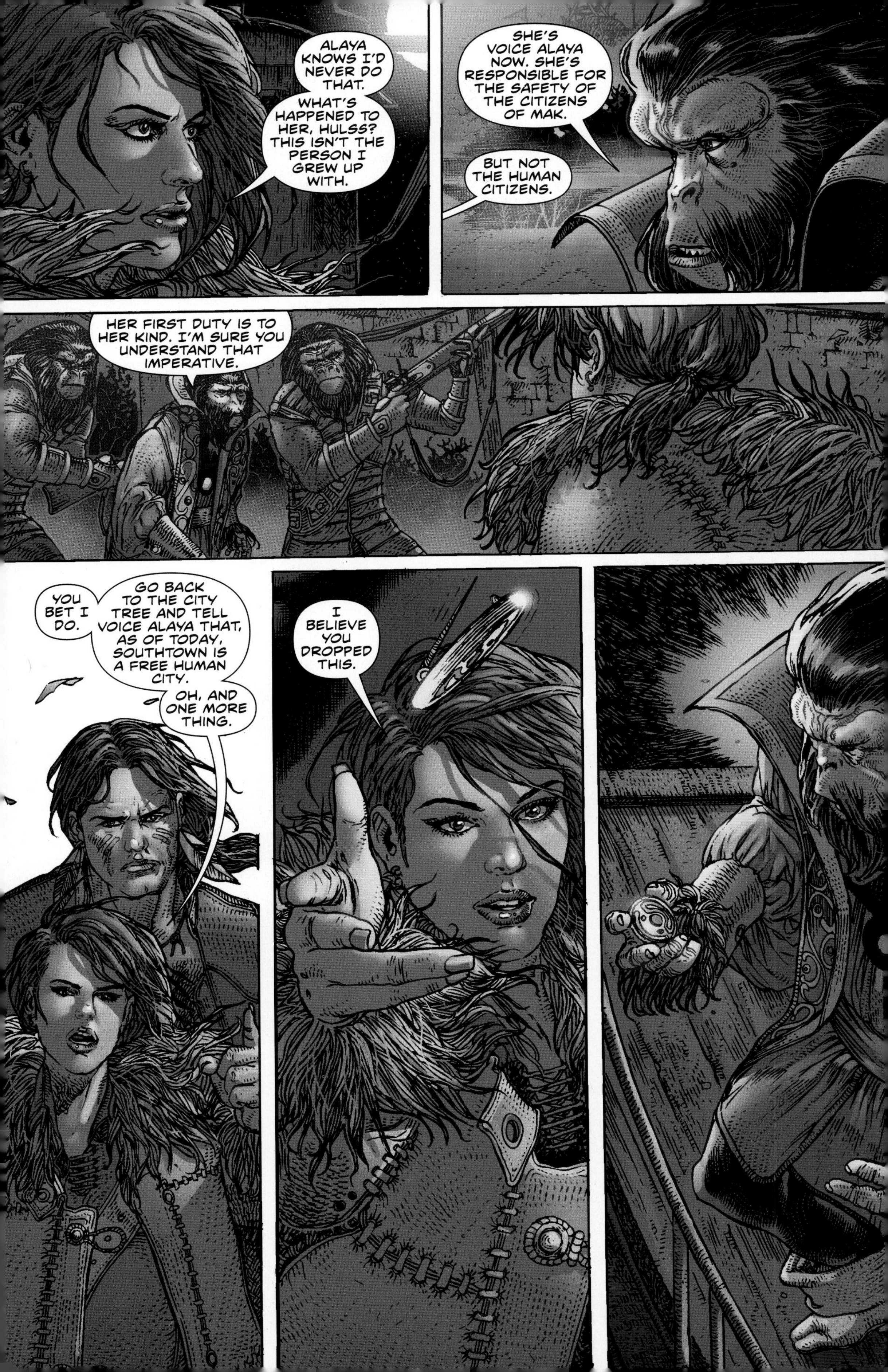
ALAYA KNOWS I'D NEVER DO THAT.
WHAT'S HAPPENED TO HER, HULSS? THIS ISN'T THE PERSON I GREW UP WITH.
SHE'S VOICE ALAYA NOW. SHE'S RESPONSIBLE FOR THE SAFETY OF THE CITIZENS OF MAK.
BUT NOT THE HUMAN CITIZENS.
HER FIRST DUTY IS TO HER KIND. I'M SURE YOU UNDERSTAND THAT IMPERATIVE.
YOU BET I DO.
GO BACK TO THE CITY TREE AND TELL VOICE ALAYA THAT, AS OF TODAY, SOUTHTOWN IS A FREE HUMAN CITY.
OH, AND ONE MORE THING.
I BELIEVE YOU DROPPED THIS.

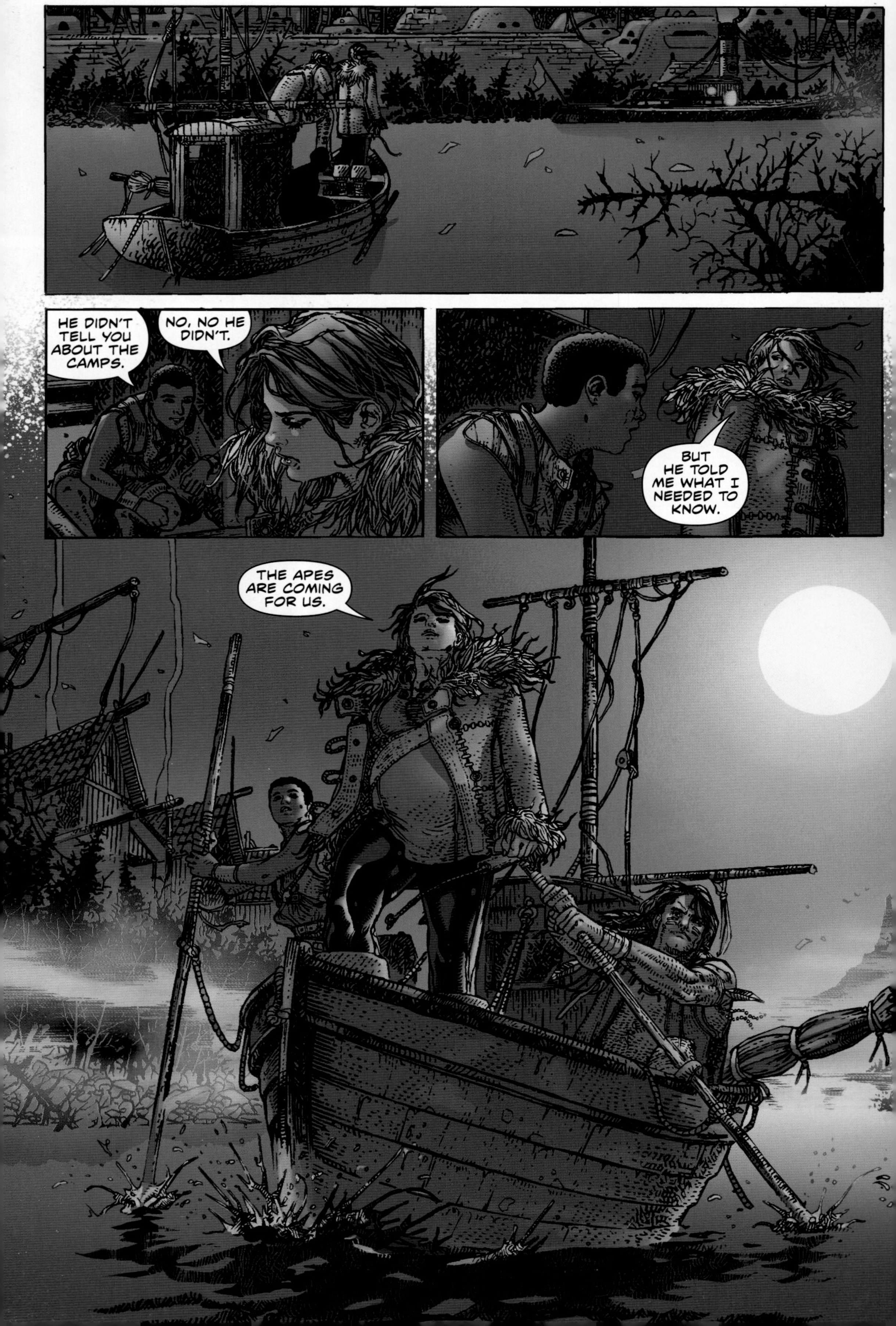
HE DIDN'T TELL YOU ABOUT THE CAMPS.
NO, NO HE DIDN'T.
BUT HE TOLD ME WHAT I NEEDED TO KNOW.
THE APES ARE COMING FOR US.

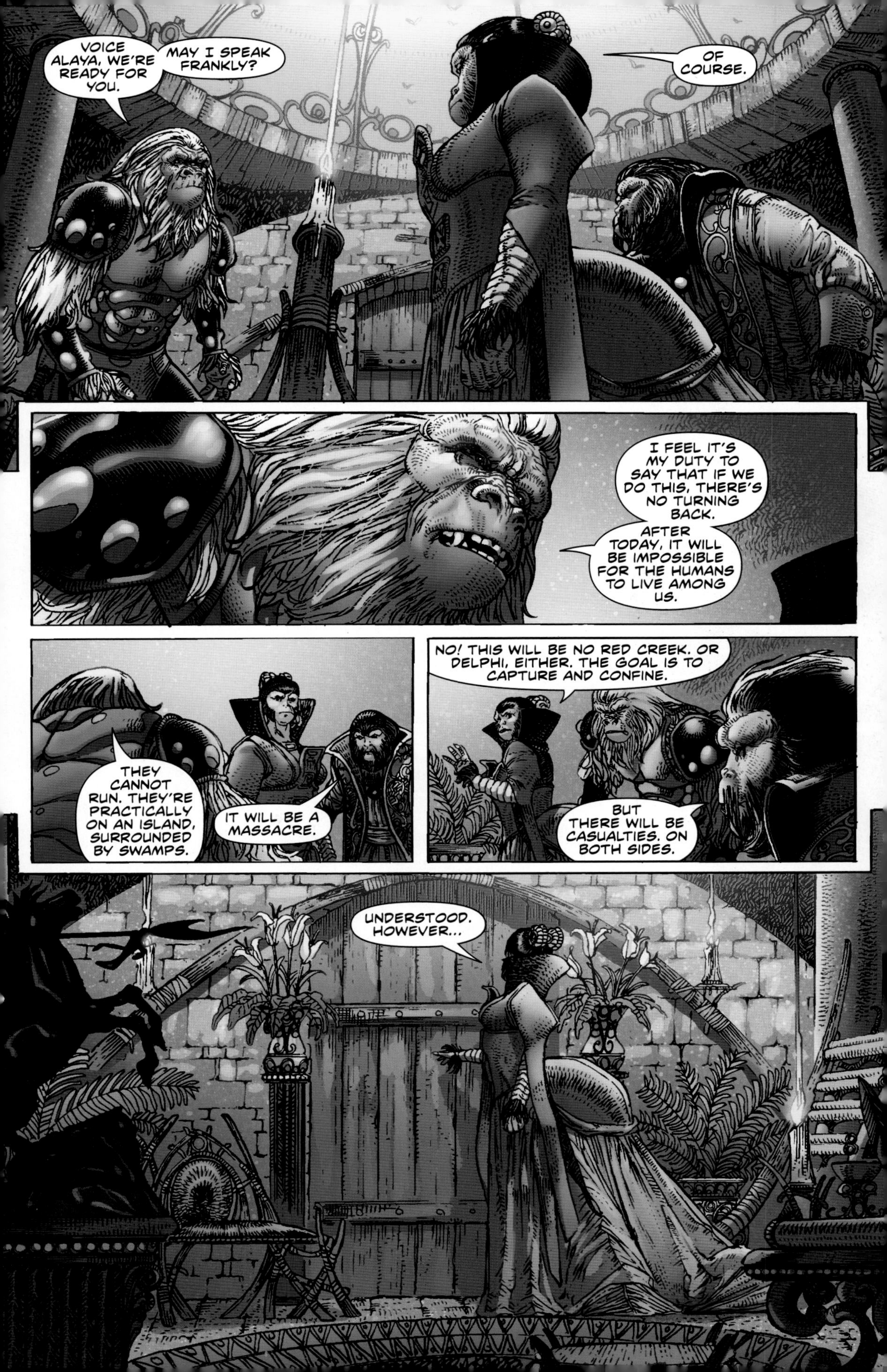
VOICE ALAYA, WE'RE READY FOR YOU.
MAY I SPEAK FRANKLY?
OF COURSE.
I FEEL IT'S MY DUTY TO SAY THAT IF WE DO THIS, THERE'S NO TURNING BACK.
AFTER TODAY, IT WILL BE IMPOSSIBLE FOR THE HUMANS TO LIVE AMONG US.
THEY CANNOT RUN. THEY'RE PRACTICALLY ON AN ISLAND, SURROUNDED BY SWAMPS.
IT WILL BE A MASSACRE.
NO! THIS WILL BE NO RED CREEK. OR DELPHI, EITHER. THE GOAL IS TO CAPTURE AND CONFINE.
BUT THERE WILL BE CASUALTIES. ON BOTH SIDES.
UNDERSTOOD. HOWEVER...

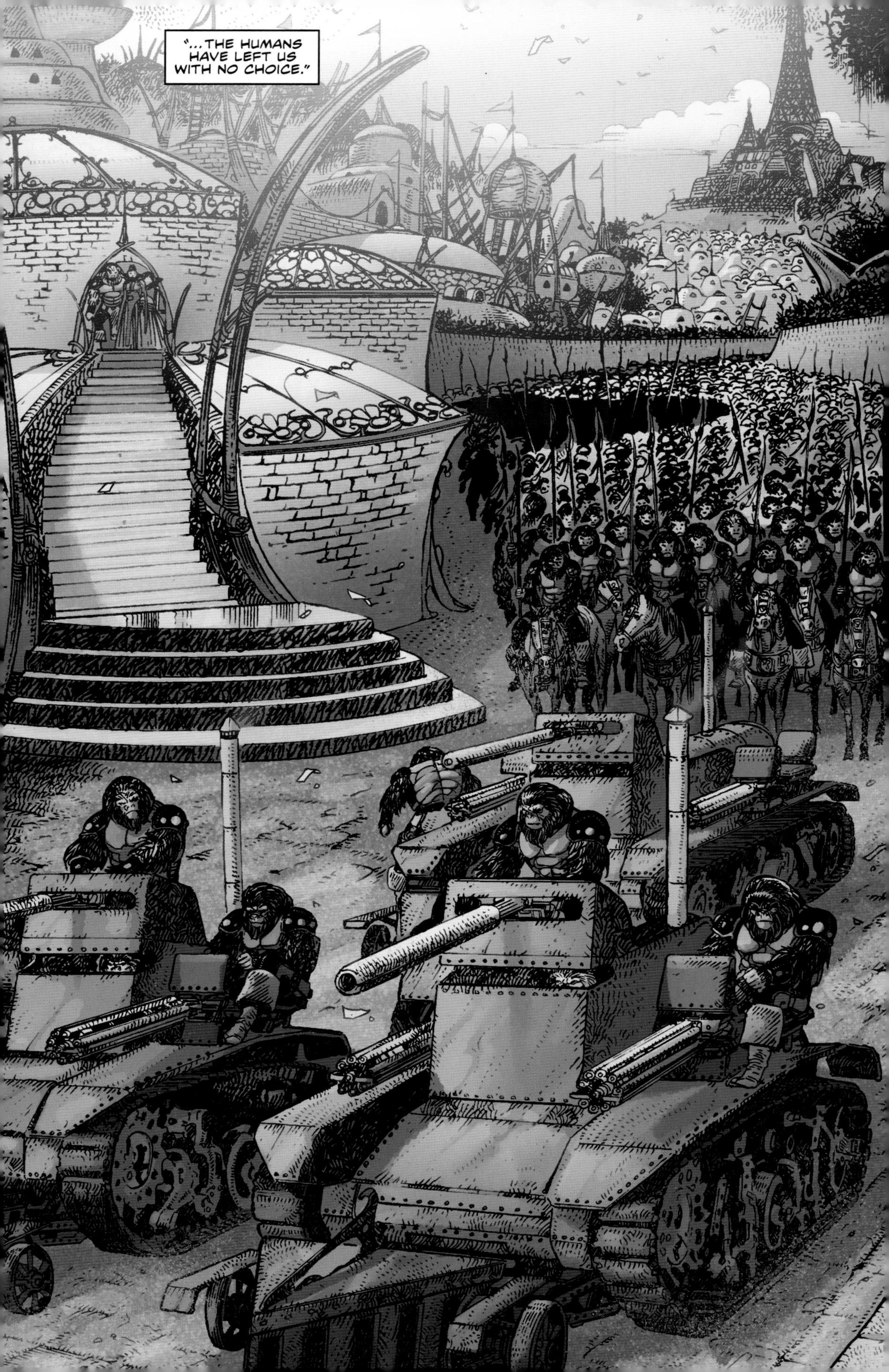
"...THE HUMANS HAVE LEFT US WITH NO CHOICE."

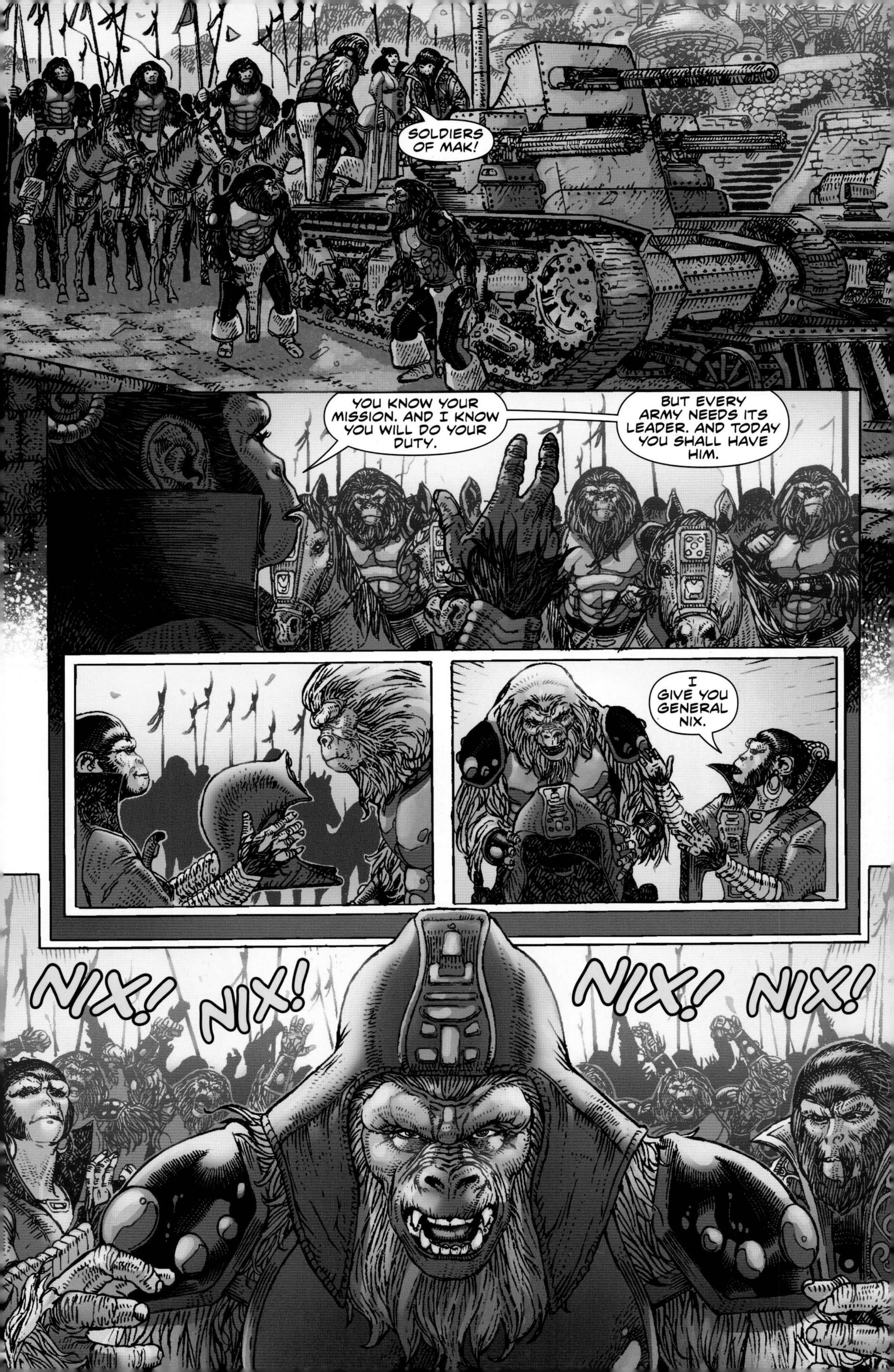
SOLDIERS OF MAK!
YOU KNOW YOUR MISSION. AND I KNOW YOU WILL DO YOUR DUTY.
BUT EVERY ARMY NEEDS ITS LEADER. AND TODAY YOU SHALL HAVE HIM.
I GIVE YOU GENERAL NIX.
NIX! NIX!
NIX! NIX!

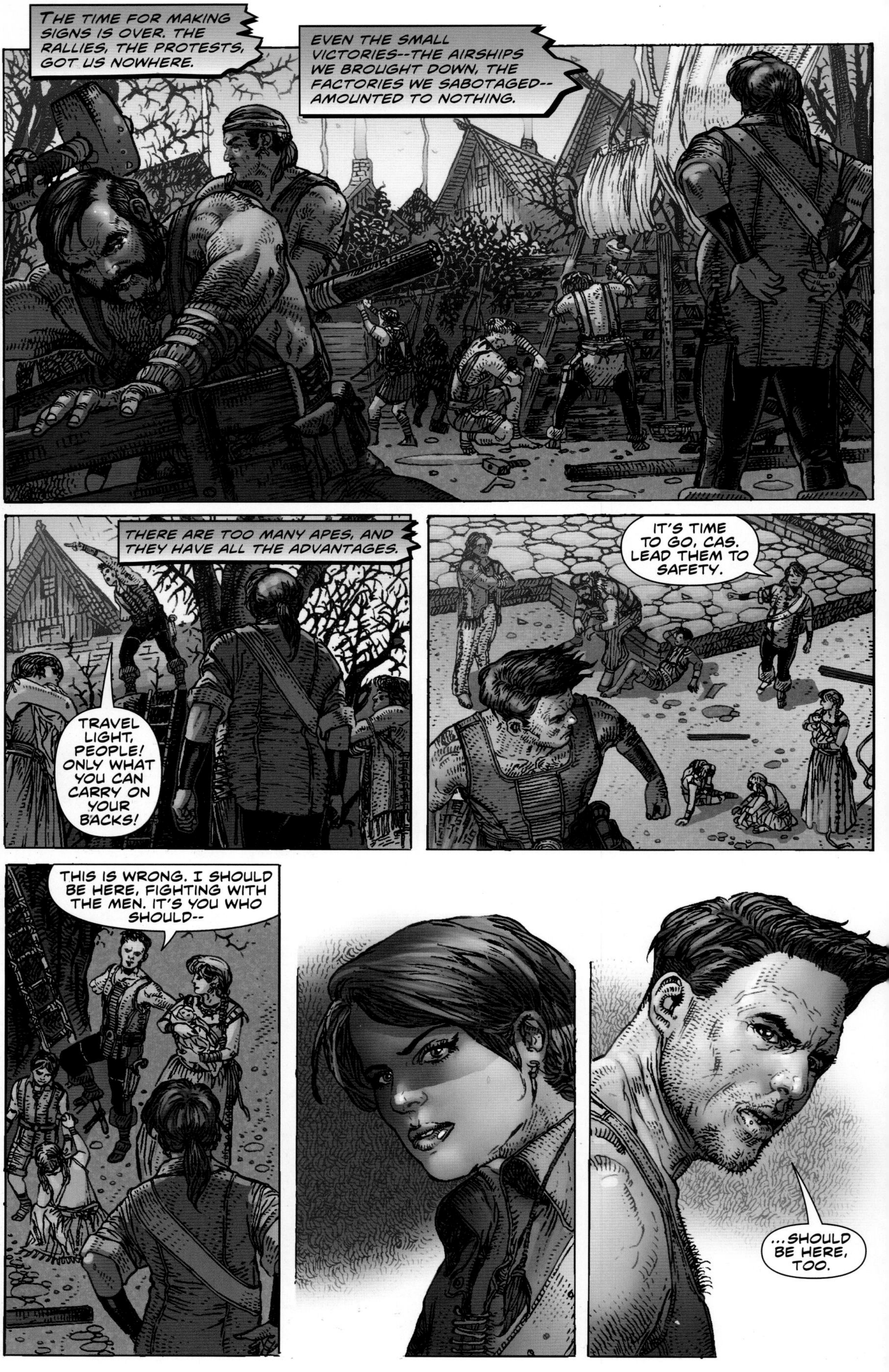
THE TIME FOR MAKING SIGNS IS OVER. THE RALLIES, THE PROTESTS, GOT US NOWHERE.
EVEN THE SMALL VICTORIES--THE AIRSHIPS WE BROUGHT DOWN, THE FACTORIES WE SABOTAGED--AMOUNTED TO NOTHING.
THERE ARE TOO MANY APES, AND THEY HAVE ALL THE ADVANTAGES.
TRAVEL LIGHT, PEOPLE! ONLY WHAT YOU CAN CARRY ON YOUR BACKS!
IT'S TIME TO GO, CAS. LEAD THEM TO SAFETY.
THIS IS WRONG. I SHOULD BE HERE, FIGHTING WITH THE MEN. IT'S YOU WHO SHOULD--
...SHOULD BE HERE, TOO.

CAS, WITH BAKO GONE I'M DEPENDING ON YOU.

THESE PEOPLE NEED A LEADER.

ME? A LEADER?

OOH, NOW HE'S MR. MODEST. YOU'VE ALWAYS LIKED BOSSING PEOPLE AROUND, HUSBAND.

TAKE CARE OF THE PEOPLE, AND THE NEW WEAPONS, TOO.

JUST UNTIL BAKO COMES.

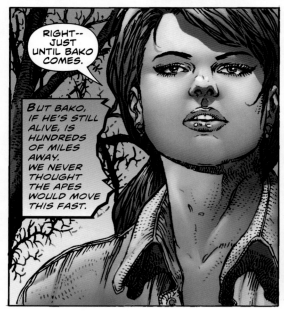

RIGHT-- JUST UNTIL BAKO COMES.

BUT BAKO, IF HE'S STILL ALIVE, IS HUNDREDS OF MILES AWAY. WE NEVER THOUGHT THE APES WOULD MOVE THIS FAST.

THE BRIDGES, MAYOR! THE MACHINES ARE ON ALL THREE BRIDGES!

WHAT DO YOU MEAN, MACHINES?

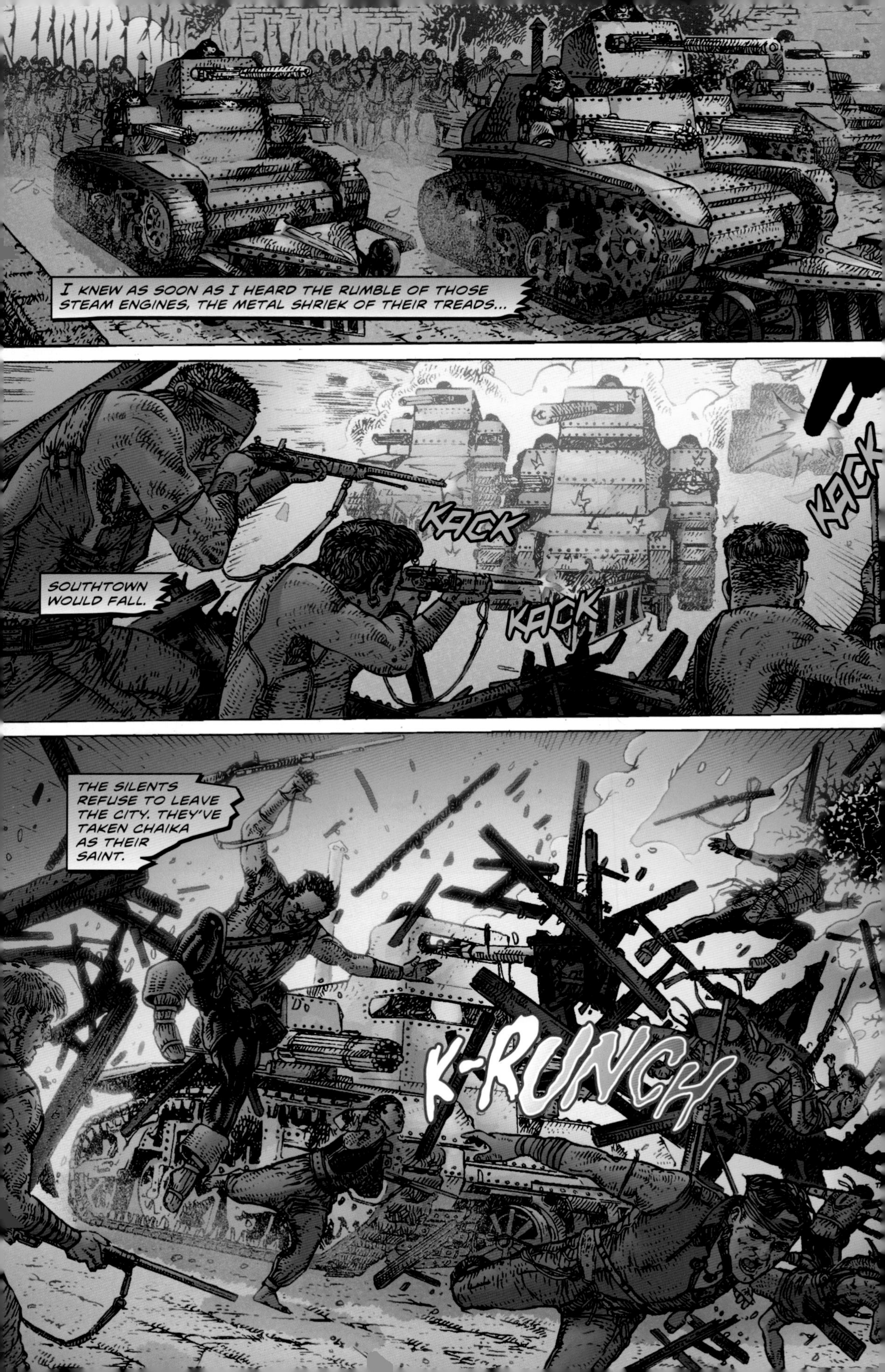
I KNEW AS SOON AS I HEARD THE RUMBLE OF THOSE STEAM ENGINES, THE METAL SHRIEK OF THEIR TREADS...
SOUTHTOWN WOULD FALL.
KACK
KACK
KACK
THE SILENTS REFUSE TO LEAVE THE CITY. THEY'VE TAKEN CHAIKA AS THEIR SAINT.
K-RUNCH

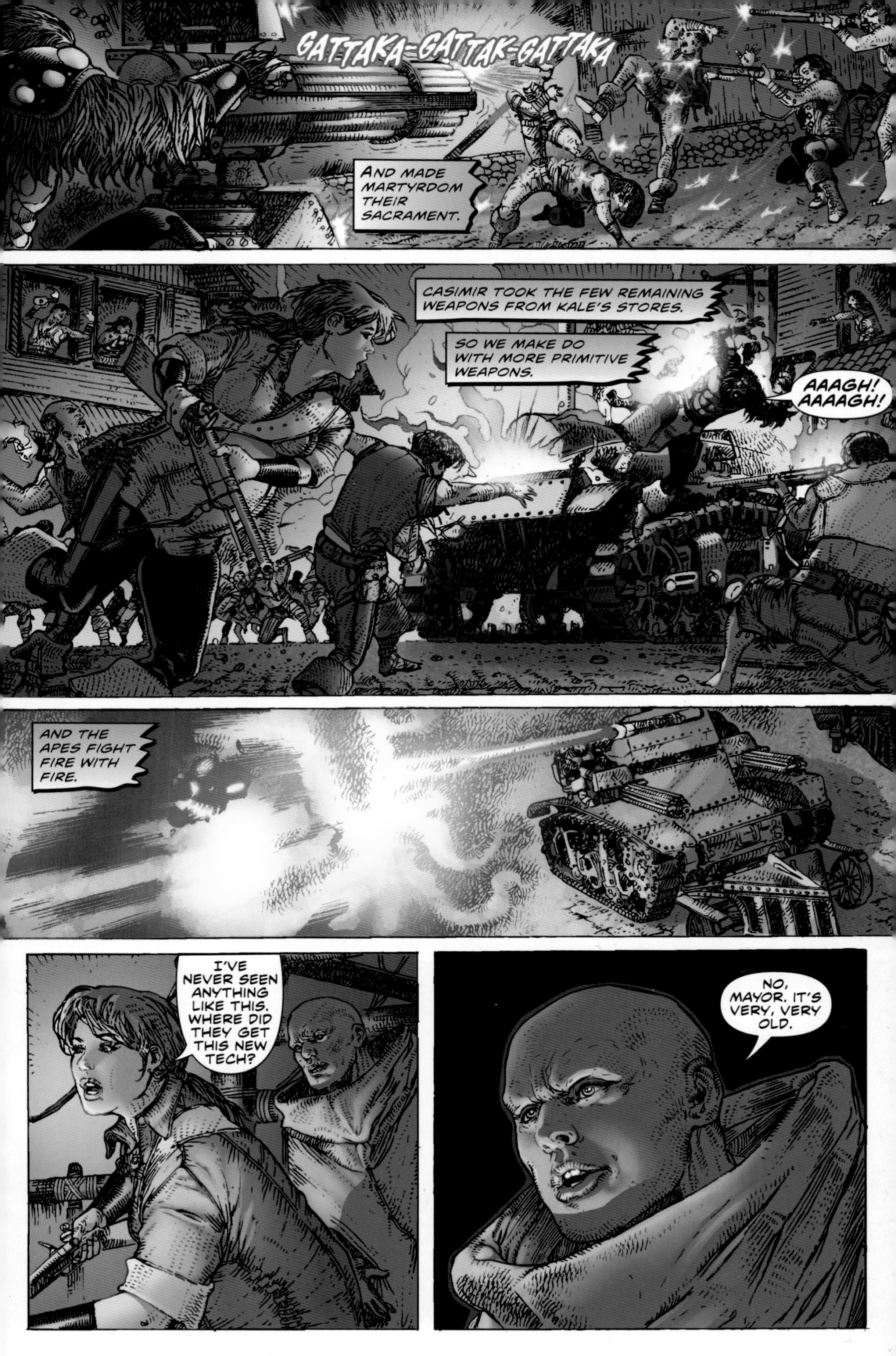
GATTAKA-GATTAK-GATTAKA
AND MADE MARTYRDOM THEIR SACRAMENT.
CASIMIR TOOK THE FEW REMAINING WEAPONS FROM KALE'S STORES.
SO WE MAKE DO WITH MORE PRIMITIVE WEAPONS.
AAAGH! AAAAGH!
AND THE APES FIGHT FIRE WITH FIRE.
I'VE NEVER SEEN ANYTHING LIKE THIS. WHERE DID THEY GET THIS NEW TECH?
NO, MAYOR. IT'S VERY, VERY OLD.

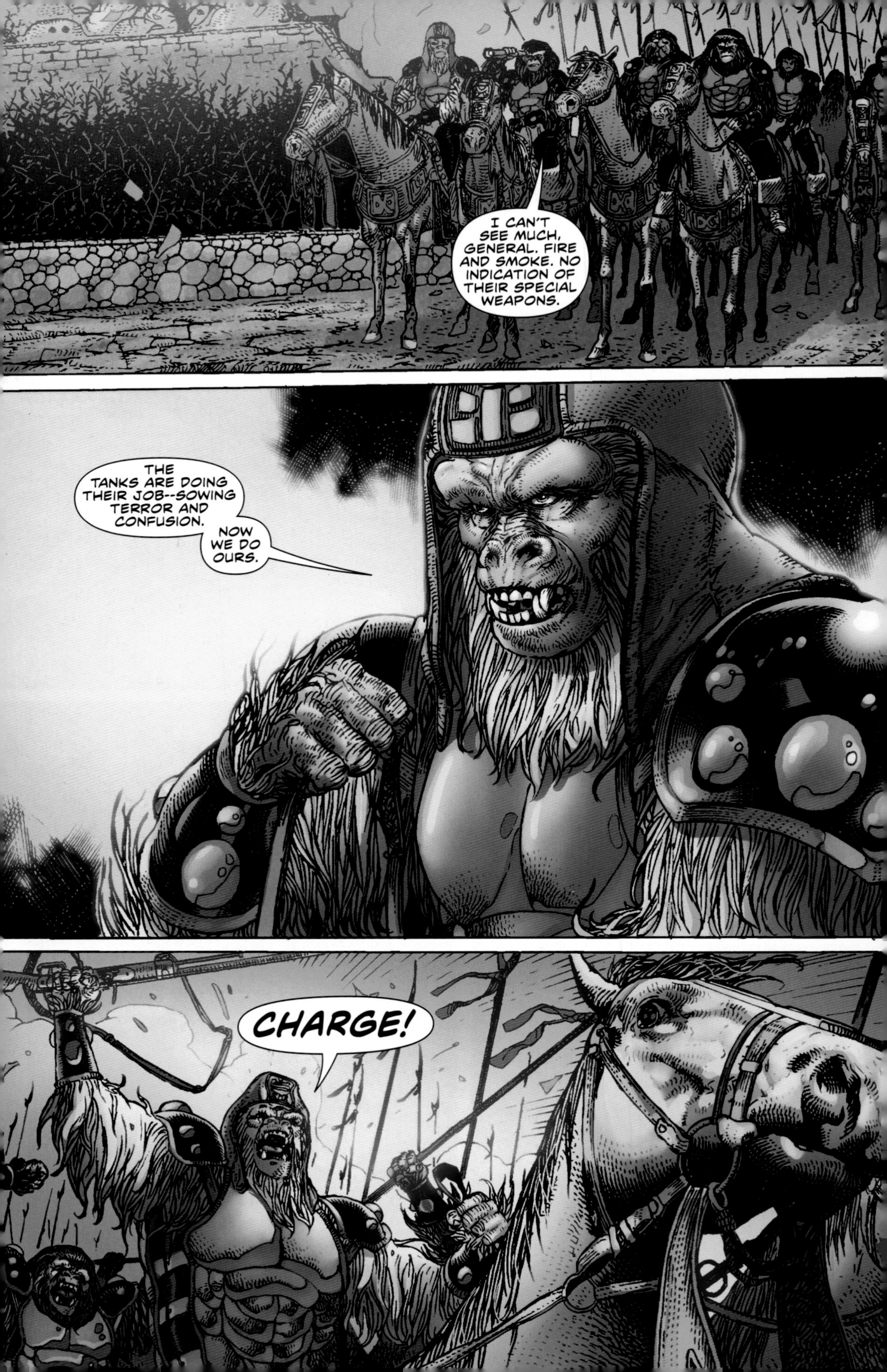
I CAN'T SEE MUCH, GENERAL. FIRE AND SMOKE. NO INDICATION OF THEIR SPECIAL WEAPONS.
THE TANKS ARE DOING THEIR JOB--SOWING TERROR AND CONFUSION.
NOW WE DO OURS.
CHARGE!

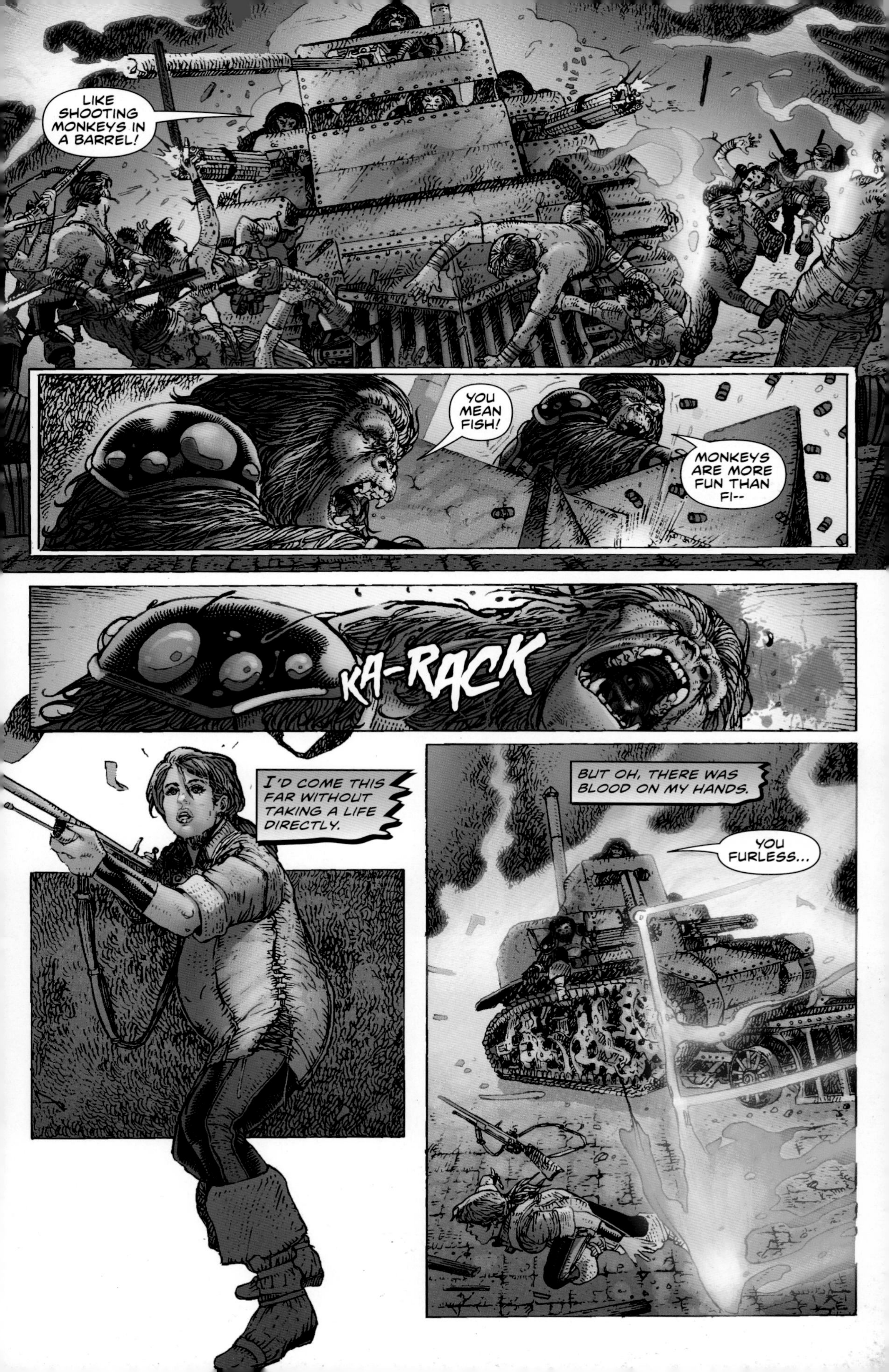
LIKE SHOOTING MONKEYS IN A BARREL!
YOU MEAN FISH!
MONKEYS ARE MORE FUN THAN FI--
KA-RACK
I'D COME THIS FAR WITHOUT TAKING A LIFE DIRECTLY.
BUT OH, THERE WAS BLOOD ON MY HANDS.
YOU FURLESS...

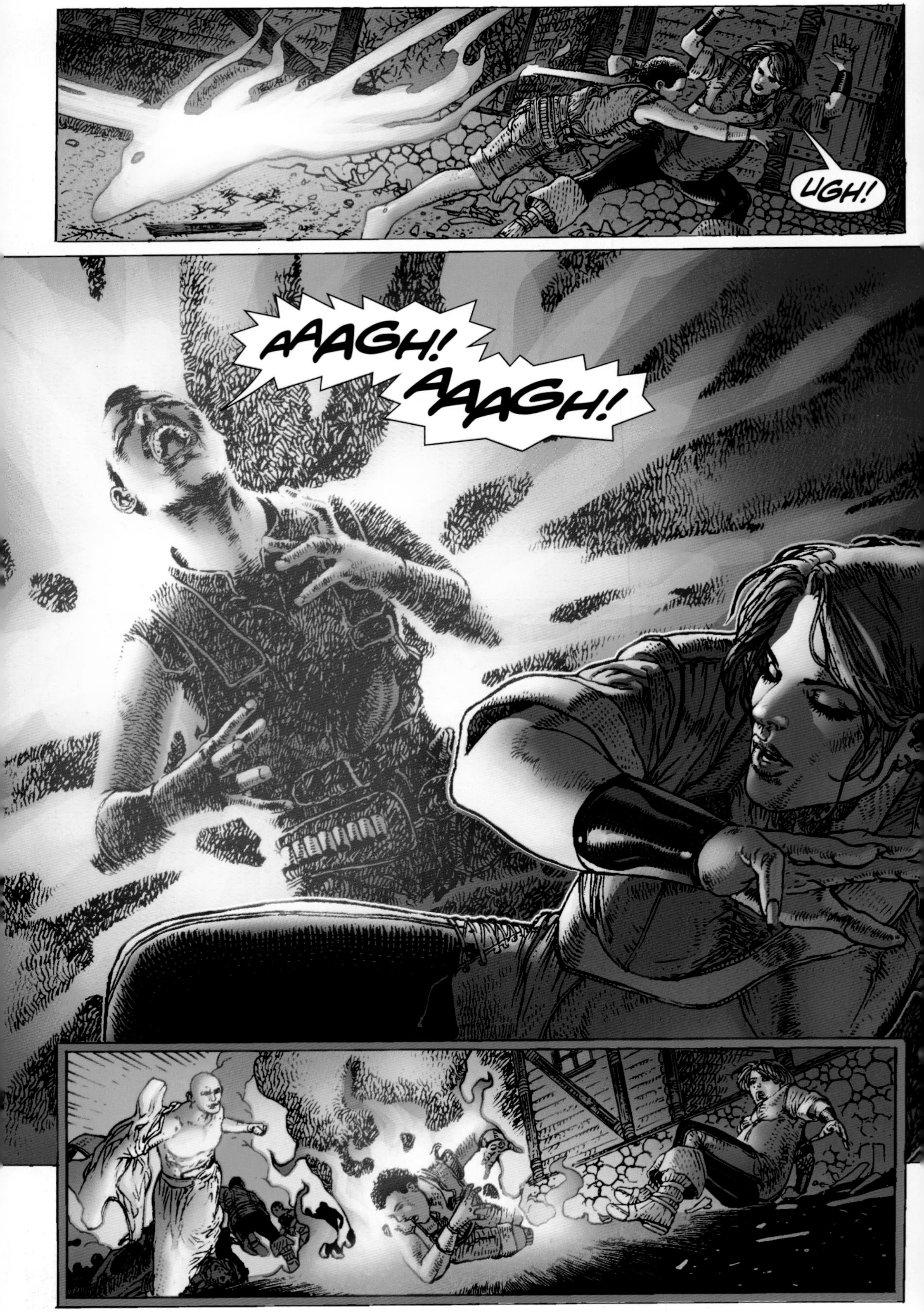
UGH!
AAAGH!
AAAGH!

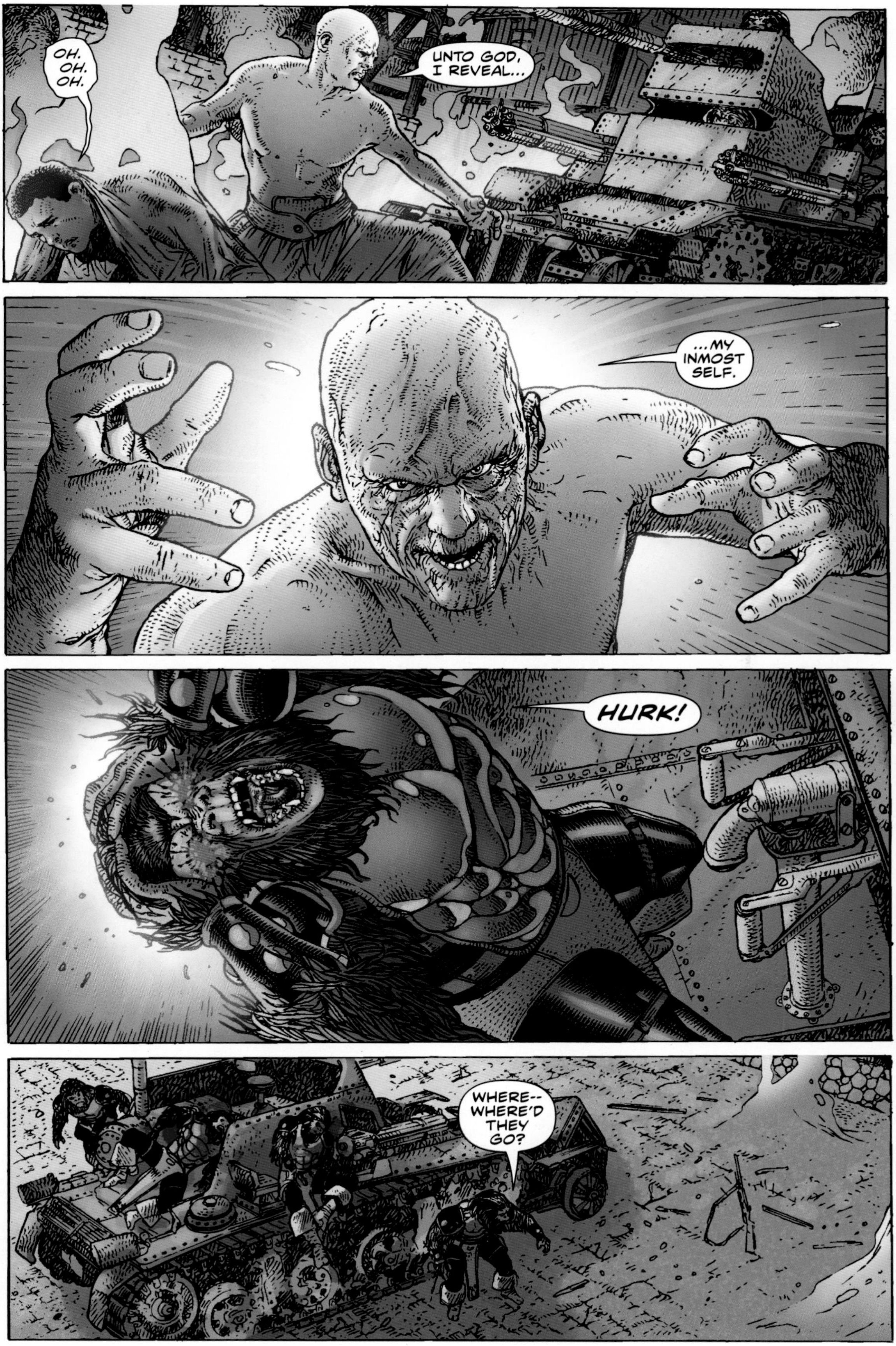
OH. OH. OH.
UNTO GOD, I REVEAL...
...MY INMOST SELF.
HURK!
WHERE-- WHERE'D THEY GO?

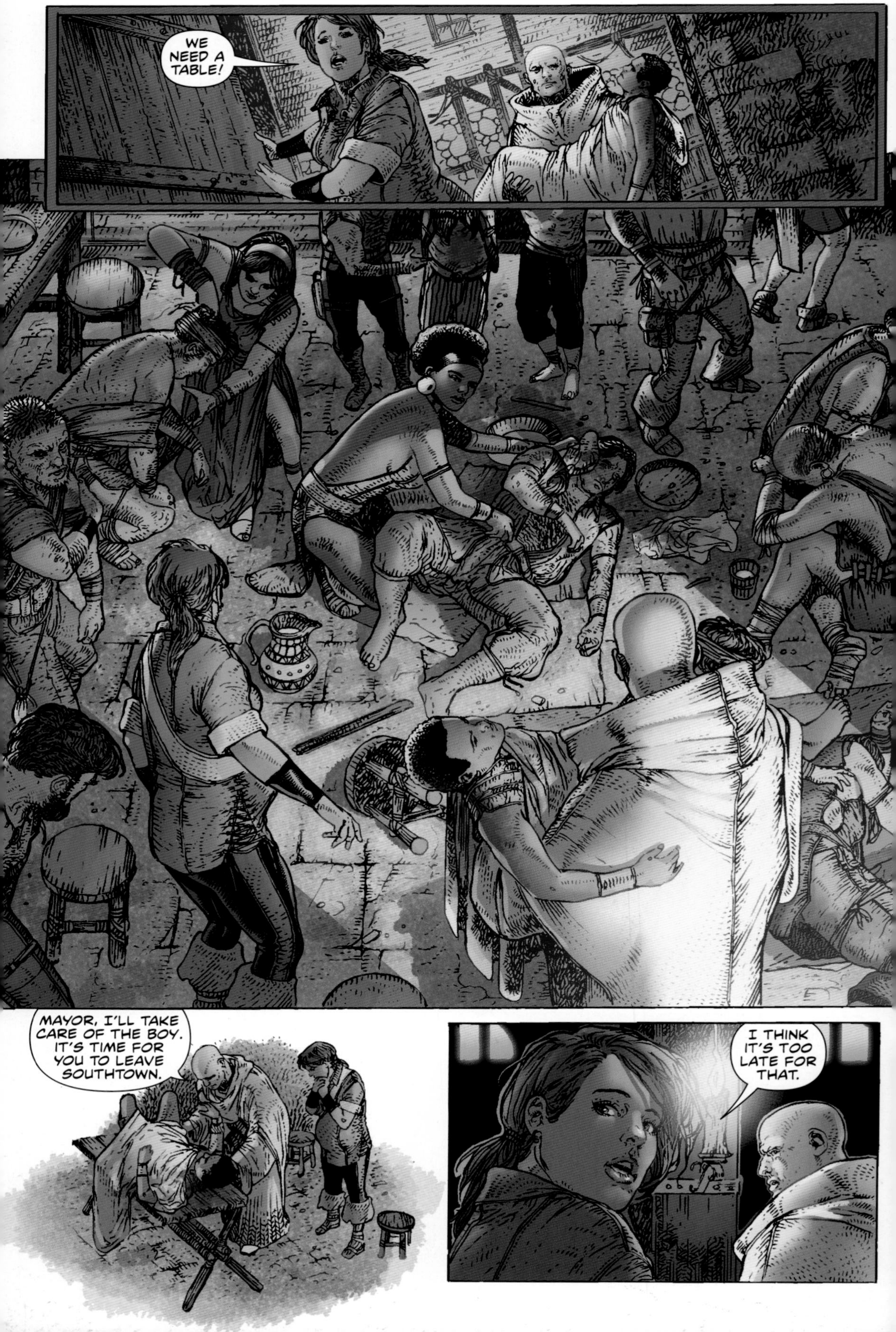
WE NEED A TABLE!
MAYOR, I'LL TAKE CARE OF THE BOY. IT'S TIME FOR YOU TO LEAVE SOUTHTOWN.
I THINK IT'S TOO LATE FOR THAT.

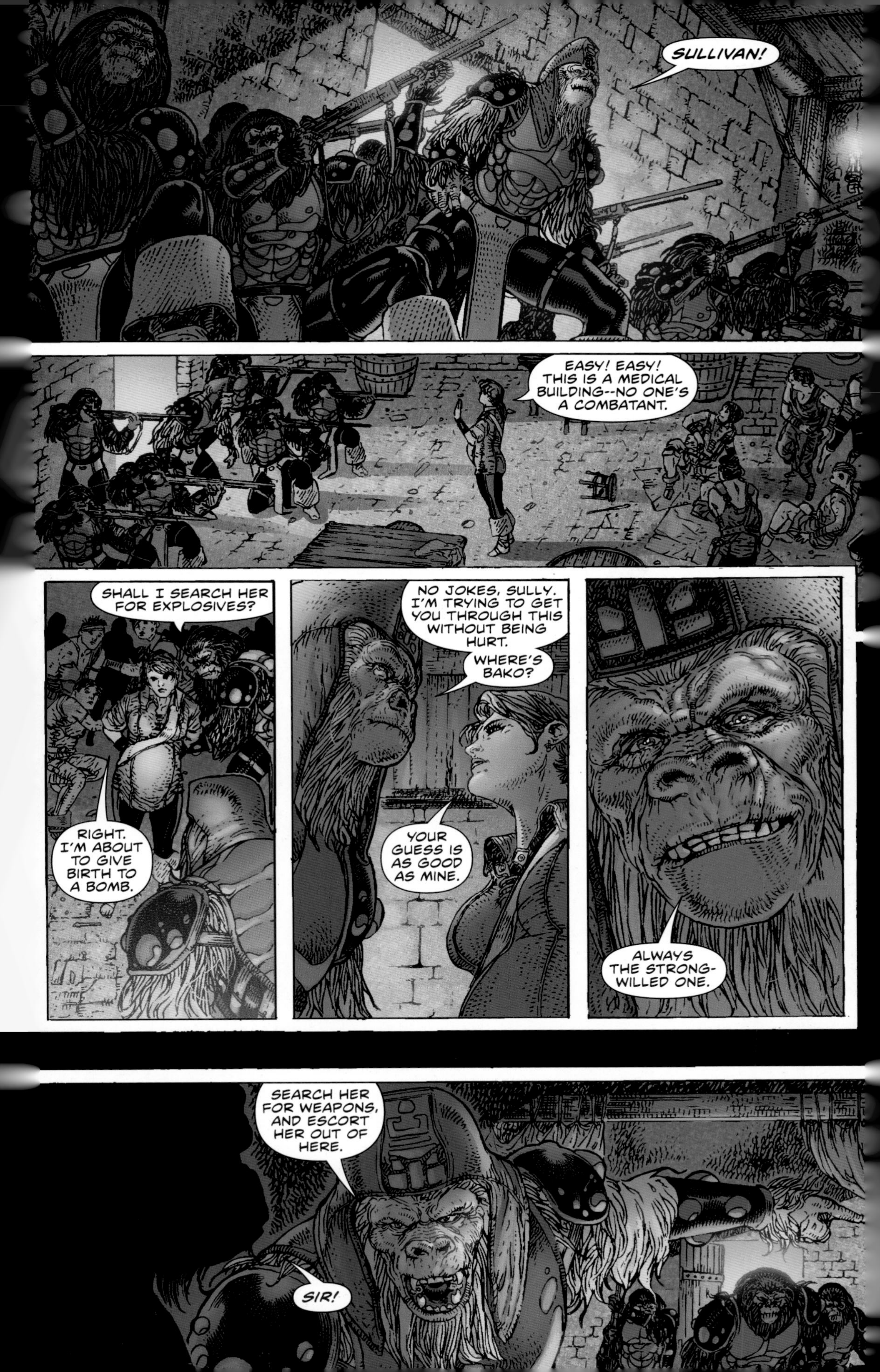
SULLIVAN!
EASY! EASY! THIS IS A MEDICAL BUILDING--NO ONE'S A COMBATANT.
SHALL I SEARCH HER FOR EXPLOSIVES?
RIGHT. I'M ABOUT TO GIVE BIRTH TO A BOMB.
NO JOKES, SULLY. I'M TRYING TO GET YOU THROUGH THIS WITHOUT BEING HURT.
WHERE'S BAKO?
YOUR GUESS IS AS GOOD AS MINE.
ALWAYS THE STRONG-WILLED ONE.
SEARCH HER FOR WEAPONS, AND ESCORT HER OUT OF HERE.
SIR!

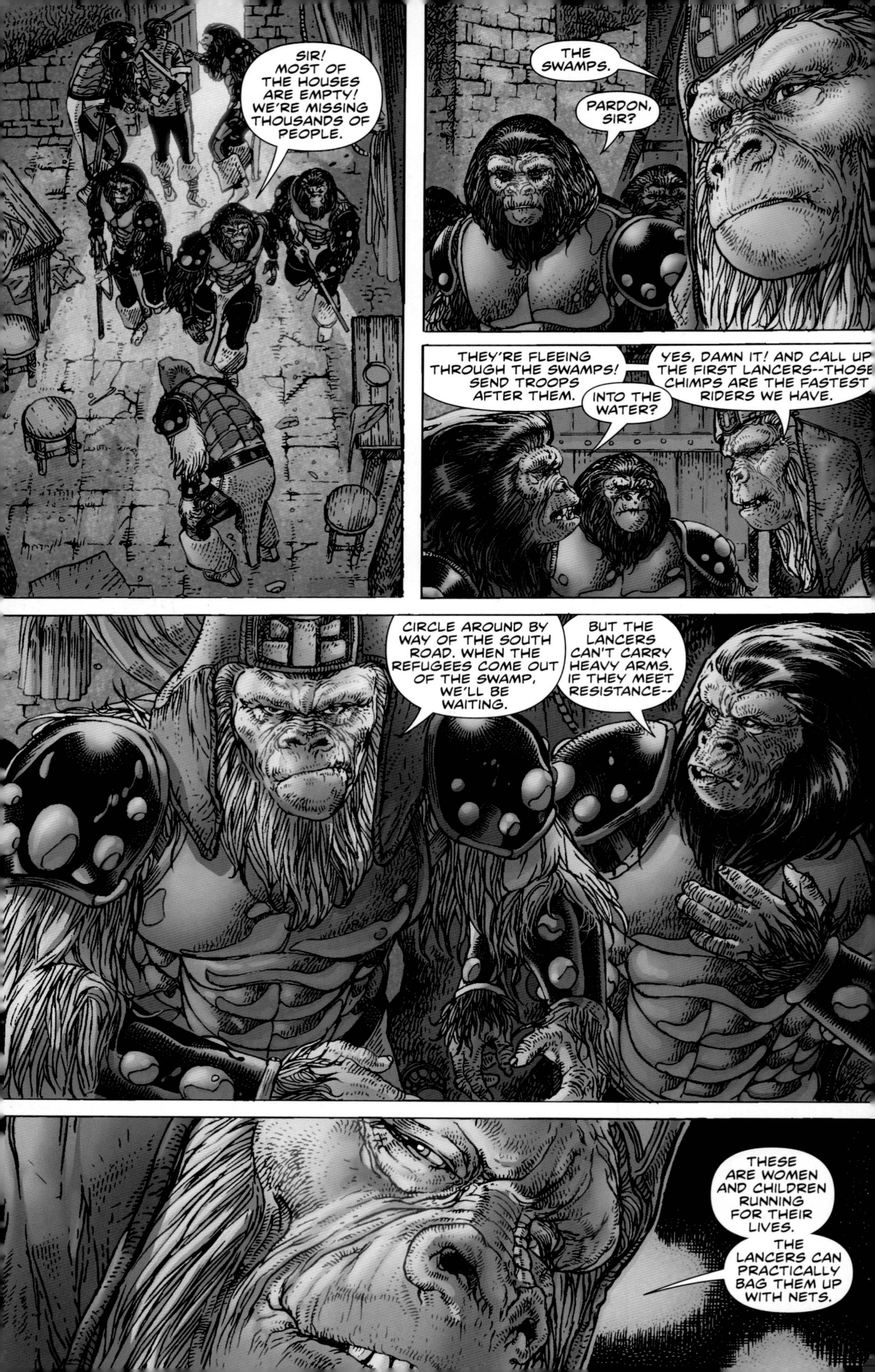
SIR! MOST OF THE HOUSES ARE EMPTY! WE'RE MISSING THOUSANDS OF PEOPLE.
THE SWAMPS.
PARDON, SIR?
THEY'RE FLEEING THROUGH THE SWAMPS! SEND TROOPS AFTER THEM.
INTO THE WATER?
YES, DAMN IT! AND CALL UP THE FIRST LANCERS--THOSE CHIMPS ARE THE FASTEST RIDERS WE HAVE.
CIRCLE AROUND BY WAY OF THE SOUTH ROAD. WHEN THE REFUGEES COME OUT OF THE SWAMP, WE'LL BE WAITING.
BUT THE LANCERS CAN'T CARRY HEAVY ARMS. IF THEY MEET RESISTANCE--
THESE ARE WOMEN AND CHILDREN RUNNING FOR THEIR LIVES.
THE LANCERS CAN PRACTICALLY BAG THEM UP WITH NETS.

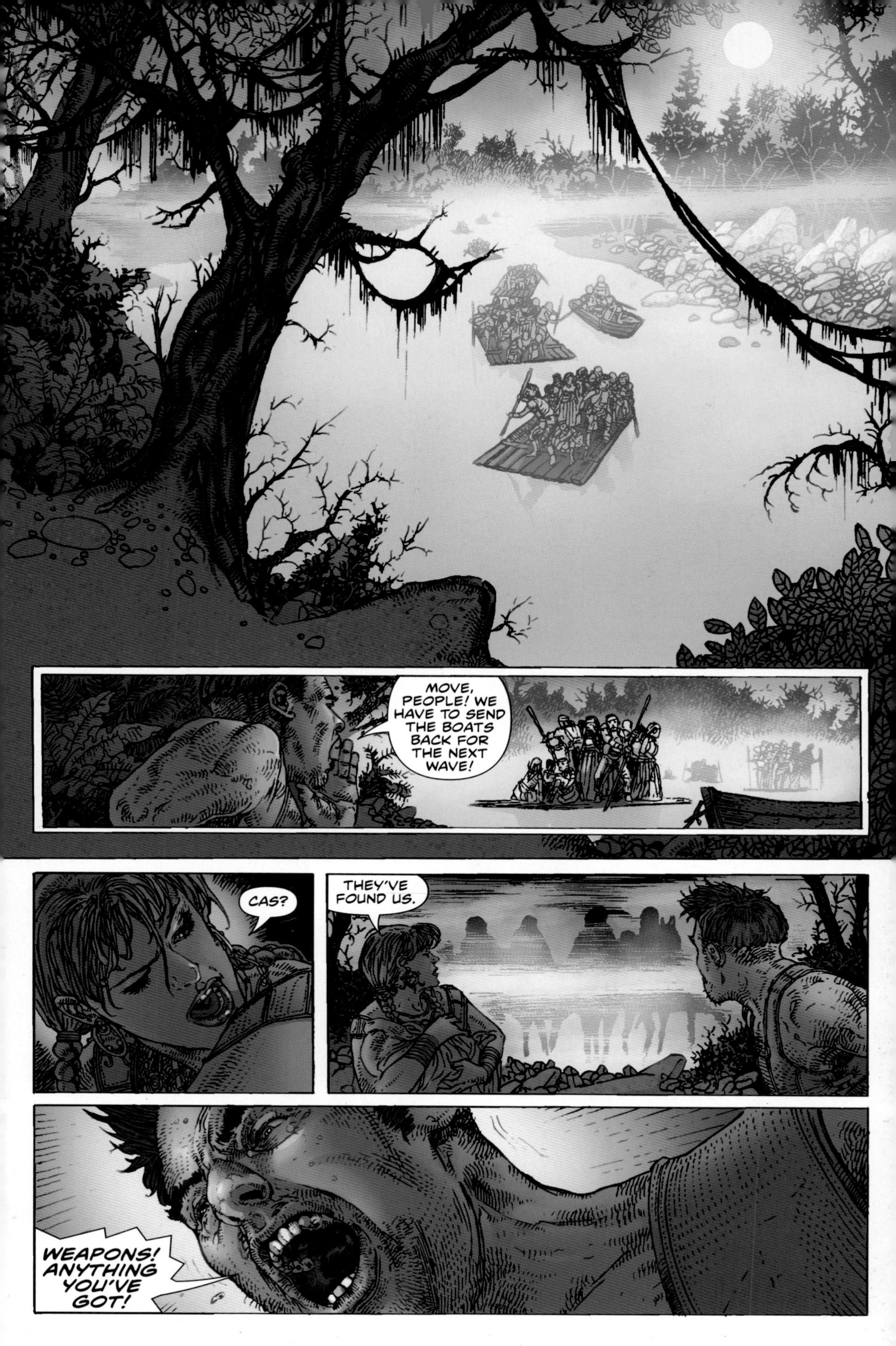
MOVE, PEOPLE! WE HAVE TO SEND THE BOATS BACK FOR THE NEXT WAVE!
CAS?
THEY'VE FOUND US.
WEAPONS! ANYTHING YOU'VE GOT!

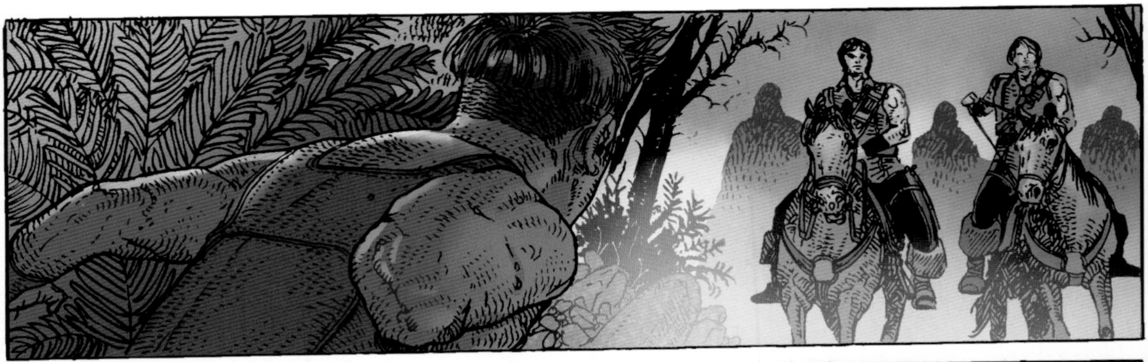

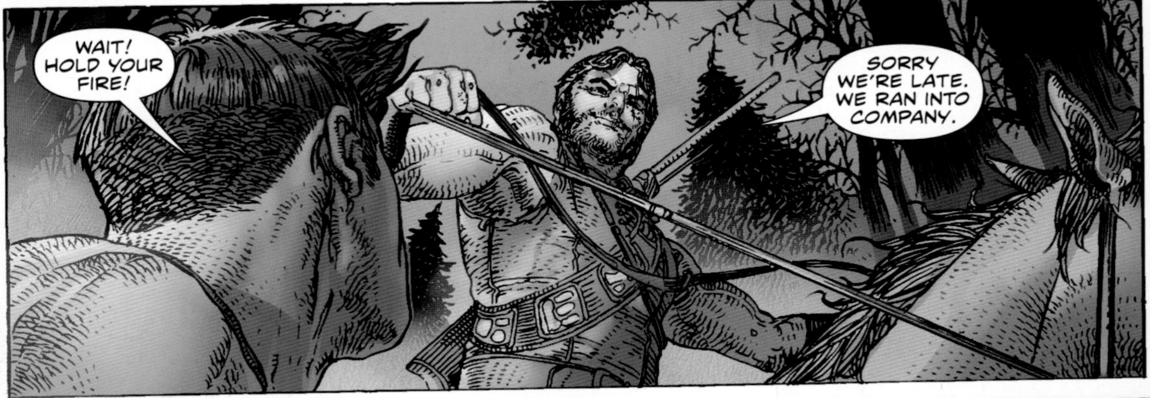
WAIT! HOLD YOUR FIRE!
SORRY WE'RE LATE. WE RAN INTO COMPANY.

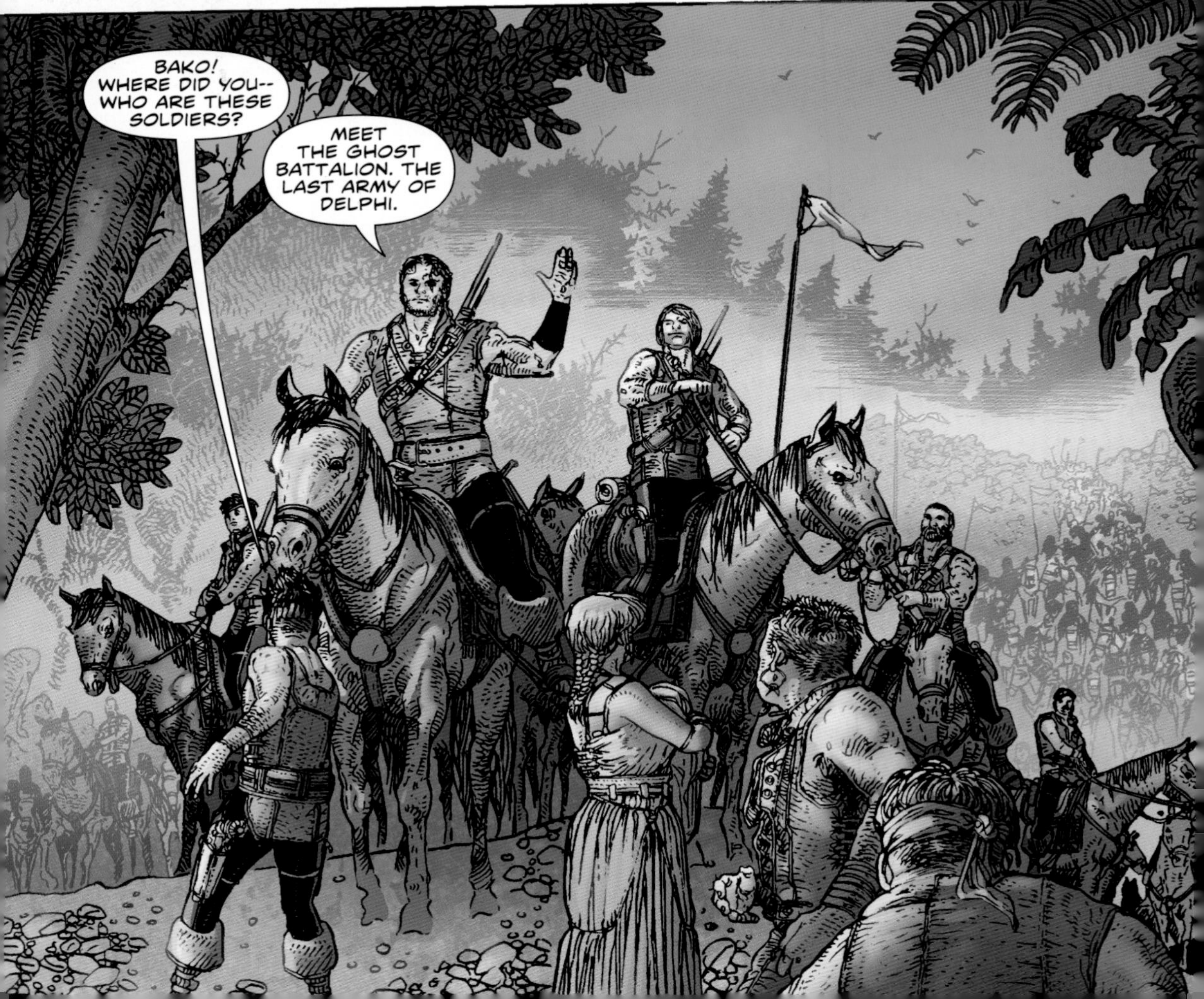
BAKO! WHERE DID YOU-- WHO ARE THESE SOLDIERS?
MEET THE GHOST BATTALION. THE LAST ARMY OF DELPHI.

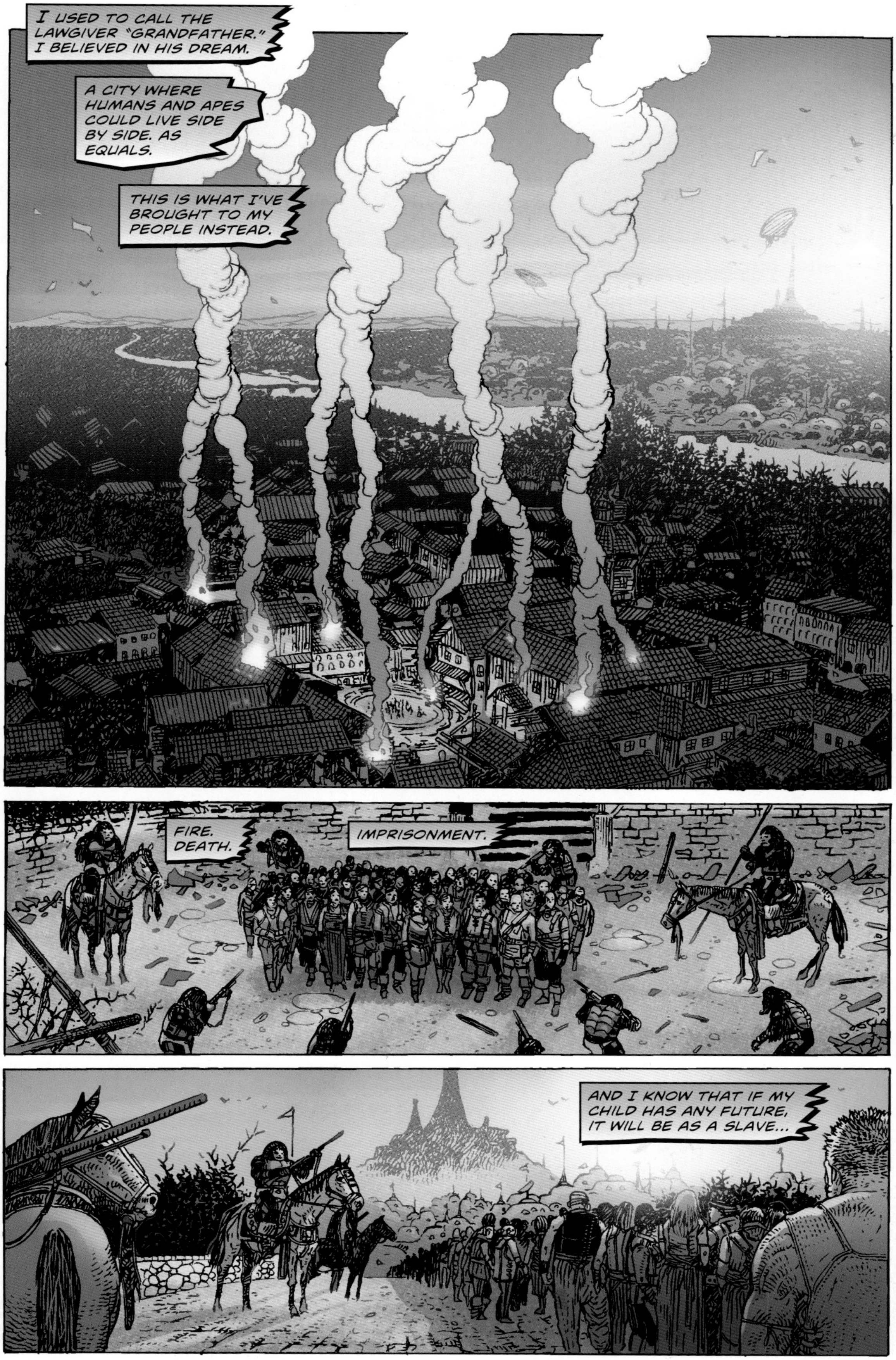

I USED TO CALL THE LAWGIVER "GRANDFATHER." I BELIEVED IN HIS DREAM.
A CITY WHERE HUMANS AND APES COULD LIVE SIDE BY SIDE. AS EQUALS.
THIS IS WHAT I'VE BROUGHT TO MY PEOPLE INSTEAD.
FIRE. DEATH.
IMPRISONMENT.
AND I KNOW THAT IF MY CHILD HAS ANY FUTURE, IT WILL BE AS A SLAVE...

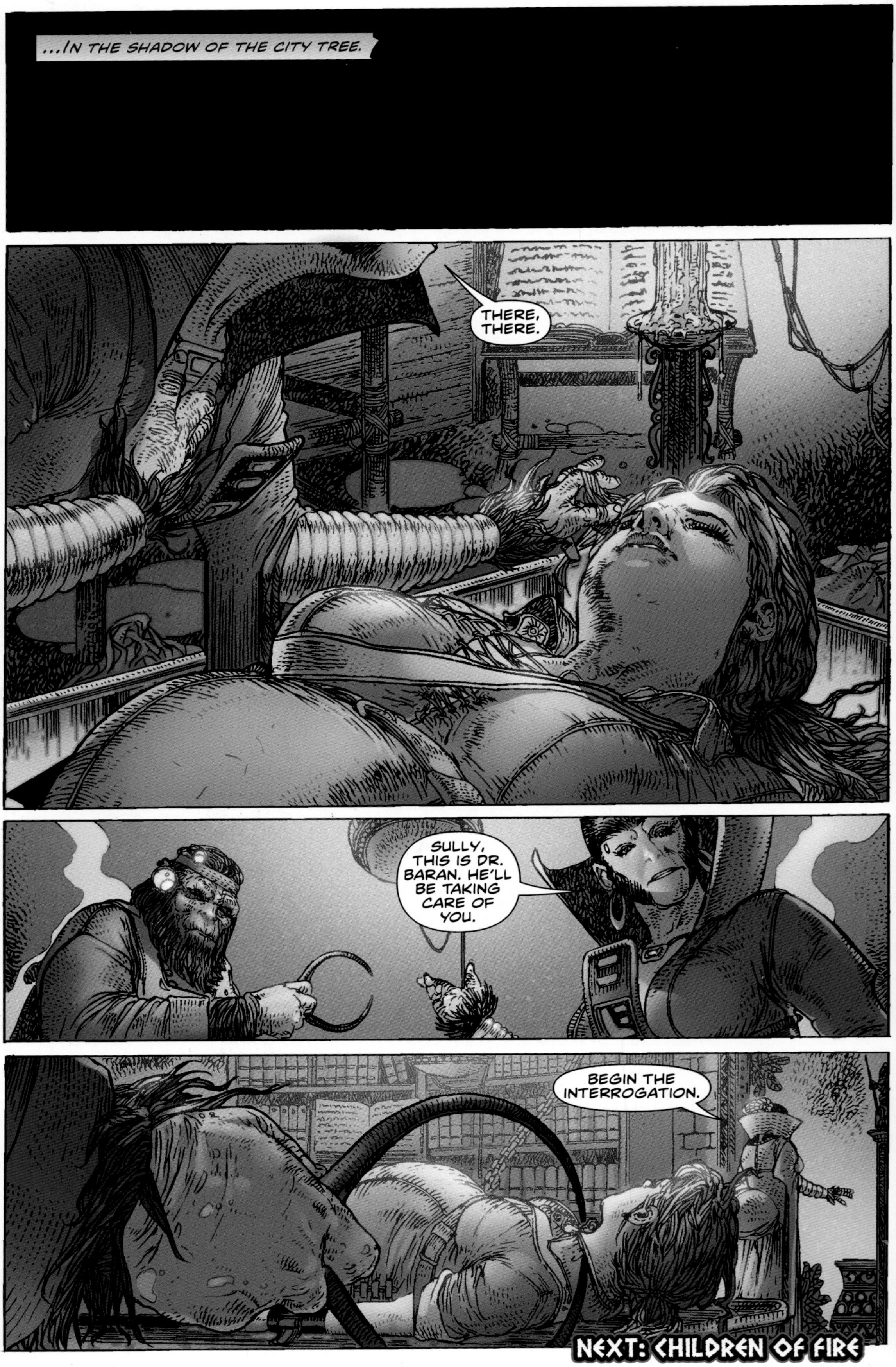
...IN THE SHADOW OF THE CITY TREE.
THERE, THERE.
SULLY, THIS IS DR. BARAN. HE'LL BE TAKING CARE OF YOU.
BEGIN THE INTERROGATION.
NEXT: CHILDREN OF FIRE

# COVER GALLERY

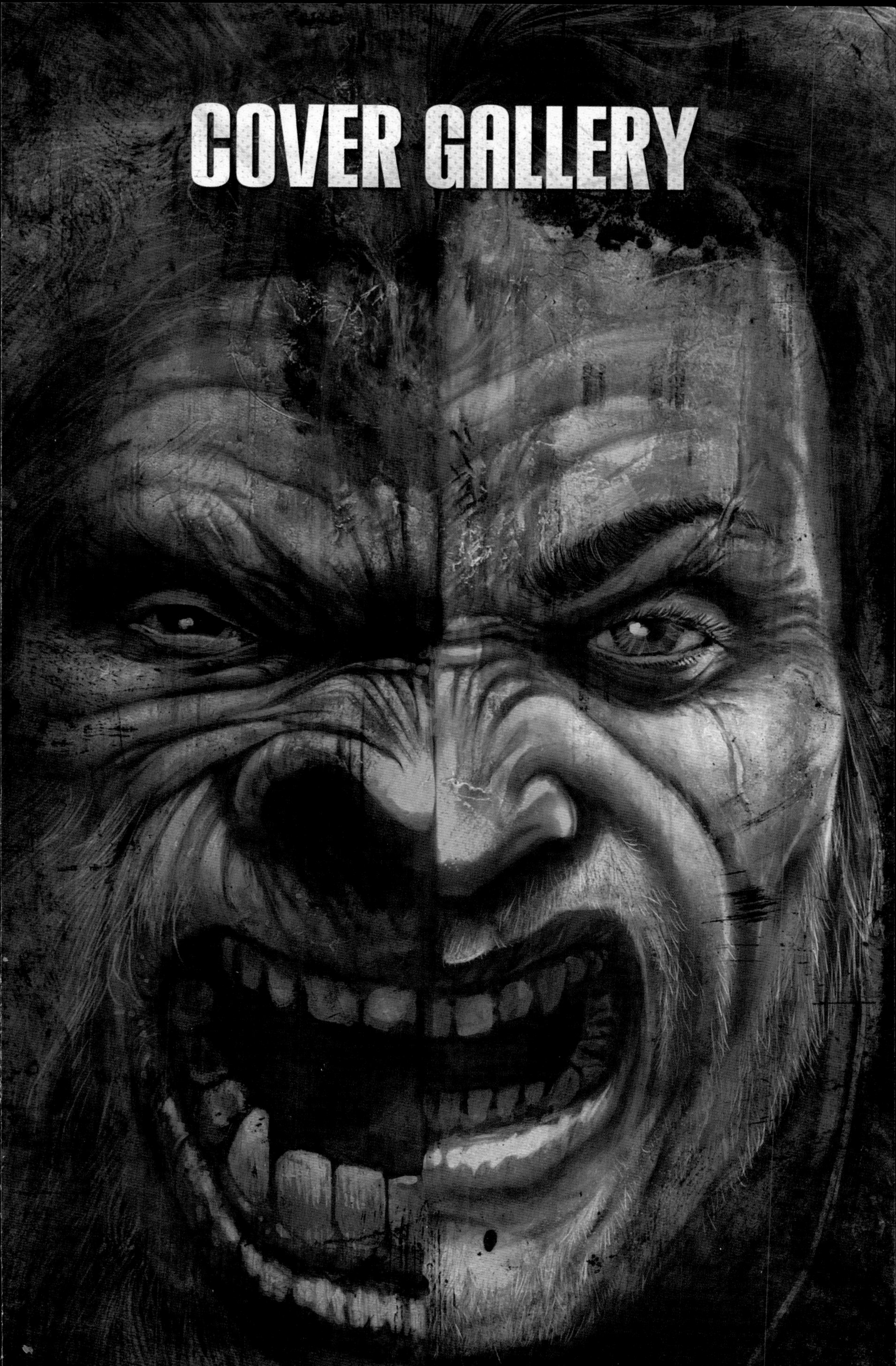

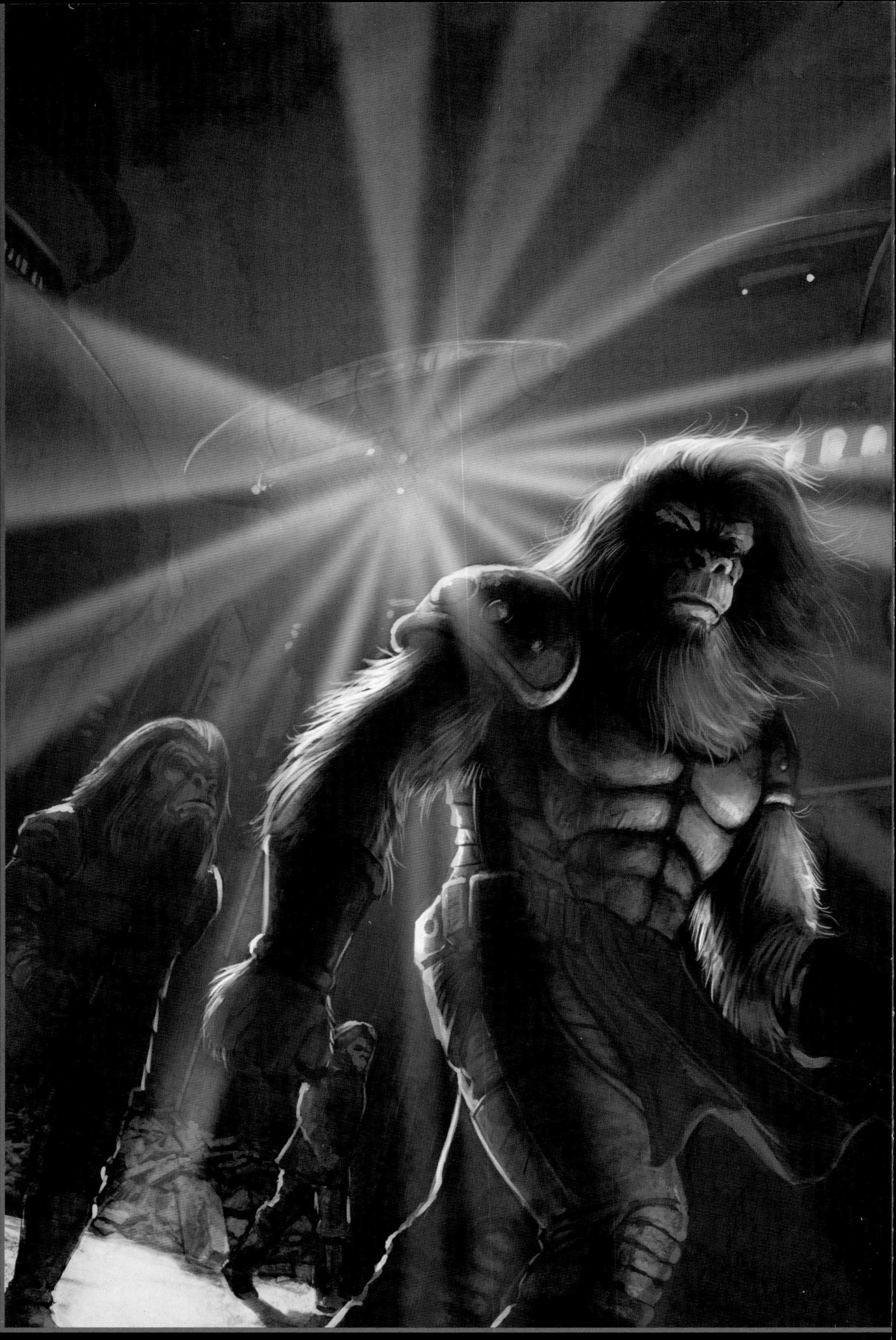

ISSUE 5A: SCOTT KEATING

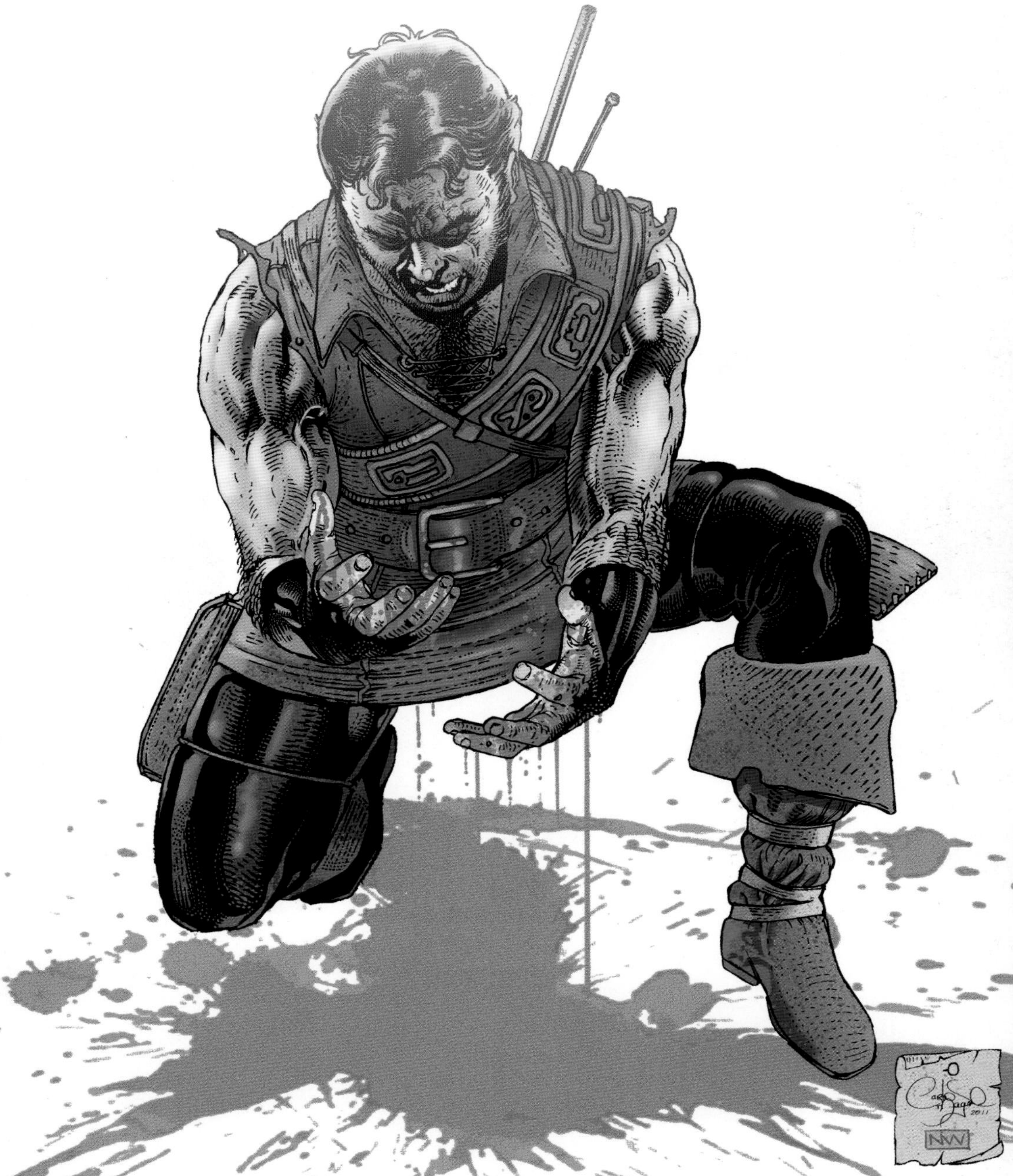

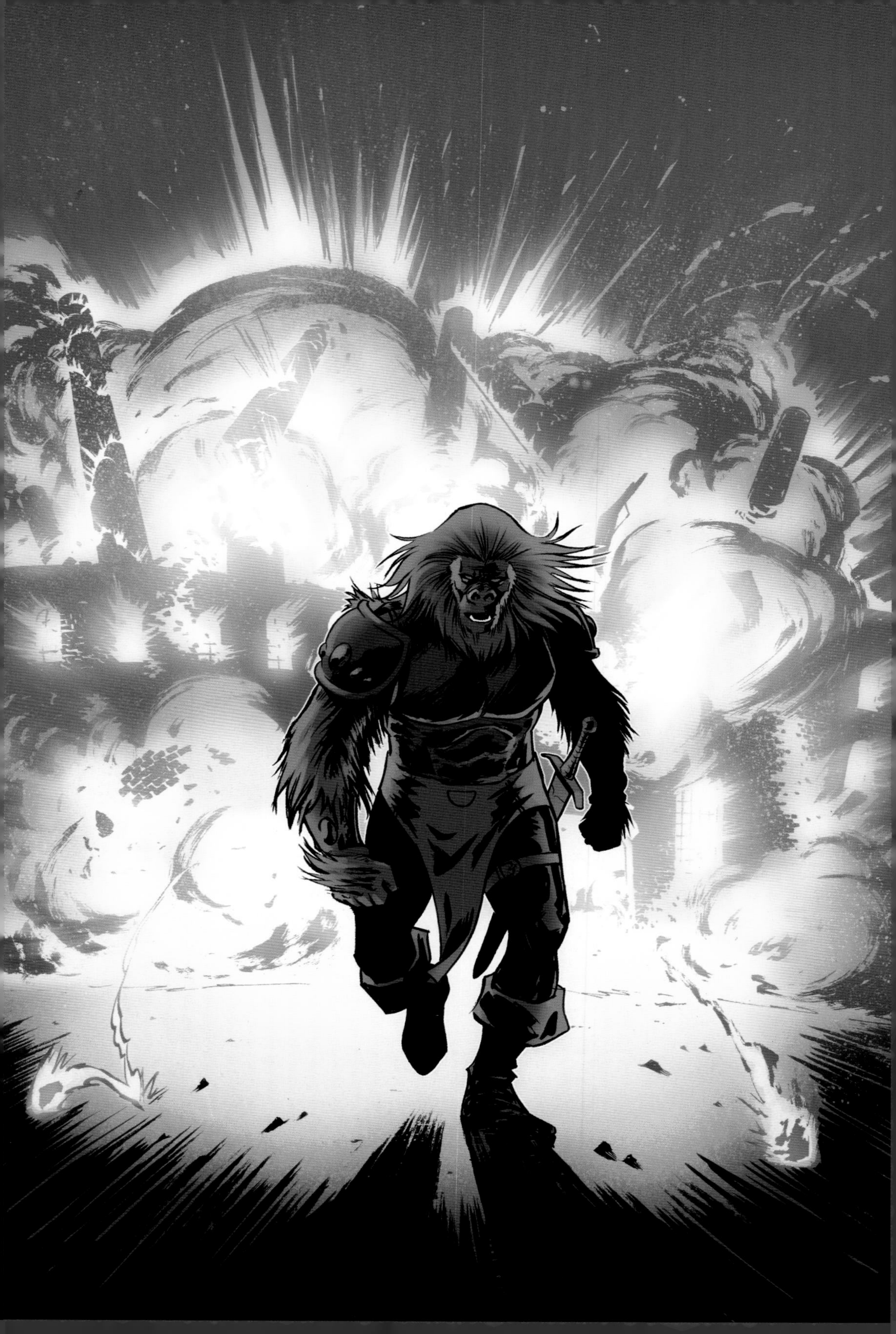

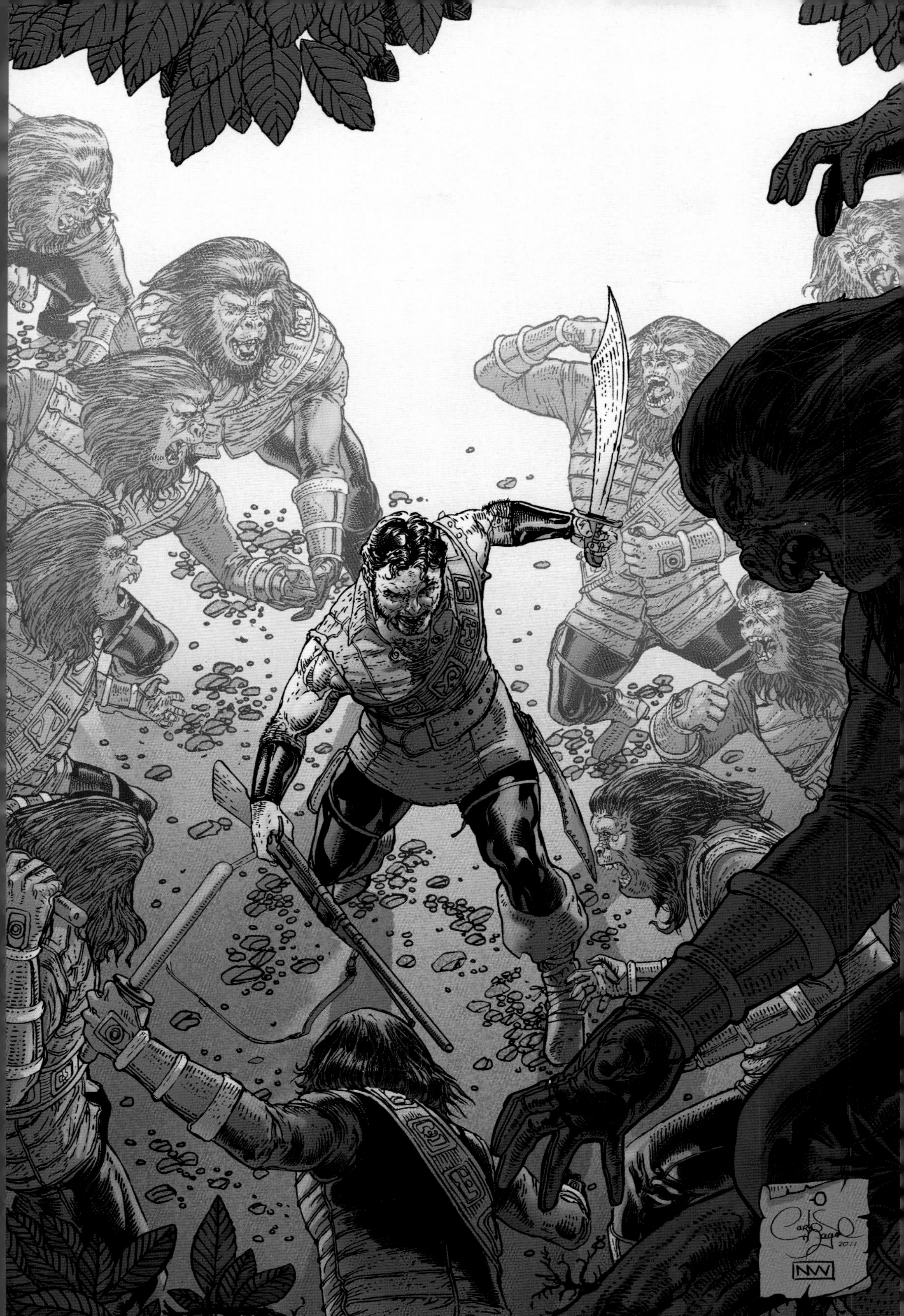

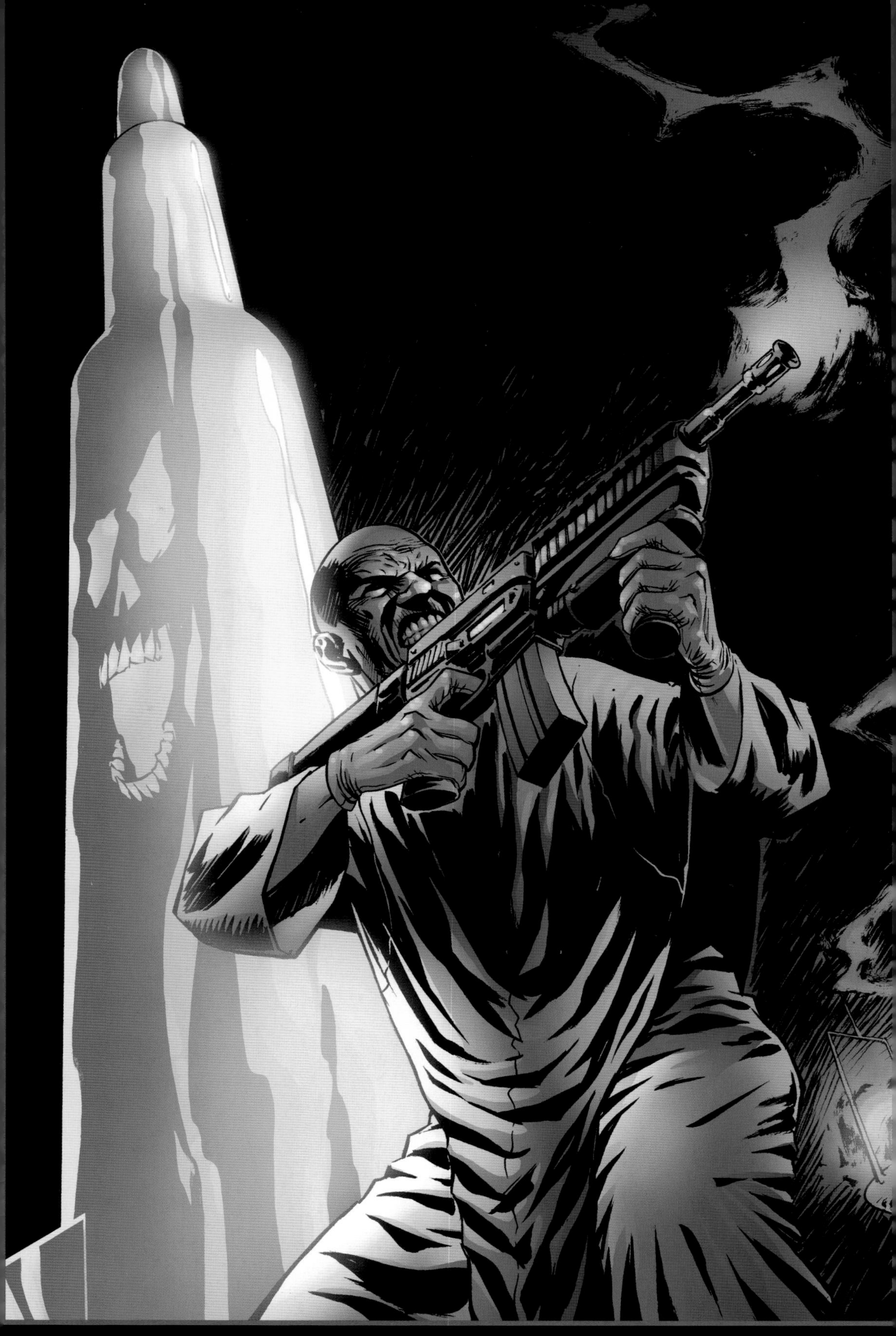

COVER 6B: DAMIAN COUCEIRO

WITH NOLAN WOODARD

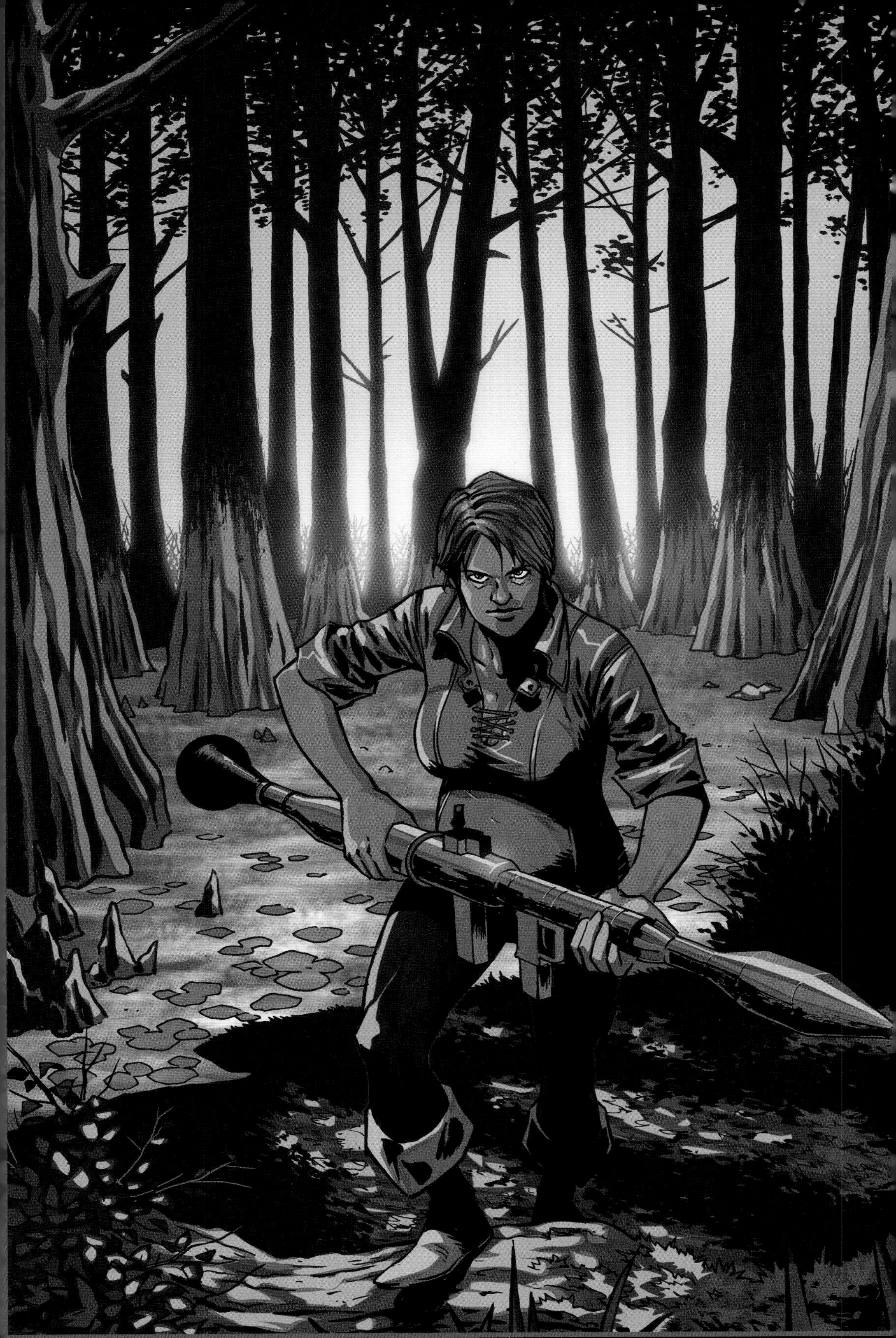

COVER 6C: DAMIAN COUCEIR

WITH ANDER ZARAT

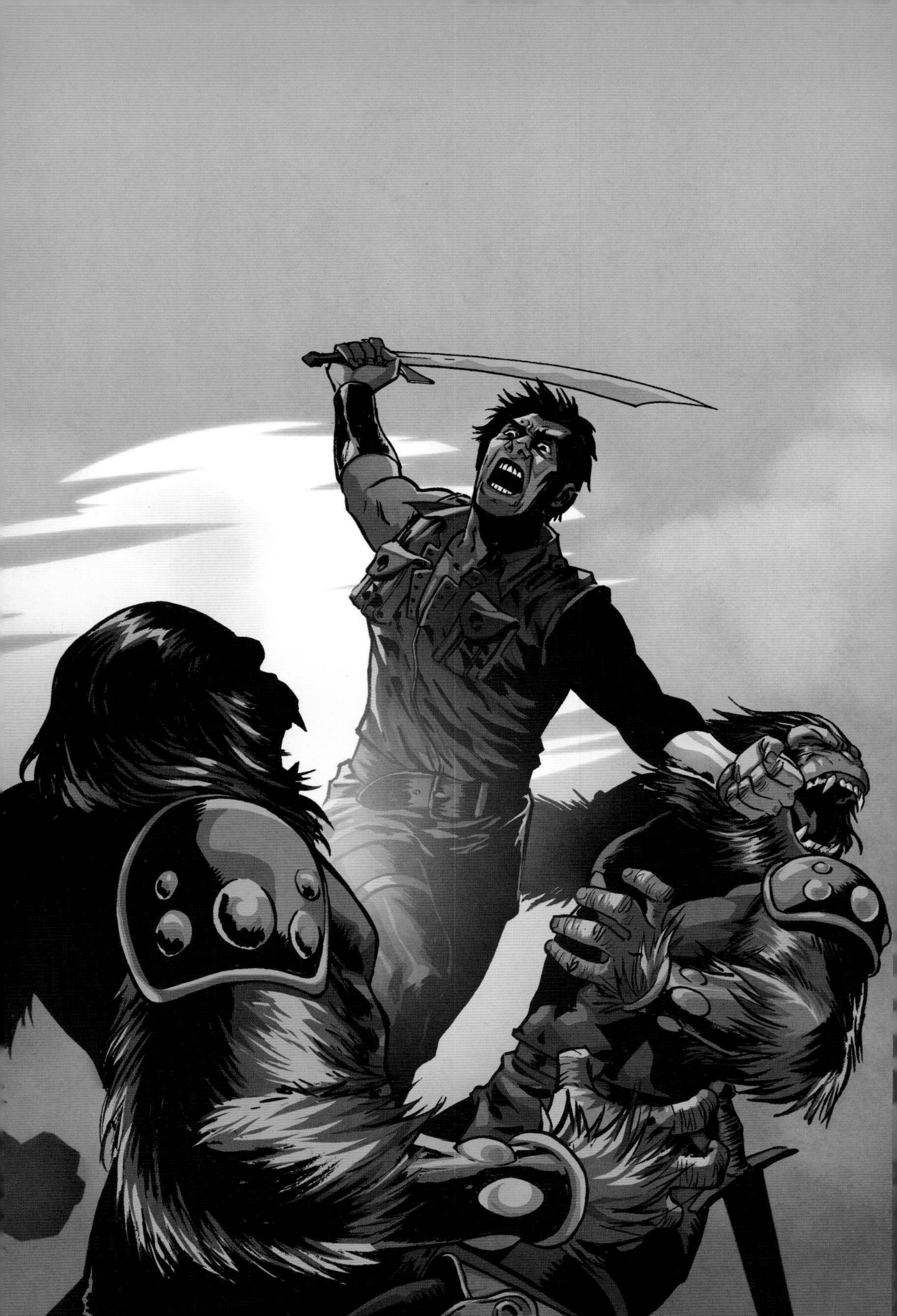

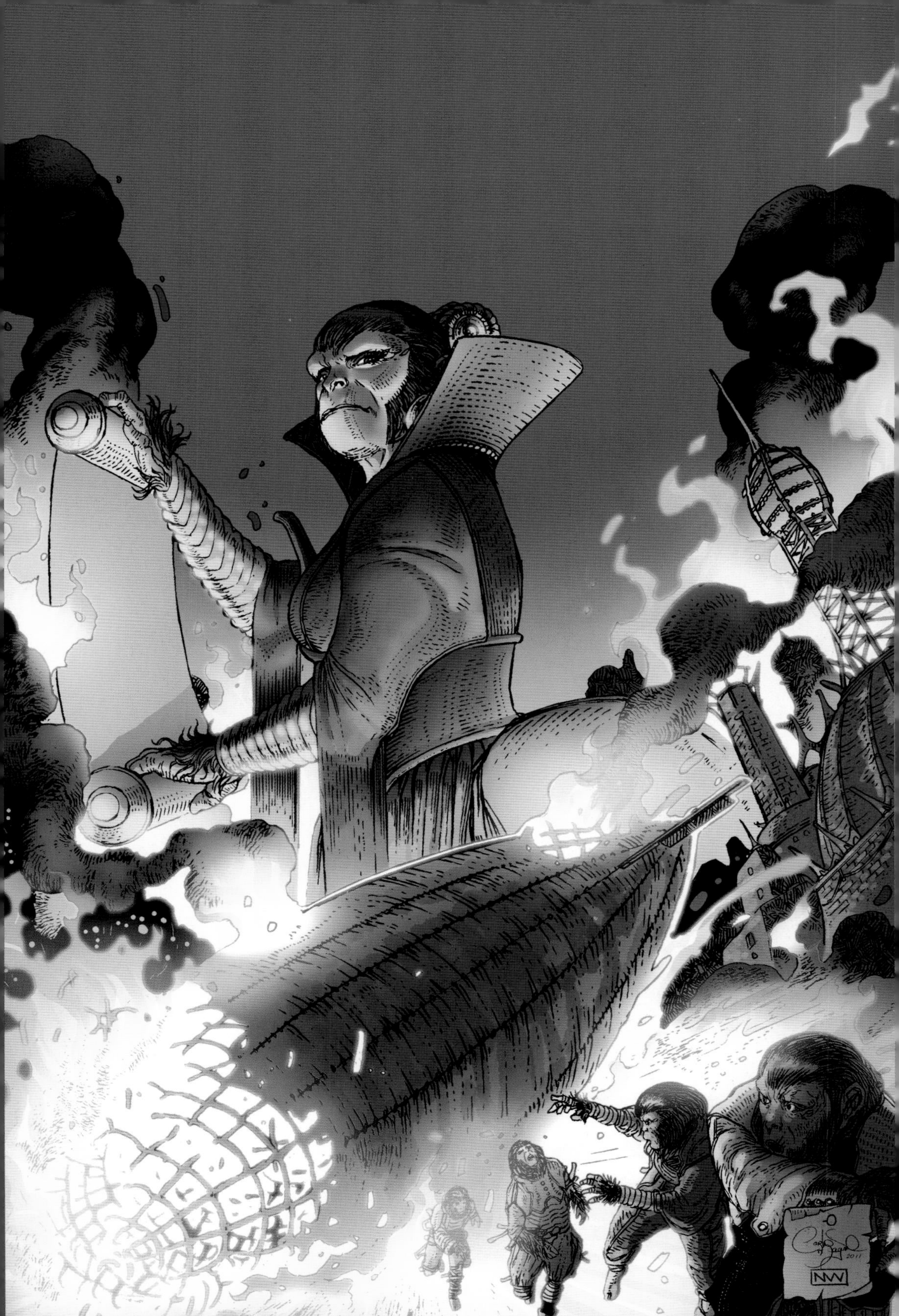

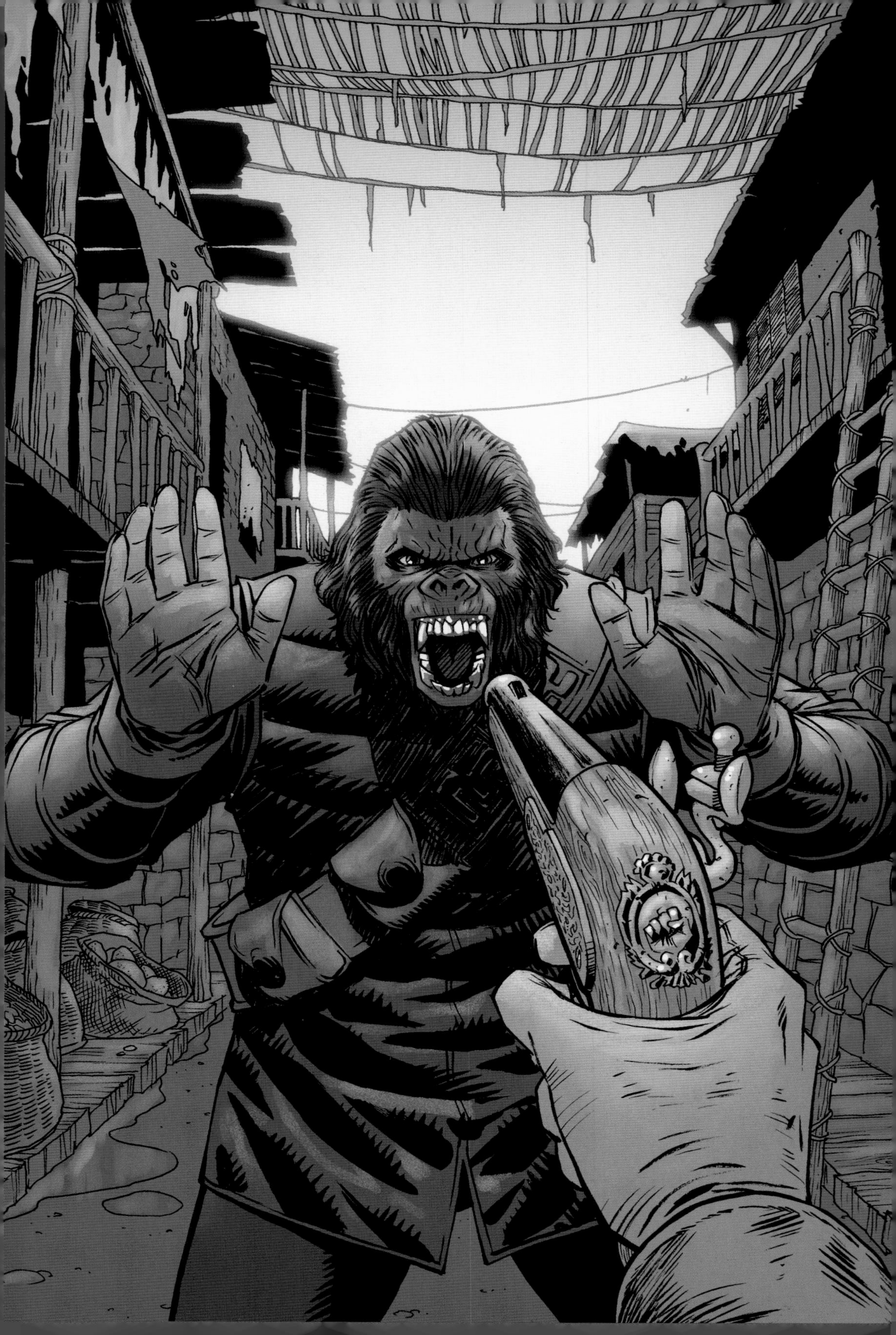

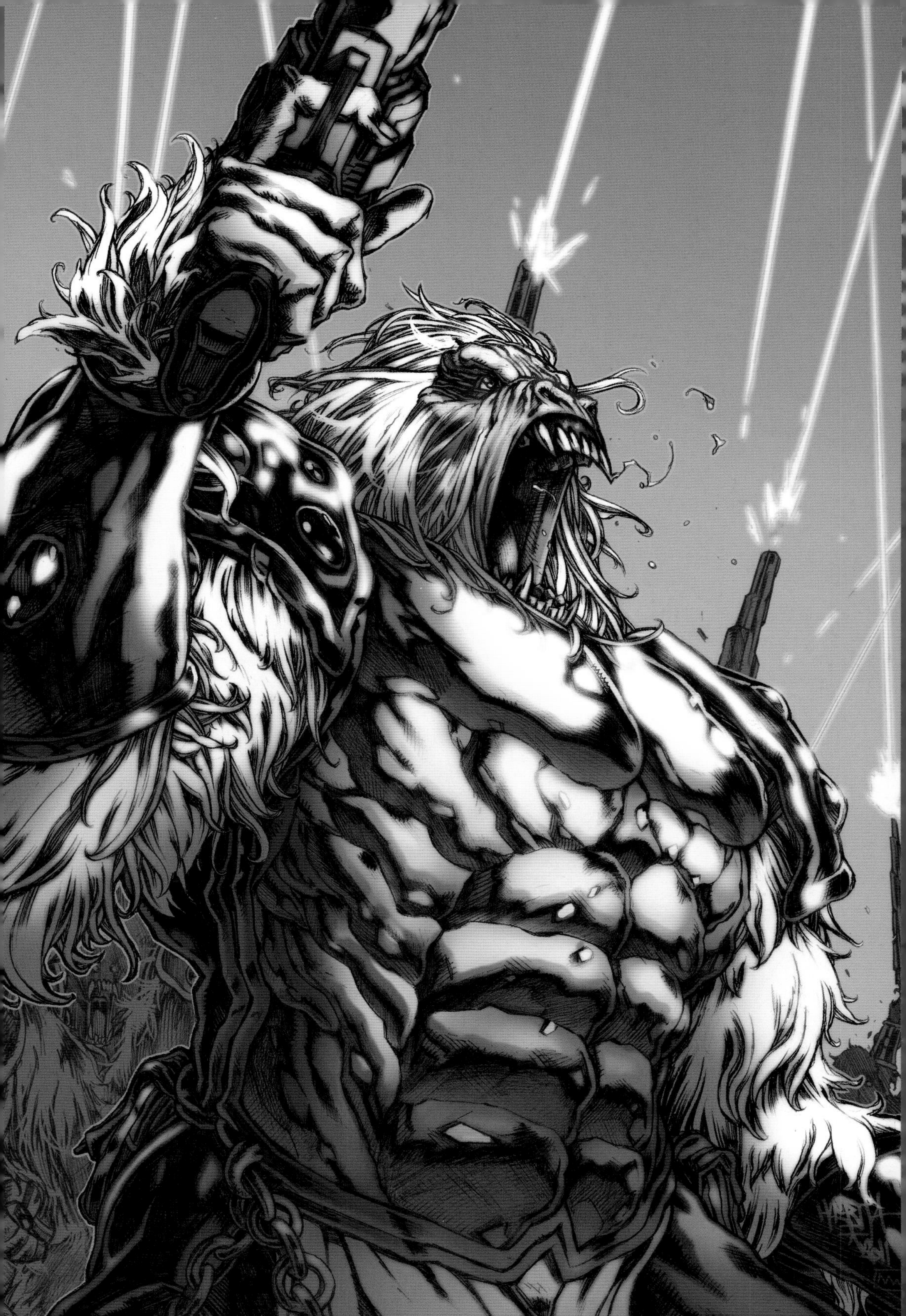

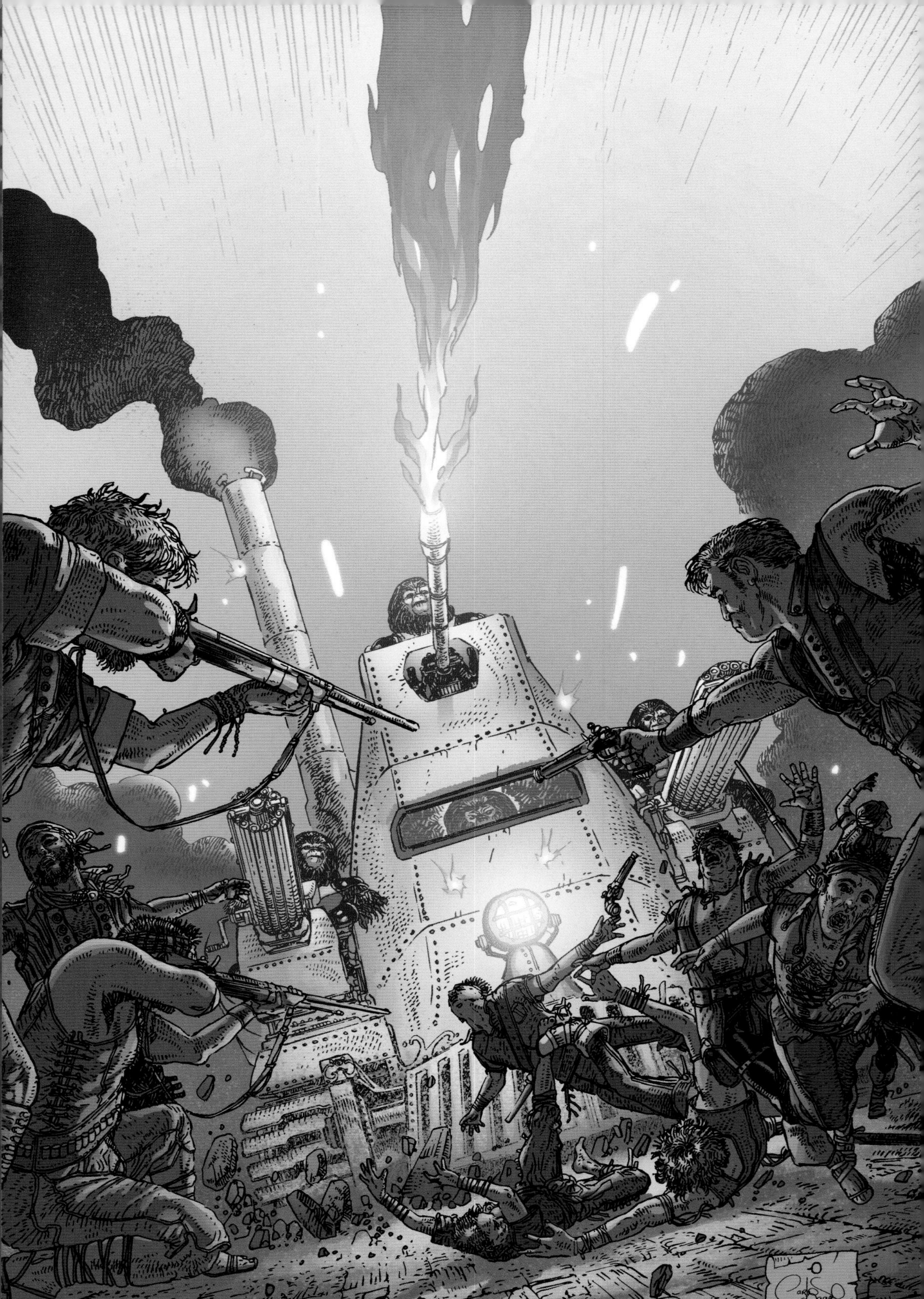

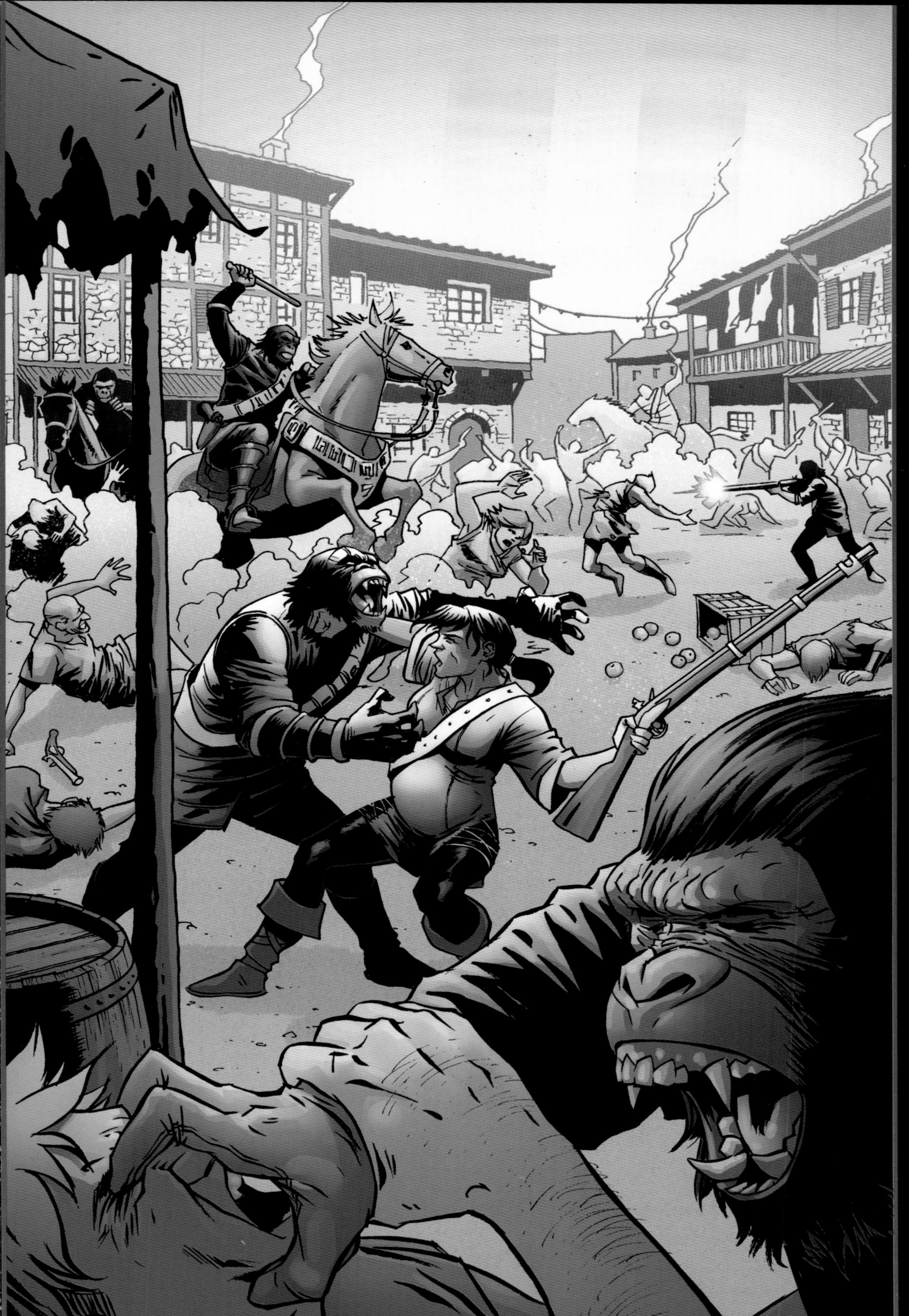

COVER 8B: DAMIAN COUCEIRO

WITH NOLAN WOODARD

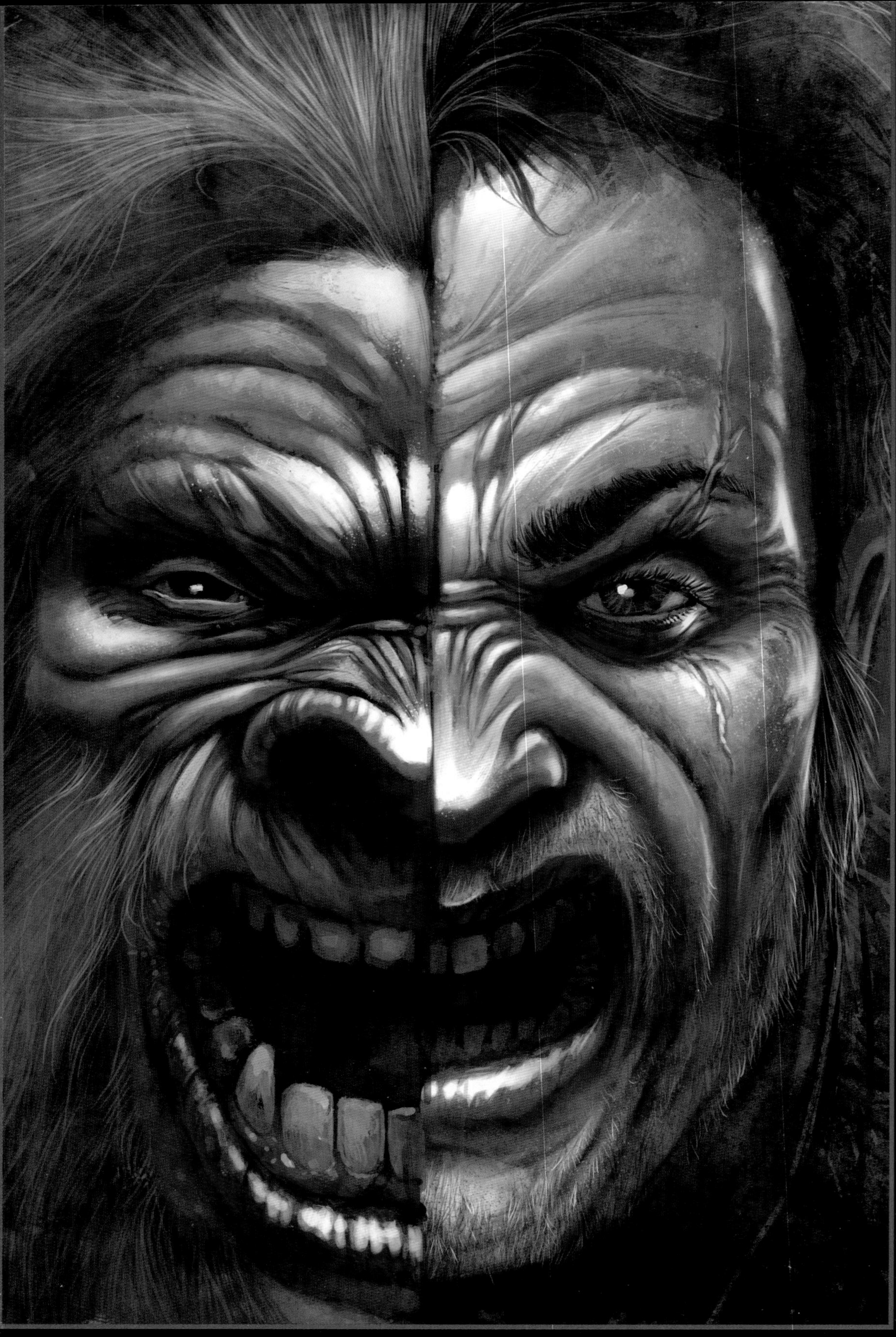

COVER 8C: SCOTT KEATING